What Will We Do If We Don't Experiment On Animals?

What Will We Do If We Don't Experiment On Animals?

Medical Research for the Twenty-first Century

Jean Swingle Greek, DVM
C. Ray Greek, MD

Printed in Victoria, Canada

A cataloguing record for this book that includes the U.S. Library of Congress Classification number, the Library of Congress Call number and the Dewey Decimal cataloguing code is available from the National Library of Canada. The complete cataloguing record can be obtained from the National Library's online database at: www.nlc-bnc.ca/amicus/index-e.html
ISBN 1-4120-2058-1

TRAFFORD

This book was published *on-demand* in cooperation with Trafford Publishing.
On-demand publishing is a unique process and service of making a book available for retail sale to the public taking advantage of on-demand manufacturing and Internet marketing.
On-demand publishing includes promotions, retail sales, manufacturing, order fulfilment, accounting and collecting royalties on behalf of the author.

Suite 6E, 2333 Government St., Victoria, B.C. V8T 4P4, CANADA
Phone   250-383-6864   Toll-free   1-888-232-4444 (Canada & US)
Fax   250-383-6804   E-mail   sales@trafford.com
Web site   www.trafford.com   TRAFFORD PUBLISHING IS A DIVISION OF TRAFFORD HOLDINGS LTD.
Trafford Catalogue #03-2637   www.trafford.com/robots/03-2637.html

10   9   8   7   6   5   4   3

*We dedicate this book to the scientists
and institutions that are searching for the cures.*

CONTENTS

Acknowledgments

In writing this book we made use of many websites and other data sources from companies actively exploring nonanimal research modalities. We are pleased to acknowledge their assistance and believe these companies will do very well in the future as their products outperform products from companies that base their research on the animal model. We thank all the companies mentioned for the information they provided and for the steps they are taking to insure medical progress.

This book was made possible, in part, by a grant from the National Anti-Vivisection Society. We have enjoyed our relationship with NAVS and Peggy Cunniff, NAVS' director, and look forward to continuing that relationship.

The diagrams of DNA, RNA, DNA chip technology and so forth are reproduced here courtesy of the National Human Genome Research Institute as indicated in most of those diagrams. The SNP diagram is reproduced courtesy of Dr. Gill-Garrison. Affymetrix provided the picture of their GeneChip, which we think will change the way medicine is practiced.

Many people critiqued and/or contributed material for the book and we owe all of them far more than a thank you in the acknowledgments: Walter Bass, Paula and Richard Bird, Beata and Andy Gajek, Clare Haggarty, Larry Hansen, Nancy Harrison, Anja Heister, Patricia Herzog, Suzette Naylor, Mark Rice, Jill Russell, Niall Shanks, and Jerry Vlasak.

Kathy Archibald and Rick Bogle provided valuable editing and research assistance in addition to priceless friendship.

Finally we want to give a special thanks to Rita Vander Meulen for her assistance in this endeavor.

Introduction

We have written two books explaining why animal models are no longer sufficient to answer the questions of modern day biomedical research. In this book, we outline the present and future of biomedical research. Also, we include small sections on the use of animals in other areas of science, as we are frequently asked about them.

This book divides biomedical research into disciplines like epidemiology, *in vitro*, technology-based, human-based research with human tissue, genomics, drug discovery and development and so on. These divisions are artificial; epidemiology, a human-based research modality, uses technology and even *in vitro* research to analyze data and to draw conclusions. Genomics is human-based, uses technology, is mainly an *in vitro* type of research and involves human tissues. You will read in the drug discovery chapter about technology, human tissues and other research modalities that may have their own chapter elsewhere in the book. This is the nature of biomedical research. We have tried to divide the book into chapters that emphasize the research modality in question but there must be overlap, as no area of biomedical research stands alone just as no body part exists independent of the others.

Except where we are clearly discussing history, the data and examples we use are very recent. Most of the information in this book is straight out of the medical headlines. This is particularly true of the examples that start some chapters. Each example is based on actual situations but is not itself an actual case. By giving many examples of the topic, be it clinical research, *in vitro* research, epidemiology, and so forth, we wish to impress the reader that these fields of research are the ones actually providing breakthroughs in present time. How often has your attention been grabbed by headlines that screamed: "Cancer Cured", only to read on and find that the alleged cure had been wrought in nude mice? What happens to all these "cures"? The mythical land of animal-based-breakthroughs just doesn't exist. In each section we provide many examples of the kind of research we are discussing and provide even more at www.curedisease.com. The examples we provide will probably be unknown to most and that is why we are producing them in such volume. This is the research that is changing the world, not the flash-in-a-pan animal experiments.

If the reader grows tired of reading the myriad examples, please keep in mind that many of the people who ask the question: "What will we use if we don't use animals?" simply don't understand the sheer volume of nonanimal-based research going on. That is why we wrote this book. Some will understand the concept after just a few examples but, in our experience, others will need all the examples to finally understand that the animal model is a very insignificant percentage of research methods and how productive these nonanimal research methods are.

Some may be disappointed that we do not offer a one to one replacement for currently used animal models. In other words, we do not present animal test or model X and say "replace it with Y." As we have shown in our previous works, the animal model is no longer adequate for modeling human disease or testing drugs, hence, the *paradigm* needs to be replaced. If the paradigm is incorrect, it is highly unlikely that useful data will come from experiments based upon it. (For example, basing research on the old notion of four bodily humors will probably not yield useful data.) Empirical evidence such as we have presented confirms this. Discussing individual animal tests or animal models has, to a great degree, already been done. The purpose of this book is to show the myriad testing and research options available today that are scientifically viable, not to outline why animal test X should be replaced by nonanimal test Y. If animal test X is not efficacious then it should be abandoned, regardless of what else is out there simply because it does not work.

Further, we readily acknowledge that not all the things we learn from animal models can be learned without them. The experimental procedure of using a sterotactic device to implant electrodes in the brain of a monkey to map the monkey's brain, obviously cannot be done in humans. But this point is immaterial. This type of research, while providing very interesting data about the brains of monkeys, does not consistently translate to the brains of humans. Hence, a replacement is not needed for this model as, again, it provides no benefit for humans suffering from Alzheimer's, Parkinson's, schizophrenia and so forth. To suggest that we need to find a way to derive this data from humans or else we should continue to use monkeys is fallacious. We *do* need to learn more about the brain and diseases of the brain but, 1) monkey brains will not provide this data and 2) we have good options for learning about the human brain (with more on the horizon) and it is these options we discuss in this book.

Using animals in biomedical research is like watching, from the deck of a cruise ship, a child drowning in the ocean. The child obviously needs assistance. The animal-model community suggests we throw a hundred dogs into the water to drown with the child. This will not save the child. We suggest a lifejacket. This book is about lifejackets.

Chapter *1*

Replacing the Animal Model in Biomedical Research and Education

To the old, the new is usually bad news.
Eric Hoffer in *The Passionate State of Mind*

Susan Knickerbocker, a normally healthy and vibrant 29-year-old public relations executive, had been feeling ill for almost two weeks. She had a runny nose, fever, and chills, and was coughing up phlegm stuff every five minutes. And there was that nagging pain with every cough. Finally, at her husband Jeff's insistence, Susan made an appointment to see her internist, Dr. Shelly Lowe. Because Dr. Lowe already had Susan's medical history, she knew that Susan was allergic to seafood, had never been pregnant, and she had no family history of illnesses. At the doctor's office, Susan described her symptoms while Dr. Lowe conducted a complete physical examination, which included listening to her chest, drawing blood, and taking a chest x-ray. Sure enough, Susan had pneumonia. Dr. Lowe promptly prescribed an antibiotic that Susan's twin sister Lisa had taken last year for a similar problem. The doctor then sent Susan home, advised complete bed rest, and instructed Jeff to call her if Susan was not feeling better in the morning.

Susan died that night. Shortly after taking the first dose, Susan had gone into cardiac arrest—a lethal, adverse reaction to the antibiotic she had just been prescribed. How could this have happened? The antibiotic that killed Susan had been used by thousands of people. Even Susan's twin sister had taken the drug with no consequences. If not all humans have the same responses to all drugs, how similar are the responses when extrapolated from one species to the next? Using animals to predict human response to drugs—which is not only standard practice in the pharmaceutical industry but also a federal law—is a scientific failure.

Human-based research into the genetic factors in disease incidence and drug metabolism is providing us a new understanding of how very small gene variations between individuals of different races, ethnic groups, and even genders can make an enormous difference in a person's susceptibility to different diseases. Not only that, individual genetic variations have a powerful influence on how effective a particular medication will be—and will even predict an adverse reaction such as that experienced by Susan Knickerbocker. This information—obtained through a combination of human-based research and technological innovation—is offering astounding new opportunities to custom design a person's therapeutic protocol based on his or her genetic profile. In fact, the potential is so remarkable that it is sparking the emergence of a whole new field of biomedical research called *pharmacogenomics*, which focuses on the development of personalized medicine. In the years to come, pharmacogenomics will result in fewer adverse reactions and better outcomes for patients.

How does this relate to the animal model (animals are used as models to predict human responses to drugs and also as models of human diseases) and its failure as a scientific paradigm? Consider that the antibiotic Susan's doctor prescribed killed Susan, but was beneficial to her twin sister. With differences in response so dramatic in two individuals who have virtually identical genetic profiles, what does this portend about attempting to extrapolate data on human response based on studies in rodents, monkeys, dogs, cats, and other species? Disaster. In this book, we will demonstrate why the animal model never really worked to begin with, and why, given recent developments in genetics and technology, it has now become the ultimate millstone in biomedical research today. We will explain how traditional human-based biomedical research modalities are offering cures and preventions to disease. We will describe some remarkable new technologies that offer real hope—not the hype that often surrounds "breakthrough" animal experiments—for suffering patients and their families.

If you were planning a trip from New York to Paris, would you paddle a canoe across the Atlantic or fly in a jet like the recently retired Concorde? The canoe *might* get you there, although the chances of safe passage would be astronomically against you. And even if you managed to reach your destination, it would have taken you much, much longer than the airline flight, and you would most likely have had a variety of unanticipated difficulties along the way. A similar argument can be put forth for animal experimentation in biomedical research. There was a time in the distant past when a canoe, however limited its capabilities, was all we had. But those days are long gone. Today, about $30 *billion* of taxpayer money is earmarked for biomedical research every year and even more from charities and foundations. Much, if not most of it, is used for experiments on animals or experiments using animal tissue. Given the poor track record of animal-based research, which we will discuss in greater detail in the next few pages (and which is explored at great length in our previous books, *Sacred Cows and Golden Geese: The Human Cost of Animal Experiments* and *Specious Science: How Genetics and Evolution Reveal Why Medical Research on Animals Harms Humans*) it seems abundantly clear that there are far better ways to distribute these funds if we really want to find more effective treatments and cures for human disease.

It boils down to this: How do you want *your* money to be spent? For our part, we'd much rather put a researcher in a jet than in a canoe.

The Challenge and Opportunity: A Better Way Through Non-Animal Modalities

Despite the inherent problems with the animal model, billions of dollars continue to be spent in experiments on animals every year in the United States. The use of animals can be divided into two general categories: 1) living, intact animals and 2) tissue obtained from animals. These two general categories can be broken down further as follows:

1.   Animals are used as models to study human disease.
2.   Animals are used as test subjects (e.g., to test drugs for efficacy and side effects, and to test chemicals to determine if they cause cancer, birth defects, or other conditions).
3.   Animal tissues are used as spare parts (e.g., heart valves) for human patients or as ingredients in vaccines and drugs.
4.   Animals are used as living incubators for substances that are used in medicine, such as insulin for diabetic patients or monoclonal antibodies.
5.   Animal tissue and living animals are used to study basic physiological principles (e.g., animals were used to discover some of the very basic principles about anatomy and physiology).
6.   Animals are used in dissection exercises in life science classrooms and for training medical doctors in some procedures.
7.   Animals are used as a modality for ideas; as heuristic devices.
8.   Animals are used to gain knowledge for the sake of knowledge as an end in and of itself.
9.   Animals are used to study a disease or condition for the benefit of the same species, but not the benefit of the individual animal being studied. Now is a good time to point the difference between the terms *experimentation* and **research** as they are used in biomedical research. The global term *Research* **can be divided into** research (small r) and experimentation. Both are examples of *Research* in the general sense of the word, but to be more specific, one uses a modifier in front of the word research e.g., human-based research or animal-based research. Animal-based research can be for the benefit of the animal—in which case it is called *animal research*, or for the benefit of others in which case it is called *animal experimentation*. The same rhetorical distinction can be made with human-based research. Research or studies conducted in order to benefit someone other than the individual upon whom it is being conducted is referred to as *experimentation*. Medical research conducted on monkeys in hopes of finding a cure for AIDS is an example of animal experimentation.

The term *research* is used when the study or experiment has the potential for good, or at least minimal or no harm, for the subject upon whom the research is being conducted. Hence *human research*, such as occurs every day in university teaching hospitals is ethical and appropriate but *human experimentation*, without the consent of the individual involved, such as occurred in the Tuskegee syphilis experiments on Black men, is not ethical. Animals are also used in *research*, such as in clinical trials for potential new cancer drugs, just as humans are. Animals are used in *experiments*, both for the supposed benefit of humans and the benefit of other animals. In this book, we will be using the word *animal experiments* to mean the use of animals to benefit humans, or advance knowledge, or for some other purpose during which the individual animal subject is harmed in some way. We will leave aside further discussion of the use of animals for the benefit of the same species since that is an ethical, not a scientific, issue.

Our thesis focuses exclusively on the animal model as a method of *scientific* investigation, production, and education. We will prove that: animal models are no longer necessary in biomedical research; they slow down drug approval and divert resources from more valid avenues of inquiry; indeed in extreme cases our dependence on the animal model has resulted in human death and suffering; they should be replaced with the myriad modern-day and traditional research modalities that do lead to success; when animals can be used successfully, as in the production of insulin, the production of monoclonal antibodies, or to demonstrate basic anatomical or physiologic principles, that other, better ways exist to accomplish that goal; and finally, that animals are not necessary for training physicians or educating high school students. In other words, there are alternatives to using animals even when the animal model accomplishes what it was meant to accomplish (for example, demonstrate the anatomy of mammals or produce insulin for diabetics). There are far better ways of conducting biomedical research, education, drug and device production, and medical training.

Like most endeavors, there are a wide variety of ways to approach medical research. The ever-increasing costs in this field make it a matter of life and death that we channel our resources such that the maximum benefits are reaped. Money is tight, and every project that is funded diverts research dollars from competing studies. Like using a bullet to cure your brain cancer, there is an infinitesimal probability that animal experimentation might work, but less risky and more rewarding paths are available. The bullet may shoot away the tumor leaving the rest of your brain and body intact, but the chances are that more harm than good will result.

Society need not fear that the abandonment of the animal model will hinder medical progress; in fact, science—and the patients awaiting life-saving treatments and cures—will be far better served, both in the short- and long-term. As we will see, modern-day science has a vast array of tools and technologies at its disposal to replace a paradigm that never worked well in the past and certainly doesn't work today. These tools and technologies range from clinical research to *in vitro* technologies using human tissue, to molecular modeling, and many others. It is our contention that greater focus on these non-animal modalities, both in terms of scientific interest and in funding, will accelerate, rather than hinder medical progress.

False Hype and Feigned Hope:
How Animal-Modeled Research Harms Humans

Although the focus of this book is nonanimal research modalities, we will begin with a brief discussion of some of the inherent problems of using animals as human stand-ins for medical research. This subject is discussed in much greater depth in our previous books to which interested readers are referred.

Is there objective evidence that the use of animals as models for humans in biomedical research is hopelessly flawed and has often worked to the detriment, of human health? Consider the following:

- The National Cancer Institute (NCI) tested 12 anti-cancer drugs on mice that are currently being used successfully in humans. The scientists took mice that were growing 48 different kinds of *human* cancers and treated them with the 12 drugs. They found that 30/48 times, the drugs were ineffective in the mice. In other words, 63 percent of the time, the mouse models with human tumors inaccurately predicted human response.[1]

- In a study that spanned over ten years and has not yet been repeated, the Food and Drug Administration (FDA) began in 1976 to follow all the new medications it released for side effects. In that study, the FDA found that out of 198 new medications, 102 (52 percent) were either recalled or relabeled secondary to side effects not predicted in animal tests.[2] A similar study examined six drugs, the side effects of which were already known in humans. The study found that animals correctly predicted 22 side effects, but incorrectly identified 48 side effects that did not occur in humans, while missing 20 side effects that did occur in humans. This means that the animal models were incorrect 68/90 times, or 76 percent of the time.[3] More recent research indicated that a new drug has a one in five chance of being relabeled or recalled due to serious adverse reactions.[4] This, despite the fact that all new medications have undergone extensive animal testing prior to being released to the public.

- In August 2001, Mark Levin, Ph.D. and CEO of Millenium Pharmaceuticals, presented data at the Drug Discovery Technology Conference in Boston, MA regarding the inadequacy of current animal models in drug testing. In the study he presented, 28 potential new drugs were tested in rats for liver toxicity. Eleven of these drugs were shown to be toxic, while 17 were shown to be safe. Twenty-two of the 28 potential drugs advanced into human clinical trials, and the results revealed that of the 11 drugs that had been shown to be toxic in rats only two were toxic in humans, while six were safe. Of the 17 drugs that were safe in rats, eight were found to be safe in humans, while six were found to be toxic to humans (see Figure 1.1). Levin concluded that this basically means the animals were about as accurate as "a coin toss."

Figure 1.1

28 Drugs Tested for Hepatotoxicity			
17 were safe in Rats		11 were toxic in Rats	
22 Advanced to Trials in Humans			
8 were safe in Humans	6 were toxic in Humans	2 were toxic in Humans	6 were safe in Humans

- In the *Handbook of Laboratory Animal Science Volume II: Animal Models*, the authors state:

> The case of the huge 25-year screening program, undertaken by the prestigious U.S. National Cancer Institute, illustrates the kind of dilemma possible: in this program, 40,000 plant species were tested for anti-tumor activity. Several of the plants proved effective and safe enough in the chosen animal model to justify clinical trials in humans. In the end, none of these drugs was found useful for therapy because of too high toxicity or ineffectivity in humans. This means that despite 25 years of intensive research and positive results in animal models, not a single antitumor drug emerged from this work. As a consequence, the NCI now uses human cancer cell lines for the screening of cytotoxins.

- Of 20 compounds known not to cause cancer in humans, 19 *did* cause cancer in animals[5] while of 19 compounds known to cause oral cancer in humans, only seven caused cancer in mice and rats using standard NCI protocol.[6]
- Of 22 drugs tested on animals and shown to be therapeutic in spinal cord injury, none were effective in humans.[7]
- The American Heart Association (AHA), the American College of Emergency Physicians, the American College of Cardiology (ACC), the European Resuscitation Council, the Heart and Stroke Foundation of Canada, the Institute of Critical Care Medicine, the Safar Center for Resuscitation Research, and the

Society for Academic Emergency Medicine stated the following in the journal *Circulation*:

1) concerning animal experiments into cardio-pulmonary resuscitation, "Unfortunately, the results of one lab may not be reproducible in another lab or in human trials."

2) for cardiac arrest, "high doses of epinephrine therapy significantly improved survival in most animal models but does not improve survival in humans."

3) "species differ in response to anesthesia and drugs, and may require different doses to produce the same physiological response."

4) "differences in metabolism, physiological function, response to ischemia, hypoxia, hypercarbia...return to spontaneous circulation...[are seen] in rats, dogs and pigs."

5) rats, dogs and pigs show "anatomical differences [in] myocardial blood supply, pre-existing collateral circulation, sensitization to arrhythmia...shape of chest."[8]

• Although aptiganel (a n-methyl-D-aspartate (NMDA) receptor blocker, manufactured under the brand name Cerestat), was effective at providing brain protection against stroke in animal models, large clinical studies revealed no positive effects and possibly some harm when it was given to humans.[9] More patients who received the drug died than those who did not, and more side effects were observed in the group receiving aptiganel than in the control group. No benefits were seen in patients treated with aptiganel. In contrast to humans, rats given aptiganel showed a decrease in brain damage by up to 70 percent. According to the Associated Press, "Yet another experimental stroke drug that showed great promise in animals has failed in humans, with the study cut short because patients were dying or showing no improvement."[10]

• The animal model-based medical decision to give women past their reproductive years hormone replacement therapy (HRT) did not work out as the animal models had predicted.[11] As we all know by now, women receiving HRT suffered more strokes and heart attacks than their counterparts who were not taking HRT. Medical care costs continue to rise. Spending money on drugs that don't work, and that even are dangerous, just because they looked promising in animals. This report was in *USNews*:

> Marcia Stefanick knows she will not get through this October day without hearing about monkeys. The Stanford University medical professor is addressing a major meeting of researchers and physicians at the National Institutes of Health, detailing the recent results of what everyone calls simply "The Study." The Study is part of the massive Women's Health Initiative, and the findings are not good news. The

hoped-for health benefits of hormone replacement therapy, known universally as HRT, are not turning up. "It's clear now that there is no cardiovascular benefit," she tells her audience.

A physician approaches the microphone. He has a bone to pick: "In the monkey trials," he says, "hormones reduce heart risk and atherosclerosis if the monkeys are started on hormones early enough. Don't you think you would have found long-term benefits if the women in the trial had been younger and started hormones earlier? Are you aware of the monkey data?"

Stefanick, who has worked on most of the recent hormone trials, is struggling to conceal her annoyance. "Yes, I'm familiar with the monkey data," she says evenly. She once again goes over her newest analysis of the WHI results, showing that younger women had more risks and fewer benefits than the average women in The Study. "We've got to get our arms around this: HRT does not provide cardiovascular protection. We were wrong. We were just wrong."[12]

The journal *Science* had this to say about HRT and data obtained from animals:

The study was supposed to prove what people thought they already knew: Hormones taken by millions of postmenopausal women protect against heart disease. Instead, in July 2002 the Women's Health Initiative (WHI) abruptly ended its flagship experiment of 16,600 participants, half of whom were taking a popular estrogen and progestin combination pill and half a placebo. Those on hormones were slightly more likely to be felled by a heart attack than those on dummy pills. The headlines sent a quake through doctors' offices. An aftershock is now spreading through research labs devoted to the study of estrogen and the heart. Decades of research and hundreds of scientific papers had consistently shown that estrogen was the heart's guardian. Mice, rabbits, pigs, and monkeys displayed reduced signs of vascular damage after receiving the hormone, and genetically susceptible animals given estrogen never got heart disease. The hormone's effects on the brain and cognition appeared no less remarkable. These, too, were upended by a related WHI study... This new disconnect between patient and researcher interests has scientists jittery—nearly as jittery, in fact, as they are over the apparent contradictions between basic research and clinical data. ... Prempro, however, contains not estradiol but different estrogens from horses. (Some studies on monkeys and rabbits have found protection from heart disease with equine estrogens.) Hormone experts can't agree on whether the different compounds have different cardiac effects.

There's much debate, too, about the role of progestin, the hormone added to avert the risk of uterine cancer. Until about 5 years ago, it was rarely studied in combination with estrogen in animals. Some work hints that progestin may blunt estrogen's positive effect on vascular cells, which could render the combination useless. But studies in monkeys suggest that "it doesn't seem to be a large issue," says Thomas Clarkson of Wake Forest. Modeling heart disease in animals is an imperfect science. To mimic early-stage disease, scientists can injure a major artery. They sometimes feed monkeys extremely high-fat diets. Or they rely on genetically altered mice deficient in the enzyme ApoE. These animals develop a form of atherosclerosis, but it's unclear how closely their disease hews to the human version. Oddly enough, even mice with serious disease rarely die of it. "Most of these animals don't drop dead of heart attacks," says Banka. So researchers rely on other measures, such as improvements in arterial lesions or carotid thickness, to assess estrogen's benefits. Still, lesions aren't a surefire way to predict death from atherosclerosis in humans, who normally succumb when an arterial plaque ruptures. "These are highly artificial systems," says Jan-Åke Gustafsson, a molecular endocrinologist at the Karolinska Institute in Stockholm, Sweden.[13]

Testing on animals has shown a high degree of failure in predicting human response to medical compounds, treatments and chemicals. The animal-model paradigm is not just wasteful, it is dangerous. In addition to delaying medical progress by sending researchers down blind alleys, animal experimentation often harms human patients and volunteers as a result of unpredicted adverse reactions. As Stephen Kaufman, MD, states: "Because animal experimentation focuses on artificially created pathology, involves confounding variables, and is undermined by species differences in anatomy and physiology, it is an inherently unsound way to investigate human disease processes."[14]

Researchers struggling to develop an animal model for prostate cancer admit the limitations of the paradigm. **Tom Rosol, DVM**, a veterinarian at the Ohio State University's Comprehensive Cancer Center, who has spent almost 20 years studying the molecular intricacies of cancer metastasis, has stated, "...every time we put human prostate cancer cells in animals, they stop acting like they do in humans."[15]

The scientific board of the Alliance for Responsible Science (AFRS), in issuing a statement refuting the scientific value of animal experimentation, effectively sums up the essential problem with attempting to extrapolate relevant data from animal studies:

The very idea that one species could serve as a model for a different species ignores the basic principles of biology. Any individual species is defined by its reproductive isolation, which implies that its chromosomes cannot match, complement or recombine with those of another species. The species' genome is unique, and so is the species' genetic organization (gene sequence, location, duplication) and the control and regulation of the expression of its genes. Since the latter determines all biological activities of the species, it follows that the species' response to any external stimuli (toxic products) or to internal dysregulation (pathologies), are strictly species-specific also. These facts rigorously demonstrate that no species can be seriously considered as a biological model for another species, no matter how closely related they are in evolution.[16]

(To further illustrate how small differences can have a major impact in disease consider the following differences between individuals of different sex or race: Black women have a 50% higher incidence of breast cancer prior to age 35 than Whites. They also have a greater probability of developing aggressive tumors and have the highest incidence of pre-menopausal cancer. An article published in the prestigious *New England Journal of Medicine* in May 2001 revealed that Black people did not respond as well to medications known as ACE-inhibitors, medications routinely used to treat heart failure. One theory as to why this is the case is that Blacks have less nitric oxide, a chemical important in how ACE-inhibitors work. This theory led to the development of a medication named BiDil, a heart drug that increases the amount of nitric oxide. It appears to work very well in Blacks but when given to Whites it worked no better than a placebo, as would be expected if Whites already had adequate amounts of nitric oxide.[17] By examining the records of 786 patients and then another 1,093 women and 1,355 men, scientists found that women treated with 5-FU-based chemotherapy for colorectal cancer, had more severe stomatitis and leukopenia compared with men.[18] There is more evidence that men and women do not react exactly the same way to medications.

Among 10 medications withdrawn from the US market between 1998 and 2001, eight had more severe side effects in women than in men. The 10 drugs were Pondimin, which led to valvular heart disease; Redux, which also led to valvular heart disease; Rezulin, which led to liver failure; Lotronex, which led to ischemic colitis; Seldane, which led to a life-threatening heart condition known as Torsades de Pointes (TdP); Posicor, which lowered heart rate and caused drug interactions; Hismanal, also caused TdP; Propulsid, also caused TdP; Raxar, also caused TdP; and Duract which led to liver failure. All but Raxar and Duract were more toxic to women.[19] There is no requirement that clinical trials include women.

If humans differ so much between groups such as race or sex, how can we possibly expect animals of a different species to predict disease or drug response? Genomics and the other human-based research modalities described in this book will lead to personalized medicine that will benefit all groups of people.)

Unlike animal studies, the great advances in science that have given us the high standard of medical care we enjoy today are the result of human-based research, most notably clinical observation, epidemiology, post-mortem examinations, human tissue research, genetics, *in vitro* research, pathology, and advances in technology. Technology-based research has given us computer and mathematical modeling and CT and MRI scanners. The specialization of physicians, nurses, and hospitals, along with reforms in public sanitation, has increased the length and quality of life. In the not-too-distant future, drug prescriptions will be customized to a patient's individual genetic profile, thus eliminating adverse drug reactions, such as the adverse reaction that killed Susan Knickerbocker. Susan had most of the same genes as her twin sister, but one of the genes the twins both had was not expressed in Lisa, but was expressed in Susan. This gene's product interacted with the antibiotic in Susan's body and caused the fatal drug reaction. A DNA profile from a blood sample could have identified the danger. These are the research modalities and tools we will describe in this book.

Animal experiments have diverted funds from reliable approaches to medical research that have, time and again, proven their tremendous value in easing human suffering and prolonging life. Penicillin, cyclosporin, heart valve replacement, the statins, antidepressant medications, and many other important medicines and tools were delayed because of misleading test results in animals. People died as a result of these delays. Vaccines and drugs such as fen-phen and Rezulin, which tested safe in animals killed humans, while cigarette smoking, environmental poisons such as asbestos and glass fibers, and high cholesterol were originally advertised to be safe in humans based on tests in animals.

For too long, the public has been duped into believing the notion that animal experiments save human lives...a notion endlessly reinforced by the daily media parade of "breakthroughs" that make the news every day, but that never seem to actually work in humans. Animal experiments do serve some interests—most notably the interest of those who make their current or future living conducting them—but they most certainly do not serve the interests of human patients. In our previous publications, we have documented myriad instances of the use of the animal model resulting in human harm, as well as the many, many times when the animal model simply got it wrong.

We, and others, have pointed out that the theory of evolution and molecular biology predict that animal models will be very poor models of human disease. In light of modern scientific thought and the mass of empirical data, the burden of proof lies with those who claim the animal model is productive. In science, the burden of proof falls on the claimant, not the critic. Therefore, we ask those who claim that animal models are valid to "show us the data" that supports their case. They have not been able to do. We suspect that they will not be able to do so in the future as such data seems not to exist. (For more on *why* the animal model fails in modern-day biomedical research, see *Brute Science* by Hugh LaFollette and Niall Shanks. Routledge 1996)

Why, Then, Does Animal Experimentation Continue?

The scientific evidence demonstrating the lack of predictive value in animal studies is overwhelming. But the reasons that animal experimentation continues have little, if anything, to do with science or concern for human patients. Instead, the vested interest groups, comprised of individuals and corporate entities that have career advancement, prestige, and the bottom line to look after, protect the animal experimentation industry under the guise of protecting human health. For example, why do researchers announce, with such confidence, breakthroughs in animals knowing that these breakthroughs may fail in humans? Fran Visco, president of the National Breast Cancer Coalition said: "... scientists receive media training and are scripted by their hospitals. There are so many agendas here [at a meeting of cancer researchers]: fame, patient referrals, fund-raising, pharmaceutical grants, academic advancement."[20]

Certainly, you would not be hard pressed to find scientists in research institutions across the world who continue to support animal experimentation solely on the basis of intellectual inertia. Even the most disciplined and ambitious among us are often plagued by a certain resistance to change—it's simply human nature.

Then there are the busy clinicians (physicians who work directly with patients), who assume that what they were taught in medical school about animal experiments is true—and have neither the time nor inclination to challenge the notion. The rare students who challenge the status quo are quickly slapped down by their instructors.

Academia has its hand in this too. PhDs are promoted, and thus more highly compensated, based on the number of papers they publish in academic and scientific journals. Conducting animal experiments is a convenient and highly effective way for these researchers to gain career prestige and job security, and for the universities who employ them to obtain lucrative research grants. There is a *quid pro quo* relationship between research institutions and those giving the grants.

In June of 2003, Congress started investigating possible ethics violations and conflict of interest, by officials at the National Institutes of Health, with special emphasis on former National Cancer Institute Director Richard D. Klausner, current executive director of global health at the Bill & Melinda Gates Foundation in Seattle. Congress is concerned that NIH employees accepted cash awards from universities or other institutions that received NIH funding; mainly for giving lectures at the university. Those awards can pose conflict-of-interest concerns when they are given to a person who has some control over the granting of federal funds to the institution giving the award.[21]

Allegedly, Klausner accepted an Arizona cancer center's invitation to give the center's annual Waddell Award lecture and in return received $3,000 and travel reimbursements. The Arizona center received $42 million in NCI research grants in 2001-02, more than twice the amount it received five years previously, raising its rank to 23rd on the NCI's list for 2001-02.

Animal experimentation is big business. Tens of millions of animals are used in research in the United States alone each year. The equipment and materials necessary to maintain them, such as cages, feed, and instrumentation—not to mention the animal breeders who produce the animals purchased for experiments—adds up to huge revenues, and of course, profits. Millions more are used in high-school dissection classes.

The role of pharmaceutical companies, which develop and manufacture drugs, is based largely on self-induced regulations vis-à-vis the federal government and cost containment. The U.S. government, under the guise of protecting its citizens, mandates by federal law animal testing as a way to determine the safety and effectiveness of pharmaceutical drugs. For pharmaceutical companies, which are vulnerable to liability suits when a drug harms or kills a patient, animal testing is a relatively simple and inexpensive way to provide evidence in court that they have done what is required to ensure a drug's safety.

More money for government regulation is coming from industry, and industry is in turn gaining more control over the process of drug regulation and what it takes to get a drug to market. According to the *Washington Post*, in 2001 alone, the pharmaceutical industry spent $75 million on lobbying—more than any other sector. According to the Pharmaceutical Law and Policy Report, because of the pharmaceutical industry's lobbying efforts, many members of Congress are afraid to directly challenge the industry. According to *ABC News*, the drug industry has enormous influence in Washington. The pharmaceutical industry has more registered lobbyists than the number of senators and members of the House of Representatives combined. According to Robert Pear and Richard A. Oppel Jr. of the *New York Times*:

> In the last six years [1996-2002], according to Public Citizen, the group founded by Ralph Nader, the [pharmaceutical] industry has spent close to $500 million on lobbying, including 600 lobbyists that includes about two dozen former members of Congress. The industry has directed much of its largess to lawmakers who control the fate of legislation affecting prescription drugs.

Again, according to Public Citizen, the drug industry, in 2002 employed 675 Washington lobbyists, many with revolving-door connections, and the top 10 drug companies made $36 billion in 2002 which was more than half of all profits netted by Fortune 500 companies:

Public Citizen found that the drug industry hired 675 different lobbyists from 138 firms in 2002 – nearly seven lobbyists for each U.S. senator, according to federal lobbying disclosure records. The industry spent a record $91.4 million on lobbying activities in 2002, an 11.6 percent increase from 2001....Public Citizen's new report, The Other Drug War 2003, exposes the drug industry's lobbying barrage. Among its findings:

Drug industry lobbying ranks include 26 former members of Congress. All told, 342 lobbyists (51 percent of those employed by the industry) have "revolving door" connections between K Street and the federal government. The Pharmaceutical Research & Manufacturers of America (PhRMA), which represents more than 100 brand-name prescription drug companies, shelled out $14.3 million last year, a 26 percent increase from 2001 and nearly double what the group spent in 2000. PhRMA hired 112 lobbyists in 2002, 30 more than the year before....

Since Public Citizen began tracking the drug industry's lobbying activities in 1997, the industry has spent nearly $478 million lobbying the federal government. In that same period, the top 25 pharmaceutical companies and trade groups gave $48.6 million to federal campaigns. Well over $100 million more went to paying for issue ads, hiring academics, funding nonprofits and other activities to promote the industry's agenda in Washington. All told, the drug industry has spent nearly $650 million on political influence since 1997.

The success drug companies have enjoyed in protecting high prescription prices is reflected in annual profitability rankings recently published by *Fortune* magazine. In a year when the stock market remained listless and company after company was wounded by accounting scandals, the 10 drug companies in the Fortune 500 maintained nearly the same level of total profits in 2002 as in 2001. According to Public Citizen's report, "2002 Drug Industry Profits:" As a group, the 10 drug companies in the Fortune 500 saw $35.9 billion in profits in 2002, a drop of 3.5 percent from 2001. By comparison, all companies in the Fortune 500 suffered a combined loss of 66.3 percent in profits from 2001 to 2002. The pharmaceutical industry soared past other business sectors – raking in profits five-and-a-half times greater than the median for all industries represented in the Fortune 500. Profits registered by the 10 drug companies on the list were equal to more than half the $69.6 billion in profits netted by the entire roster of Fortune 500 companies – when all losses are subtracted from all gains. "The drug industry contends that it needs high prices to finance the discovery of new, innovative drugs," Clemente said. "But a closer look shows that drug-makers make far more money in profits than they spend on research and development."[22]

A whistle-blower recently revealed how extensively doctors were involved in promoting unapproved uses of a Warner-Lambert drug called Neurontin. The company paid dozens of doctors hundreds of thousands of dollars to lecture to other physicians about how Neurontin, an epilepsy drug, could be prescribed for uses besides epilepsy despite the fact that Neurontin had not been approved for these uses. One physician, Dr. B. J. Wilder, a former professor of neurology at the University of Florida, received more than $300,000 for such lectures while six other doctors received more than $100,000 each.[23] (For more on the interaction between the FDA and industry, see the Appendix.)

There's an old saying, he who pays the piper calls the tune. Industry now provides about 70% of all funding for clinical drug trials.[24] Many university departments are entirely underwritten by corporations[25] and over 50% of the advisors to the FDA have financial ties to industry.[26] The May 30, 2003 issue of the *British Medical Journal* was devoted entirely to the problem of the pharmaceutical industry's powerful influence over the positive outcome of research projects. The authors of an article in the *New England Journal of Medicine*[27] provide a striking example of the problem. The authors' ties with companies that make antidepressant drugs were so extensive that it would have used too much space to disclose them fully in the *Journal*. The Journal had a difficult time even finding an editor to write about the article. As a result of this and other such problems the *New England Journal of Medicine* relaxed its longstanding rules on conflict of interest so that it could publish evaluations of new drugs by researchers with financial ties to the manufacturers because it cannot find enough experts without financial ties to drug companies.[28] Recently the *New England Journal of Medicine* was forced to publish a disclaimer along with an article that reported on a new drug. Every single member of their review board had a financial relationship with the company that produced the drug.

A 1998 study in the *New England Journal of Medicine*[29] compared the authors' financial relationships with industry together with their published positions about the safety of calcium channel blockers. Authors who had financial relationships with pharmaceutical companies were significantly more likely to reach supportive conclusions than authors without such industry affiliations. One study reported that lead authors in 1 of every 3 articles published hold relevant financial interests, while another reported that approximately two thirds of academic institutions hold equity in "start-up" businesses that sponsor research performed by their faculty.[30]

The pharmaceutical industry's share of the total amount invested in biomedical research was 32% in 1980 but soared to 62% in 2000, while the amount coming from the federal government plummeted. It also appears that life science companies are increasingly involved with academia. A 1996 survey[31] found that 92% of firms supported academic research and that approximately one fourth of investigators have industry affiliations. Other recent studies have revealed a statistically significant association between industry financial sponsorship and pro-industry conclusions. In other words, money talks.

Madison Avenue is also actively engaged in helping create the next generation of blockbuster drugs. Ad agencies are buying or investing in companies engaged in the actual science of drug development, including organizing clinical trials. Some ad agencies also own companies that ghostwrite scientific journals and develop medical education courses – all designed to promote the perceived need for "new and better" drugs to fight human disease.

According to NOW with Bill Moyer,[32] Joe Torre, chief executive of the ad agency, Torre Lazur-McCann Healthcare Worldwide, stated: "We've launched over 65 new pharmaceutical products." And to help launch even more products, Torre Lazur early this year bought its own clinical research firm, Target Research Associates so the agency no longer merely markets new drugs, it now studies the benefits and dangers of experimental drugs. Torre continued: "We provide services that go from the beginning of drug development all the way to the launch of your products." This means an ad agency can submit data to the FDA that will determine if the drug is approved. A case in point was the new pain reliever Bextra. The Food and Drug Administration approved Bextra for mild pain like arthritis, but not for acute pain. Six months later a private research company - Scirex - partly owned by The Omnicom Group, released a new study showing that Bextra did relieve acute pain from dental surgery. While Bextra cannot be advertised for acute pain, doctors are now freely prescribing it for that purpose.

So, what does all of this have to do with animal testing?   Pharmaceutical companies are in the business of making and marketing drugs. The easiest way to make sure you obtain the results you want is to use animal models. Experiment on enough species and you will find the result you want: that your drug is safe or that your competitor's is not. It is also the cheapest. Drug discovery and development costs approximately $800 million. Only about 1-2% of that is due to experiments on animals.

According to the journal *Drug Discovery and Development*: "The major costs incurred by a drug company are for clinical trials and marketing. The amount of money spent on initial discovery and development is only about 2 to 5% of the total cost of getting the drug to market"[33] Testing drugs on animals (part of that 2-5%) is much cheaper than conducting clinical trials on humans and it is only when new drugs are tested on many, many humans that effects and side-effects are revealed. By testing on animals, pharmaceutical companies establish liability protection, can get their product to market more rapidly, and do not have to conduct more extensive and hence more expensive human trials.

The true effects and side effects of drugs are not revealed until human clinical trials are performed. But since clinical trials cost about two-thirds of that $800 million, drug companies (and, now, their marketers) are reluctant to do what physicians have wanted for decades—extend and broaden clinical trials. That would lessen profits.

While being relatively inexpensive, animal tests—as mentioned above—give drug companies liability protection. When a pharmaceutical company is sued, they demonstrate to the jury that the drug was tested in animals where it performed well and was shown to be safe. Most juries do not understand the intricacies of drug development and, thus, believe the animal data to be irrefutable. Consequently, monetary settlements are often low in proportion to the injury caused by the drug. Animal testing of drugs has, therefore, proven to be a wise investment for the drug company.

Dr. Lemuel A. Moye, a physician at the University of Texas School of Public Health, who served from 1995 to 1999 on an FDA advisory committee, described the FDA officials:

> They've lost their compass and they forget who it is that they are ultimately serving. Unfortunately, the public pays for this, because the public believes that the FDA is watching the door, that they are the sentry.

As Gina Kolata reported in the *New York Times,* September 16, 1997, on the diet drug fen-phen:

> Why weren't these problems [heart valve abnormalities] noticed before? Dieters in Europe had used Dexfenfluramine for decades. Dr. Friedman [an FDA official] said he could only speculate. No one had initially thought to examine patients' hearts, he said, because animal studies had never revealed heart abnormalities and heart valve defects are not normally associated with drug use.

While there are no doubt legions of researchers employed by pharmaceutical companies who fully understand the flaws in the animal model—after all, they are the ones conducting the experiments themselves—no one is willing to blow the whistle on the system that provides their paycheck and economic security. Moral compromises are a part of life.

Medical and scientific journals rely on advertising dollars from pharmaceutical companies and the advertising of companies that make products for research on animals. This may explain why it is so hard to get an anti-pharmaceutical or anti-animal model argument published in a medical journal and why it is so easy to get things published like: "What Was Good Enough for Galen is Good Enough for Us"[34] (Galen was the father of the animal model), and "millions of lives have been saved because of animal testing,"[35] and "animal activists are politically shrewd and have more money than we [those with a vested interest in the animal model] do."[36]

And so pharmaceutical companies are quite content to move new drugs to market more quickly based on animal testing; to save money on development by relying on animal testing; and to shield themselves from lawsuits by hiding behind animal testing. It all adds up to a vicious circle of self-protection, with no one willing to step forward with the truth. Meantime, the public is duped into believing that animal experimentation leads to the cures and treatments that save lives, when in actuality, the continued reliance on the animal model sidetracks discovery and misguides the public about what is beneficial and safe.

By holding science back, it contributes to the suffering and death of untold numbers of humans.

The case of Susan Knickerbocker is hardly unique. Severe adverse reactions to prescription drugs kill about 100,000 Americans every year. In 1994, adverse drug reactions were the fourth leading cause of death in the United States, killing more people than all illegal drugs combined and costing the general public over $136 billion in health care expenses.[37]

For years, researchers have known, even if they haven't publicly admitted, that the animal model's lack of predictive value is one reason behind the high number of adverse drug reactions reported in human clinical trials and in the subsequent release of a dangerous or useless drug into the general population. But it was not until relatively recently that we have truly understood exactly *why*.

It turns out that it's all in the genes.

Chapter *2*

Darwin and DNA: New Findings in Genetics Negate the Value of the Animal Model

It has not escaped our notice that the specific pairing we have postulated immediately suggests a possible copying mechanism for the genetic material.
J. D. Watson and F. H. C. Crick in *Nature* April 2, 1953

Bryan Turner, a geneticist from the University of Birmingham in Britain said: "The important thing is not just what genes you have, but what you do with them."[38] Modern evolutionary biology combined with molecular biology shows us that the differences between species with regard to how organisms operate at the cellular level—the level at which disease occurs—are far more significant than the similarities, thus invalidating the animal model. Evolutionary theory, the central organizing principle of modern biology, provides the reason why the results of experiments on animals cannot be reliably extrapolated to humans. Evolution is why it *appears* we can use animal models, but explains why we cannot.

According to evolutionary theory, first proposed by the British naturalist Charles R. Darwin in his seminal work, *The Origin of Species* (1859), all living things on earth evolved from a single life form that inhabited the earth about 3.5 billion years ago. Over thousands of millions of years, this single life form developed gradually, or *evolved*, into multiple species through a branching process known as *speciation*. Because of their common heritage, which can be traced to that single life form, all species share certain characteristics. Those species with a more recent common ancestor will be more closely related. For example, the common ancestor of humans and reptiles lived about 300 million years ago, while the common ancestor of humans and chimpanzees lived far more recently—between 4 million and 10 million years ago.

When Darwin put forward his theory of evolution, he observed that the characteristics of organisms might change during the process of being passed on to offspring. However, because the principles of genetics were not yet known, he could not explain how or why these changes occurred. Today's *Modern Synthesis* incorporates our new knowledge of molecular genetics and offers a theory to explain how evolution works at the level of genes and populations, whereas Darwinism was concerned mainly with individuals. This is a major paradigm shift and those who fail to appreciate it find themselves out of step with the thinking of evolutionary biologists. Many instances of such confusion can be seen in the newsgroups, in the popular press, and in the writings of anti-evolutionists.[39]

Chromosome

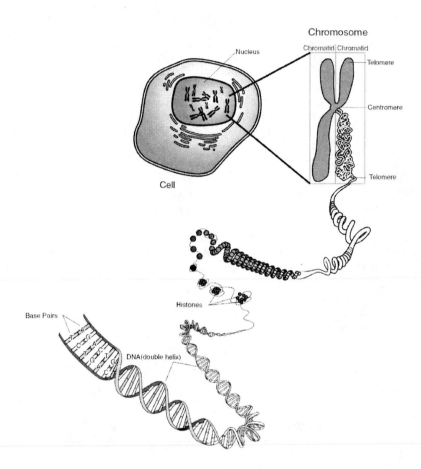

Figure 2.1

As a result of these and other developments, scientists began to understand the molecular processes involved in evolution. Today, it is our knowledge of how evolution operates at the molecular level that ultimately demonstrates the invalidity of the animal model. To fully appreciate how this is so, and how the non-animal methodologies are breaking new scientific ground, let's review some basics involving cell biology and genetics.

Cell Biology In A Nutshell

What is life—at least, biologically and chemically speaking? All living things are made up of cells, and more complex living beings, from horses to humans, are made up of many billions of cells. Each of these cells has its own special function; for example, nerve cells carry messages to the brain, while muscle cells control the movement of the body. The cell is the basic unit of life; it is the smallest structural unit of living organisms that is able to grow and reproduce independently. And each one is as alive as the plant, animal, or person it is part of. In its own way, a cell is born, it breathes, it takes in food, it eliminates waste, and, eventually, it dies. The structure of a cell is built chiefly of proteins, which in turn are made up of substances called amino acids. As such, proteins are critically important in building, maintaining, and repairing tissues in the body.

Proteins have a role in virtually every biological process that occurs in our bodies, and thus are essential for life. They instruct the body to build more cells and destroy others. They regulate all aspects of metabolism. They aid in respiration. They act as chemical messengers between different cells and parts of the body. They regulate the movement of substances in and out of cells and within they break food down so the body can absorb it. Just as each type of cell has a different function, so do proteins. Enzymes, for example, are a type of protein that speeds up chemical reactions. Albumin, a protein in the blood, helps maintain the body's fluid balance by keeping fluids in the blood instead of allowing them to seep into the tissues. Antibodies are proteins in the blood that help protect the body from disease. Several proteins can contribute to a single function, or one protein can serve several functions.

The nucleus is the control center of each cell—in other words, it directs all the cell's activities. Within the nucleus are the chromosomes (see figure 2.1 "chromosome") - long, threadlike strands made up of deoxyribonucleic acid (DNA), tightly coiled and packaged with proteins (see Fig 2.2 "DNA"). Genes are segments of DNA that encode instructions that enable a cell to produce a protein (see Fig 2.3 "Gene"). Every cell has tens of thousands of genes, and the difference between all forms of life lies in the genes. A single gene may explain why some people are sprinters and others are long distance runners.[40] A genome is a set of all the genes a species has on its chromosomes.

Deoxyribonucleic Acid (DNA)

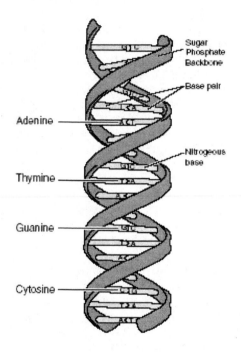

Figure 2.2

Gene Advanced

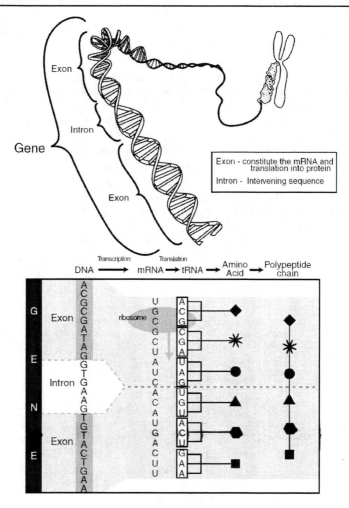

Figure 2.3

Most people are familiar with the famous double helix, or spiral staircase, that illustrates a strand of DNA (see figure 2.2). But what does it really illustrate? The sugar-phosphate backbone of the helix holds the all-important bases in position like the teeth of a rungs of a ladder. There are four types of nucleotide bases in DNA—adenine (A), guanine (G), thymine (T), and cytosine (C). These are always paired together—adenine with thymine (AT) and cytosine with guanine (CG). Together, these are called base pairs. The chains of phosphates and sugars form the sides of the "staircase," while the base pairs are the "steps" that hold the chains together. In humans, DNA molecules typically have more than 100 million base pairs.

Thus, the genome contains the complete set of instructions for making the proteins that an organism needs to survive. Each cell has 46 chromosomes of double-stranded DNA. Each chromosome is made up of 50 to 250 million bases of DNA. While it is true that every cell contains 100% of an organism's DNA, different cells need different proteins, so different genes are activated or 'expressed' in different cells. The cell will activate whatever gene it needs otherwise, the gene will be turned off. Some genes stay turned off for the entire life of an individual, while others are turned on almost continuously. (This in part because cells differentiate into types in response to chemical/environmental signals. Two cells may be genetically identical yet differ in type, because different genes are activated in each cell. The problem of differential gene activation is the problem of gene regulation, a matter studied by evolutionary-developmental biologists)

Gene expression is the process by which a cell makes a protein according to the instructions carried by a gene. It is a two-step process. The first step is known as transcription, and the second is translation (see figure 2.4 "RNA" and 2.5 "mRNA") for a diagram of the following). Transcription involves RNA, a close chemical cousin of DNA. Like DNA, RNA consists of long chains of nucleotide units. But, unlike DNA, which is only found in the nucleus, RNA may be found throughout the cell. During transcription, a cell makes an RNA copy of one of the DNA strands of a gene. Part of the DNA spiral staircase uncoils and splits, with one side of the staircase serving as a template for lining up the RNA bases. An RNA strand called messenger RNA (mRNA) is formed. The mRNA then travels out of the nucleus into the cytoplasm of the cells to the cell's protein factories, which are structures called ribosomes. In the translation step of gene expression, the ribosomes "read" the code in the mRNA and link amino acids in the order the mRNA dictates.

Just as the arrangement of the letters of the alphabet determine which words are made, so the order of A, T, G, and C determines which proteins are made. Proteins are composed of one or more chains of amino acids, of which there are 20 in common use (see figure 2.6 "Amino acid" and 2.7 "Protein"). Various combinations of these amino acids are linked to form long chains known as polypeptides.

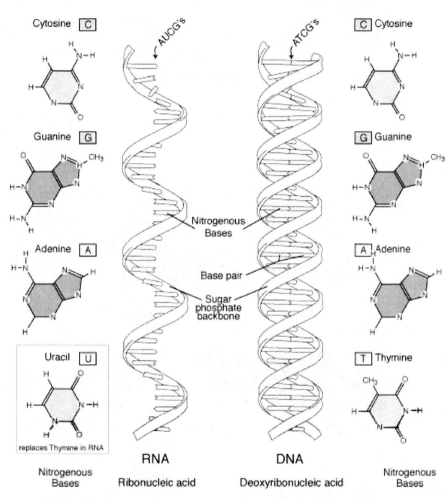

Figure 2.4

mRNA

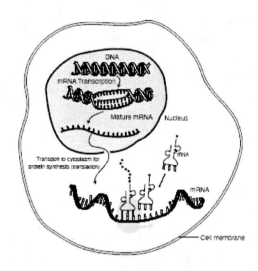

Figure 2.5

National
Institutes
of Health

National Human Genome Research Institute
Division of Intramural Research

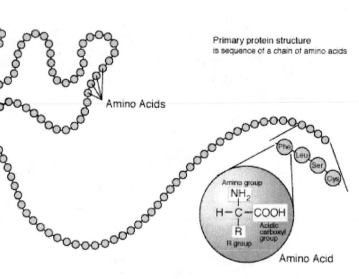

Primary protein structure
is sequence of a chain of amino acids

Amino Acids

Figure 2.6

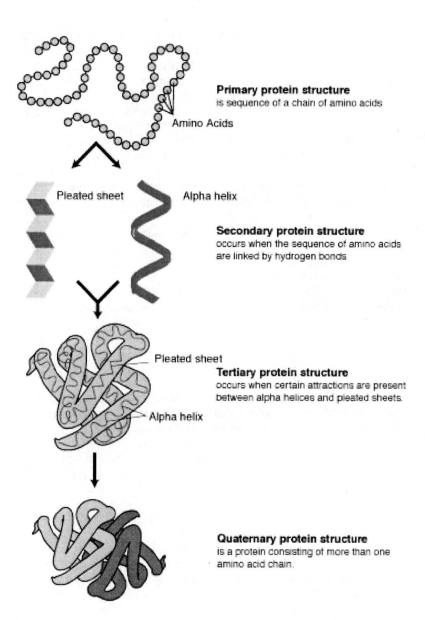

Primary protein structure
is sequence of a chain of amino acids

Amino Acids

Pleated sheet   Alpha helix

Secondary protein structure
occurs when the sequence of amino acids
are linked by hydrogen bonds

Pleated sheet

Tertiary protein structure
occurs when certain attractions are present
between alpha helices and pleated sheets.

Alpha helix

Quaternary protein structure
is a protein consisting of more than one
amino acid chain.

Figure 2.7

The cause of most human diseases lies in the proteins the body makes, the regulation of these proteins, and the protein-protein interactions. Today, the goal of medicine is to make drugs that target the dysfunctional protein and only the dysfunctional protein. And we have some already, including imatinib mesylate, ZD1839, and trastuzumab.[41] As of this writing, there are over 100 drugs based on the molecular understanding of cancer genes, in clinical trials.[42]

Genetic instructions are so complicated that mistakes (or 'mutations') can occur and some of them lead to disease. (Mutations, be they somatic or germline, refer to changes in the structure of DNA – deletions, insertions etc. Transcriptional and translational errors, which can also lead to disease are slightly different in nature.) As we will see in later chapters, the role of genes in certain diseases is well understood. In other instances, scientists suspect that many conditions involve a hereditary component, but have not yet identified the particular defective gene involved. In many cases, a gene with an inherited defect must be damaged in other ways before it causes illness. For example, cancer arises from defects in the genes that control cell growth and division. However, most people who develop cancer do not have inherited genetic defects. Instead, the genes have been damaged after birth by such environmental factors as chemicals, radiation, or other substances, including cigarette smoke.

More than 4,000 diseases are thought to be caused by hereditary gene mutations. However, not all genetic mutations cause disease; some mutations are "silent"—in other words, the change does not cause an abnormal protein to be produced, and therefore is not noticed in everyday life. In other cases, a genetic mutation may be so lethal that it causes a fetus to abort spontaneously. In still other instances, a mutation causes an abnormal protein to be produced, but the abnormal protein can function, just not as well as the normal protein. For example, certain alleles (a different form of the same gene) that encode the protein apolipoprotein-E have been associated with the development of heart disease and Alzheimer's disease. And there are countless other examples, as we will see in later chapters.

Why One Animal Cannot Model Another

Now, one may ask why, if virtually all disease lies in the genes, and if genes are composed of DNA, and the chemical composition of DNA is the same for all living things on earth, why can't animals be used to study human disease? After all, humans and chimpanzees share about 99.4 percent of the same genes. (Note that any two randomly generated sequences of DNA would be expected to share 25 percent homology, as there are only four base pairs.[43]) Isn't "close" good enough? Unfortunately, it is not. As we will now go on to explain, even our closest relatives do not make good models of human disease. At first glance, evolutionary similarity may appear to predict that animals can be used to model human disease. Yet ultimately, with better understanding of evolutionary biology in combination with our knowledge of molecular biology, we see why they cannot. In *Brute Science: Dilemmas of Animal Experimentation*, Hugh LaFollette and Niall Shanks pose the core ontological question:

> Since phylogenetically related species, say mammals, have all evolved from the same ancestral species, we would expect them to be, in some respects, biologically similar. Nonetheless, evolution also leads us to expect important biological differences between species; after all, the species have adapted to different ecological niches. However, Darwin's theory does not tell us how pervasive or significant those differences will be. This again brings the ontological problem of relevance to the fore. Will the similarities between species be pervasive and deep enough to justify extrapolation from animal test subjects to humans? Or will the biological differences be quantitatively or qualitatively substantial enough to make such extrapolations scientifically dubious?[44]

The answer, in large part, is supplied by Lewis Wolpert, in *Triumph of the Embryo*:

> Compare one's body to that of a chimpanzee—there are many similarities. Look for example, at its arms or legs, which have rather different proportion from our own, but are basically the same. If we look at the internal organs there is not much to distinguish a chimpanzee's heart or liver from our own. Even if we examined the cells in these organs, we will again find that they are very similar to ours. Yet we are different, very different from chimpanzees...We posses no cell types that the chimpanzee does not, nor does the chimpanzee have any cells that we do not have. The difference between us and the chimpanzee lies in the spatial organization of the cells.[45]

And as King and Wilson write about the mechanism that leads to different spatial organization of cells:

> Small differences in the timing of activation or in the level of activity of a single gene could in principle influence considerably the systems controlling embryonic development. The organismal differences between chimpanzees and humans would then result chiefly from genetic changes in a few regulatory systems....

Simply put, the difference between humans and chimpanzees (indeed, between all species) is not merely the composition of the DNA, but how the genes are *regulated*—that is, when they are turned on and off. Dog or daisy, human or hippopotamus, life at its most basic, microscopic level is made up of the same DNA units (adenine/thymine and guanine/cytosine), and they are assembled using the same process. But even infinitesimal dissimilarities in gene sequence or regulation can lead to major differences in how a living being responds to food, the environment, and medications. Further, as LaFollette and Shanks go on to say, understanding the role of regulatory genes in evolution is:

> ...crucial to proper understanding of biological phenomena. First, they focus our attention not merely on structural similarities and differences between organisms, but also on the similarities and differences in regulatory mechanisms. Second, they illustrate an important fact about complex, evolved animal systems: very small differences between them can be of enormous biological significance. Profound differences between species need not indicate any large quantitative genetic differences between them. Instead, even very small differences, allowed to propagate in developmental time, can have dramatic morphological and physiological consequences.[46]

Structural genes are responsible for building the proteins of which the body is composed. The regulatory genes turn the structural genes on and off, thus affecting the development of the embryo and the organism. Scientists are now beginning to understand that it is the regulatory genes, more than the structural genes that make all the difference between species. Gerald Weissman writes in *The Year of the Genome*:

> The problem (and in some senses the paradox) is that protein and gene sequences in the common chimpanzees and in humans are remarkably similar. In fact, human and chimpanzee proteins appear to be nearly 99 percent identical at the amino acid level, and it is widely assumed that the same percentage similarity prevails at the DNA level. Yet no one could mistake the two species as one. What these examples suggest is that only exceedingly minimal changes in genome sequences may be necessary to specific separate species, possibly with larger percentage changes in gene expression patterns. Of course, the longer any two such related lineages evolve separately from each other, the greater the genetic differences between them may become. However, in terms of the origins of unity and diversity, it is humbling as it is surprising to realize how very small the differences in the overall genome may be between two lineages as they separate from each other and thus extends our planet's biodiversity.[47]

On December 4, 2002 the international Mouse Sequencing Consortium announced the publication of the near complete (96 percent) mouse genome. It also announced that a comparative analysis of the mouse and human genomes was almost complete. This represented the first time the human genome has been compared to the genome of another animal. The study estimated that mice and humans share about 97.5 percent of their working DNA—at most just two percent less than chimpanzees and humans, suggesting that neither genome has changed much since the two species shared a common ancestor 100 million years ago.[48] The study led Tim Hubbard, head of genome analysis at the Sanger Institute in Cambridge, UK, to dismiss the significance of the 2.5 percent difference, proposing instead that the genes might in fact be all identical, and that differences between species might arise solely through divergence in the regulatory regions.[49]

Mouse researchers are heralding this event as a breakthrough, saying it will allow them to experimentally test and learn more about the function of human genes, leading to better understanding of human disease and improved treatments and cures. The theory/idea is that by 'knocking out' all the mouse genes one by one, we will discover their function and thus deduce the function of supposedly corresponding human genes. The premise is that similar genes in humans and mice will share the same functions. But, as we have seen, just because we share the same genes does not mean those genes are *regulated* the same and thus involved in the same functions. A good example would be the recent discovery that a faulty gene leads to eye tumors in some children but a similar fault in the same gene in mice leads to brain cancer, not eye tumours.

So what does this mean in terms of using the mouse to find cures for human diseases? In the harsh light of day, not much. "For all their similarities, mice are mice and people are people," says biologist Joe Nadeau.

The claim that humans and mice are the same animal at the biochemical level, but just dressed up differently, simply isn't true. Moreover, it is irrelevant to point to observed similarities in genetic makeup between species, since the details of the differences are in the (regulation of) interactions between conserved genes, (differences in the upstream regulators of such genes along with their downstream targets) not in the genes themselves—it is as though humans and mice have a common genetic keyboard on which different phenotypic tunes are being played. What matters is not the similarity with respect to the keyboard, but differences with respect to the order and timing of the pressing of the keys (keys being equal to structural genes, keys pressed on or off by regulatory genes).

Very small differences in gene sequence or regulation can lead to profound biological, physiological, and chemical differences between species. This is the most fundamental reason why using the animal model is an outmoded—and even dangerous—practice. Since living organisms are *complex* systems, related to each other in a non-linear fashion, extrapolation between them is inherently unpredictable.

There is yet another reason individual differ: epigenetics. Epigenetics is defined as: the study of the processes involved in the unfolding development of an organism. (This includes phenomena such as X chromosome inactivation in mammalian females, and gene silencing within an organism); and/or, the study of heritable changes in gene function that occur without a change in the sequence of nuclear DNA. This includes the study of how environmental factors affecting a parent can result in changes in the way genes are expressed in the offspring. Most traits are passed via DNA in the nucleus of the cell as described above but some DNA also resides outside the nucleus. This extrachromosomal DNA might further explain why identical twins differ in disease and drug response. It is well known that just because one identical twin suffers from a disease, say diabetes, the other twin might not. The genes in the nucleus are identical but the other, extrachromosomal DNA and RNA is not necessarily identical. Some believe epimutations are involved in many diseases such as diabetes, schizophrenia, and cancer among others. These genes may regulate other genes thus turning them off might stop some diseases.[50]

Implications for the Animal Model

Many years ago, before Darwin's theory of evolution, before the discovery of DNA, before scientists had access to today's technology, we were able to learn things about humans from animals. Horses have hearts, as do humans. Monkeys have immune systems, as do humans. But as the focus of biomedicine becomes increasingly fine-grained, the differences between humans and other animals outweigh the similarities. Evolutionary biology predicts and molecular biology confirms that using one species to study disease or drug response in another will be futile, if not hazardous. (In other words, animals have the same basic biological principles, but they are modulated in different ways by historical evolutionary processes. Mice and men obey the same biological principles, but they do so in different ways reflective of their unique histories. Ships float in the sea, and planes fly in the air. The laws of physics are satisfied, but ships don't float for the same reason that planes fly.)

Today, technology enables us to study human disease at the genetic level—precisely where species differentiation is most pronounced, making animal-modeled research hopelessly outdated. Even genetically engineered animals—for example, knockout mice that have had one or more of their genes removed to create a specific defect, and transgenic animals, which carry genes from another species—have failed to shed new light on human disease. Why? Because changing one or two genes out of 30,000 will not make a human out of a mouse. (The genes will interact with the mouse's other 30,000 genes and behave in a completely different way from how they perform in their natural human environment)

Entire volumes can be written on how research using mice has sidetracked real progress against cancer, but one recent example illustrates the folly of relying on the mouse model to study human cancer. Researchers at the Duke Comprehensive Cancer Center have found that a known cancer-causing gene, *Ras*, may cause cancer in humans via a different pathway than in mice. *Ras* is activated in one-third of all human cancers, and as much as 90 percent in specific cancers, such as pancreatic, so its importance cannot be overstated. Scientists have long assumed that *Ras* operates in the same way in humans as it does in mice. However, the study found that the *Ras* gene appears to use a different protein pathway, called RalGEFs, in order to transform normal human cells into cancer. Unfortunately, little is known about RalGEFs. Why? Because RalGEFs does not operate in mouse cells. According to Christopher Counter, PhD., the cancer biologist who led the research team, "The Ras oncogene appears to exert its function in humans through a pathway that was largely ignored."[51]

Such is the story of animal experimentation.

Chapter 3

Genomics, Proteomics, and the New Renaissance in Biomedical Research

"I never think of the future—it comes soon enough."
                                        Albert Einstein (1879-1955)

The date is April 26, 2010. Today, Margaret Henderson, a 39-year-old mother of two, has just completed the basics of her annual checkup with her internist, Dr. Hugh Crandell. Margaret's history medical history is unremarkable; and just like the previous year, Dr. Crandell's examination yields nothing to indicate any concern. Then, Margaret mentions that her older brother Dennis, an investment broker in his mid-40's, has just been diagnosed with colon cancer. Dr. Crandell is suddenly intrigued, and asks Margaret if any other family members have been diagnosed with colon cancer. She recalls that an aunt on her mother's side died of colon cancer some time ago, as well as an older cousin, also on her mother's side, who might also have died of the same disease. Dr. Crandell wonders whether the family has a history of familial polyposis, a rare, inherited disorder in which the rectum and colon are covered with multiple polyps. (Polyps are growths, or tumors, on a mucous membrane; polyps within the colon or large intestine may become malignant.) In cases of familial polyposis, patients and members of his or her family are closely monitored, since left untreated, the condition usually results in cancer by the time a patient is 40 years old.

After Margaret leaves Dr. Crandell's office, he requests Dennis' pathology report from his oncologist but sees no indication of familial polyposis. Because Dr. Crandell knows that other forms of colon cancer can also be inherited, he goes online to the web site *Online Mendelian Inheritance in Man*. There, he confirms that nonpolyposis colon cancers can be inherited. Dr. Crandell promptly recommended genetic testing for Margaret.

At the same time Margaret is having her blood drawn, her brother's physician calls to report that Dennis has a deleterious mutation in a gene called *MLH1*, a gene that is supposed to repair other genes. Shortly after that, Margaret's genetic testing reveals that she has the same mutation, and thus is at much higher risk not only for colon cancer, but also for endometrial cancer. As a result of these findings, Dr. Crandell recommends that, in addition to her annual pelvic exam, Margaret should have an annual colonoscopy and transvaginal ultrasound. Both these tests will detect any cancer at the very earliest stages.

Four years later, Margaret's colonoscopy reveals a precancerous lesion, which is immediately removed.

Fast forward to April 26, 2020. Born just 36 hours ago at Mercy Memorial Hospital, Adam Harwood is leaving the hospital in the arms of his elated parents. Embedded in Adam's shoulder is a tiny chip that carries his entire genome. Two months prior to his birth, Adam's genome was analyzed *in utero*, which revealed the diseases to which he is prone. Now, Adam's physicians will have the information they need to take whatever preventive measures are appropriate to prevent the diseases Adam is likely to develop. In the event that Adam needs medical treatment, his medications will be tailor-made to interact perfectly with his genes. These medications will work at the level of the genes themselves or on the proteins the genes product. As a result, Adam will receive more effective treatment with few, if any, side effects.

Both Margaret and Adam's case histories illustrate the future of genomics, and the remarkable potential this burgeoning field of research has for making a profound and positive impact on human health. In fact, not since the daring and groundbreaking work of Andreas Vesalius (1514-1564), the Flemish anatomist and physician often called the founder of human anatomy, has there been such a dramatic upheaval, in biomedical research. Vesalius is most noted for risking imprisonment and execution for performing dissections on human corpses at a time when the practice was illegal. Vesalius' work advanced the knowledge of human anatomy more than anything that preceded it, and thus the Renaissance, as it pertains to medicine, was born. In our era, mapping the human genome—in addition to being yet another example of what human-based research can accomplish, is no less an achievement, and heralds no fewer changes in the way medicine will be practiced.

New Windows to Knowledge: The Human Genome Project and the Human Proteome Project

This new Renaissance began officially in 1990, with the initiation of the Human Genome Project (HGP) as a joint, 13-year effort between the U.S. Department of Energy and the National Institutes of Health and other groups. The goals of the Human Genome Project include identifying **all the approximately 30,000 genes** in human DNA and determining the sequences of the three billion chemical base pairs that make up human DNA.[52] In June 2000, the U.S. government and the private corporation Celera Genomics jointly announced the completion of a working draft of the entire genome sequence, and initial analyses of the sequence were published in February 2001. A more polished, or high quality, version of the sequence was released in 2003. This high-quality sequence closed gaps, reduced ambiguities, and allowed for only a single error every 10,000 bases, which is the agreed-upon standard for HGP finished sequence. Geneticists agreed that this high-quality sequence is critical for recognizing regulatory components of genes.

The completion of the working draft to high quality by 2003 coincided with the 50th anniversary of James D. Watson and Francis H.C. Crick's proposal of the model of the chemical structure of DNA, which launched the era of molecular genetics. One of the first breakthroughs in the genetic basis of disease came in 1959, three years after the correct number of human chromosomes was ascertained, when Jerome Lejeune found that the disorder known as Down's syndrome, which is characterized by mental impairment and such physical features as upward-slanting eyes, a flat nose, a small head, and short hands, was caused by an abnormality in the number of chromosomes. People with Down's syndrome have 47 chromosomes instead of the normal 46, or 23 pairs. The extra chromosome occurs as a third chromosome with the pair that has been designated as chromosome 21. (Today, Down's syndrome is often referred to as Trisomy 21.) Soon after, it was discovered that Turner's syndrome and Klinefelter's syndrome were also due to chromosomal abnormalities. (Turners' syndrome is a chromosome anomaly of females in which one of the two female sex chromosomes is missing, so that there are only 45, instead of 46 chromosomes, resulting in a person having the physical appearance of an immature female, while Klinefelter's syndrome is a genetic disease in males, caused by the presence of one or more extra female sex chromosomes.) Other discoveries, such as Trisomy 13, a congenital defect that causes anatomic defects of the brain, cleft palate, cleft lip, and other physical and mental problems, and Trisomy 18, caused by an additional chromosome 18 and resulting in a number of physical and cardiovascular defects, as well as other chromosomal abnormalities, quickly followed. The ability to obtain and culture amniotic fluid and study it for chromosomal abnormalities began in 1966, thus allowing the prenatal diagnosis of Down's syndrome and enzyme disorders.

The mapping of specific genes to specific chromosomes grew exponentially in the 1980s with the birth of molecular genetics. Molecular genetics allowed three things to happen:

1.   It provided DNA problems for analysis of somatic cell hybrids so that **one** could "go directly for the gene" and not require expression of the human **gene in the** hybrid cells.
2.   It provided DNA probes (at first radioactive, later fluorescent) for *in situ* hybridization to chromosomes.
3.   Most importantly, molecular genetics provided an abundance of DNA markers that could be used for family linkage studies.[53]

In 1983, Huntington's disease, a severe hereditary disorder of the nervous system caused by an abnormal gene located on one of the pair of chromosomes designated as chromosome 4, was the first disease to be mapped through the new technique of family linkage studies using DNA markers. Recently, researchers at Johns Hopkins Medical Institutions have discovered a gene mutation that causes a condition identical to Huntington's disease, called Huntington's disease-like 2 (HDL2), which may not only help scientists better understand Huntington's, but also reveal why some diseases, like Huntington's Alzheimer's, and Parkinson's, destroy some brain cells while sparing others.[54] The implications for biomedical research in discoveries like this are monumental. As Richard Weinshilboum, MD, director of Mayo Clinic's Genomics Research Center, writes: "The genomic revolution will profoundly alter 21st century medicine and promises to provide insight into the cause, treatment and –ultimately–the prevention of diseases such as cancer, heart disease, and Alzheimer's disease."[55]

Eugene Chan, founder of U.S. Genomics, envisions a day in the not-too-distant future when rapid genome sequencing will impact every single possible element in medicine. According to Chan, who has a patent for an instrument known as the Gene Engine, with which he hopes to eventually be able to decipher an entire genome in half an hour:

> When a person is born, their genome will be scanned, analyzed, and stored. That information will then be reaccessed later. Health care will be cheaper because of the amount of preventative care by you can provide having this genetic information. Drugs will be cheaper to develop. And these new therapies are going to be so much more elegant than traditional therapies....What we're going to start seeing with genomics-based medicine is the ability to be able to customize drugs so they will be targeted only to the disease-causing cells and will have only minimal side effects. People will be making fewer doctor visits, they'll be feeling healthier, living longer, and having a better quality of life.[56]

Proteomics

Once the working draft of the Human Genome Project was completed, it became apparent that the total number of genes in the human body was approximately 30,000, rather than the 100,000 or more that had long been expected. This led to the demise of a long-held biological dogma: the one-gene-to-one-protein theory. According to this theory, each gene coded for one and only one protein. Now we know that genes code for polypeptides, which are then processed into functional proteins. Polypeptides from different genes can be spliced together in different combinations to make a variety of proteins. This new knowledge is sparking yet another renaissance of sorts—proteomics, which, according to the Human Proteome Organisation (HUPO), is the study of the function, regulation, and expression of proteins in relation to the normal function of the cell and in the initiation or progression of a disease state.[57] Because most diseases are manifested at the level of protein activity, the study of proteomics, will, as the study of genomics, have a profound impact on human health.

With all the discoveries that have occurred already as a result of the Human Genome Project, genes are in the spotlight. But what will truly alter the course of biomedical research is what the study of proteins will reveal. That's because proteins perform most life functions and comprise the majority of cellular structures. According to *Science*, "The rise of proteomics represents a change in research style that follows in the footsteps of the genomics revolution, a move towards more systematic analyses of large sets of proteins."[58]

According to the HUPO, proteomics offers huge applications, including:

• The identification of specific proteins as highly accurate and sensitive markers for diseases at a very early stage, thus ensuring their utility in a diagnostic capacity.

• The importance of under or over expression of proteins identified as disease markers in the prognosis and monitoring of therapeutic treatments.

• The insight provided by a knowledge of protein expression patterns vis-à-vis identification of toxic side effects during drug screening and lead optimization.

• The identification of proteins as valid targets for therapeutic agents, thus having an important role in the development of new therapeutic treatments.[59]

As Prof. Ian Humphery-Smith of the University of Utrecht and Glucose Proteomics, and one of the founding members of the HUPO, states:

> Proteins are central to our understanding of cellular function and disease processes and without a concerted effort in proteomics the fruits of genomics will go unrealized. The necessity of proteomics cannot be avoided...[60]

Prof. Sam Haunch from the University of Michigan had this to say about the potential of proteomics in cancer research:

> In the field of cancer research, proteomics will very likely fill an unmet need for reliable markers that allow early diagnosis to be made. Also proteomics will likely provide a multitude of novel targets for chemoprevention and therapy, as we understand the role of protein modifications and protein-protein interactions in diseases.[61]

The Human Proteome Project, which is still in its beginning stages, is to proteins what the Human Genome Project has been to genes. The Human Proteome Project will attempt to catalogue all the proteins in the human body. It will consist of two branches: profiling proteomics and functional proteomics. The profiling proteins are those that are expressed in a greater or lesser amount in a diseased condition than in a healthy normal state; thus, they serve as an identifier for the disease. Functional proteomics seeks to catalogue proteins by their function.

The proteome is defined as the constellation of all proteins in a cell. Mapping the human proteome will be a far more challenging project than mapping the genome. Whereas the genome is relatively unchanging, the proteome is much more dynamic, changing from minute to minute in response to intra- and extra-cellular environmental signals. Proteins are able to attach specific molecules to their ends; they can move around in a cell, bind with other proteins, and vary in abundance over time.[62] But the rewards will be extraordinary, if the proper investment and resources are given toward it, as Prof. Joachim Klose of Humboldt University in Germany, a researcher in the field of proteomics for more than 25 years, asserts:

> Proteome analysis will only contribute substantially to our understanding of complex human diseases like cancer and cardiovascular diseases, if a worldwide endeavor is initiated aiming at a systematic characterization of all human proteins with regard to such fundamental biological properties as tissue cell organelle specificity, developmental stage and age specificity and genetic variability among human individuals.[63]

Recent findings by researchers at Johns Hopkins Medical Institutions offer a preview of discoveries to come. In 2002, scientists there were able to determine the three-dimensional structure of a part of a protein called HER3, According to Dan Leahy, PhD., a Professor of Biophysics in Hopkins' Institute for Basic Biomedical Sciences, this will provide the first opportunity to rationally design new drugs to interfere with the HER family of proteins, possibly preventing or treating select forms of cancer. "Until we know proteins' structures, we're very limited in figuring out how a molecule or possible drug might bind...We now have a starting point to see how molecules binding to HER3 change its shape and turn it on."[64]

Another example of how new understanding of proteins will accelerate biomedical research is the discovery by scientists at London's Kings College (and their colleagues elsewhere) of a gene that prevents HIV from reproducing, but which is itself blocked by an HIV protein. This discovery has been heralded as a significant step in solving one of the great mysteries of the virus. Researchers found that a gene called *CEM15* is a natural inhibitor of HIV. They showed that a protein called Virion infectivity factor (Vif) enables *CEM15* to stop the virus from replicating. The discovery, according to virologist Roger J. Pomeranz, MD, "could start a new genre of AIDS drugs."[65]

Maps and Microarrays: Harnessing the Power of Technology for Genomics and Proteomics Research

Since there are thousands of genes coding for hundreds of thousands of proteins, analyzing them all is a complex and time-consuming task. A wide range of new technologies has been developed to accomplish this. In fact, without highly sophisticated technology, and the ability to archive into huge databases all the extraordinary amount of biological data it is generating, none of this would be possible. But, thanks to such technologies as DNA chips and other remarkable advances, scientists are now able to analyze thousands of genes simultaneously. As US President Bill Clinton stated in his 1998 State of the Union address, "Gene chips will offer a road map for prevention of illness throughout a lifetime."

Since the Human Genome Project has pointed out the similarities among humans, scientists have been trying to pinpoint which genes cause the differences.

DNA microarrays—also known as DNA chips or gene chips—are one of the revolutionary new tools that provide a means of accomplishing this through high speed genetic analysis (see figure 3.1 "Micro array"). DNA microarrays, which are manufactured using a process similar to the one used to make computer microchips, consist of a small glass plate covered in gene fragments arranged in a grid.

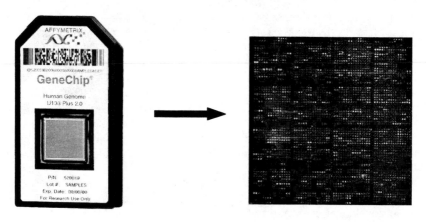

Figure 3.1

A microarray is a glass or nylon slide dotted with thousands of tiny samples of DNA, each representing a different gene. Microarrays rely on the ability of one strand of DNA to stick to another strand with a complementary sequence.

The chips enable scientists to evaluate large portions of the genome by providing a snapshot of the interactions among thousands of genes. To identify gene mutations, scientists first obtain a sample of DNA they wish to test, and a sample that does not contain a gene mutation. Then they separate the samples of DNA into single strands and cut them into smaller, more manageable segments. Next, they label the segments with fluorescent dye—the test sample with one color, and the normal sample another color. Both sets of labeled DNA are then inserted into a chip, which contains single stranded DNA sequences identical to a normal gene. The samples are allowed to hybridize, or bind, to the gene on the chip. If the test sample does not have a mutation for the gene, both sets will bind with the sequences on the chip. (Perfectly matched strands of DNA will bind more tightly than those that have mismatches.) If the test sample does contain a mutation, it will not bind properly in the region where the mutation is located. The pattern and intensity of light emitted reveals the activity of each of the genes on the chip. (See figure 3.2.)

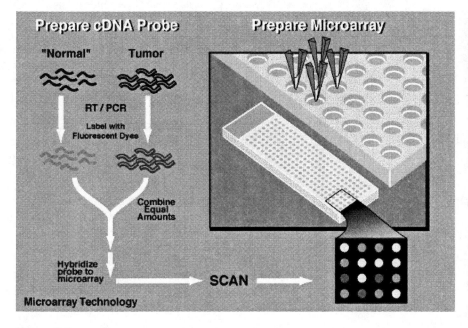

Figure 3.2

In "The Cancer Revolution" published in *New Scientist,* August 2003, Garry Hamilton described the importance of microarrays:[66]

> Charles Perou, a cancer biologist at the University of North Carolina in Chapel Hill, discovered that breast cancer can arise from several different kinds of breast cell types, not just one as previously suspected. "They are multiple cell types giving rise to similar-looking tumours that are actually biologically very different. We're finding diseases within diseases."

> ...Garret Hampton, a cancer biologist at the Novartis Research Foundation in San Diego said: "For the first time we're beginning to tell the difference between tumours that microscopically look the same. This is the key that will one day allow us to tell whether a patient with a particular sort of

tumour has a good prognosis or a poor one, and what sort of chemotherapy is appropriate."

... Until recently, evidence from tests done on lab animals suggested that metastasis is a process involving a challenging series of steps that cells can perform only after undergoing a specific and complicated sequence of genetic changes. Such cells are extremely rare - they're estimated to represent only 1 out of every 10 million primary tumour cells. Indeed biologists have come to view them as the decathletes of cancer - rare specimens that can escape the primary tumour, survive in circulation, out-fox the immune system, invade a new site, trigger the growth of new blood vessels and so on. This would explain why only 0.01 per cent of the cells that tumours constantly shed form metastases. It also suggests that the bigger tumours grow, the more likely they are to metastasise.

But results from microarray studies published in January challenge this wisdom. Working with Golub, Harvard Medical School's Sridhar Ramaswamy originally wanted to identify the genetic differences between normal primary tumour cells and metastatic cells. Surprisingly, he found that the gene signature of metastatic tumours was also present in some primary tumours. This raises the possibility that cells destined to metastasise already bear their distinctive signature at the stage when they are first detected. To test this, Ramaswamy looked for the metastatic gene signature in a separate collection of early primary lung tumour samples. He found that some of the samples carried the metastatic signatures while others didn't. When he analysed charts from the patients donating the samples, he found that the primary tumours carrying a metastatic signature were more likely to spread and kill.

Ramaswamy has proved his point by successfully predicting the likelihood of metastasis in different forms of cancer from different tissues, including breast and prostate. This suggests that the genetic mechanism driving metastasis is the same in all cancers, and not different as once thought. Together these results suggest that right from the start, cancers that are destined to metastasise are fundamentally different from those that never spread. It also indicates that the potential for cancers to spread may be less dependent on tumour size than previously thought.

Ramaswamy's findings also tie in with results from last year's study by Dutch and American scientists who used microarrays to identify genes that can act as a warning flag for metastasis when active in early breast cancer cells. Currently, all breast cancer patients undergo chemotherapy after surgery because doctors can't identify the 20 to 30 per cent who might be harbouring microscopic clumps of cancer cells that have already spread.

Being able to predict which tumours are destined to metastasise would spare many patients the toxic side effects of drugs they didn't need. With that in mind, the Dutch-American team has begun a clinical trial to see if the metastatic signature can be used to single out those patients in need of more aggressive treatment. [67]

Microarrays can be used to study and find oncogenes (cancer-causing genes), study how a disease is caused by or affects certain genes, search for the effects of a chemical on a subset of genes, or identify the gene expression pattern for a particular cell in a tissue. They are helping scientists elucidate which genes are involved in disease, as demonstrated by the work of researchers from the McKusick-Nathans Institute for Genetic Medicine at Johns Hopkins, which successfully used DNA microarrays to identify two genes that work together to cause Hirschsprung disease, an inherited intestinal disorder. Their work is the first published evidence that genome-wide scanning using DNA chips, can reveal the underpinning of disease caused by multiple genes. The scientists probed the genomes of affected children and parents from 43 Mennonite families. The researchers chose these families because Hirschsprung disease occurs in Mennonite communities in about 1 out of 500 births—a rate about 10 times higher than in the general population. They found that variations in two genes had to co-exist to cause disease in these families.[68]

DNA microarrays are also helping scientists to profile gene expression in the tumors of patients, which may help physicians decide which patients are best suited for which therapy.[69] For example, patients with diffuse large B-cell lymphoma (DLBCL) were found to have one of two differently expressed forms of a gene, which turned out to correlate with their responses to chemotherapy.[70] DLBCL is the most common type of non-Hodgkin's lymphoma in adults. About 16,000 new cases are diagnosed in the U.S. each year, and standard chemotherapy is effective in only 40 percent of patients.

Here is another example that illustrates the power and potential of DNA microarrays using human tissue: by screening four human lung cancer cell lines, scientists were able to identify a gene that suppresses lung cancer. The more the gene was activated, the less invasive was the cancer. The scientists compared normal lung tissue with lung cancer tissue obtained from 80 patients. They found that the patients who had lower expression of *CRMP-1* mRNA in the cancerous tissues were more likely to have advanced disease and worse outcomes.[71]

It is all too common today that patients with the same cancer diagnosis receive the exact same treatment, but only a percentage are cured. Clearly, there are differences in the genes between the cancers of individuals, even though they were all classified as having the same disease. In the near future, gene profiling using DNA microarray analysis may prove better at predicting the clinical status of breast cancer and other cancers. Scientists at Duke University Medical Center in North Carolina have correlated specific genes with particular categories of breast cancer - predicting which types are more aggressive and which will respond well to treatments. Studies like this will allow physicians to determine which therapy to use and to predict outcomes for individual patients.[72]

It is a long road from identifying a gene's involvement in a disease to developing a cure for that disease but it is a crucial first step. The eventual aim is to discover the fault in the gene's protein product, so that that particular protein can be targeted for repair, replacement or elimination. Alternatively, the gene itself could be the target for repair or replacement, or simply switching off.

Advances in technology, such as DNA microarrays, and the rapidly increasing amount of biological data now available to work with, are sparking the growth of companies involved in human genetics research. VARIAGENICS, for example, is one of the companies that studies genes by analyzing a drug's mechanism of action. Genes involved in drug treatment can be identified by comparing gene expression profiles of drug-treated against untreated cells or tissues.[73]

Genomics Collaborative, Inc. (GCI) is a company that maintains a large bank of human DNA, sera, and snap-frozen tissue samples. All these samples are linked to detailed medical information collected from patient populations worldwide. According to the company's web site, it has recruited over 100,000 patients, and collections continue to build for diseases involving the heart and great vessels, inflammatory disorders, metabolic disorders, various cancers, and others. GCI's mission statement illustrate both the promise and the challenge of genomics research:

> Currently, the genomics research industry can access only limited quantities of high quality genomic DNA, sera and tissue linked to well-characterized clinical data and obtained with appropriate informed consent. These constraints limit a researcher's ability to perform high throughput, large-scale analysis, despite the availability of increasingly high-powered technology and tools for analysis. Through its Global Repository™, GCI breaks this bottleneck and serves as a vital partner in elucidating the genetic pathways which lead to products directed toward complex, multiple genetic diseases prevalent in the world's populations.

> GCI currently has DNA samples from populations suffering from hypertension, type II diabetes, osteoarthritis, lipid disorders, osteoporosis, asthma, colon cancer, and coronary artery disease. GCI has obtained extensive clinical histories, detailed demographic information, family history on three generations, Gold Standard clinical diagnostic information, and drug history, including adverse events on each patient.

GCI has tissue samples from matched normal tissues and patients suffering from cancer of the:

- Breast
- Colon
- Adrenal
- Bone
- CNS
- Cervix

- Esophagus
- Gall Bladder
- Intestine
- Prostate
- Kidney
- Larynx

- Lung & Pleura
- Lymph nodes
- Ovary & Uterus
- Bladder
- Salivary Glands
- Skin

- Stomach
- Thyroid

GCI has samples from both one-time collections and longitudinal collections. Longitudinal collections enable the monitoring of such information as disease progression and therapeutic response over time. GCI seeks to correlate clinical phenotypic information, longitudinal clinical information, genotypic data, expression data, and protein characterization.[74]

Technologies such as mass spectometry as well as computer algorithms, are helping proteomics researchers catalog proteins just as genomics researchers catalog genes. Already, Gavin MacBeath and Stuart L. Schreiber of Harvard University have developed a new protein microarray that enables them to observe protein-protein interactions and protein interactions with small molecules.[75] Scientists are also studying simple organisms to gain insight into genes and their function. By finding a gene that performs a particular function in, for example, a roundworm, we are seeing what that gene did in its original form many millions of years ago prior to its being used in more complex mammals including humans. Evolution changes the function of genes as they go from species to species. But some functions are more or less preserved, and it is far simpler to discover these functions in simple organism like bacteria, yeast, worms, fruit flies, and so forth, than in mammals.

While there is little if any value in the use of the animal model for testing drugs and studying human disease, there is value in studying these simple organisms, even in a time when the mind-boggling complexities of living things on our planet are being revealed in more detail every day. No one can deny that the simplest animals can provide tentative answers to some questions concerning the most basic processes common to all animal life. While very simple organisms do exhibit basic life processes that are seen in more complex organisms, complex organisms themselves do not offer such clear demonstrations due simply to the exponential increase in factors associated with any particular biological function. That is why we challenge the validity of using complex organisms as models for human disease and drug testing, *not* the concept of using simple organisms to learn basic things about life in general.

The comprehensive genetic profiling of *Saccharomyces cerevisiae* (yeast) has proved to be a successful model for understanding the basic functions of human cells. According to an international team of researchers, this work could lead ultimately to the discovery of better drugs for the treatment of human disease, including drugs to treat fungal infections, as well as drugs that act on gene products shared by the yeast and human genomes. Human cells have the same basic cellular plan as yeast, but it is easier to genetically manipulate yeast. According to the researchers, by creating a mutant strain for a large percentage of the 6,000 yeast genes, the project now allows genetics to be practiced on a comprehensive scale.[76]

Individual Variation: Linking Genes to Human Disease

It should come as no surprise that all humans are 99.9 percent identical in terms of genetic makeup. As a species, *Homo sapiens* has been in existence for only a short time—at least in evolutionary terms. Our human ancestors first evolved in Africa a mere 250,000 years ago and migrated out of Africa into the Middle East and Europe about 40,000 years ago (according to accepted wisdom). The original members of our species included only about 10,000 people. Today, only 7,000 generations later, *Homo sapiens sapiens*—the subspecies to which all existing people on earth belong—can trace its ancestry to these 10,000 people. (The genus *Homo* consists of one living species—*Homo sapiens*—and several extinct human species that are known only through fossil remains. The chimpanzee may in the future be included in the genus *Homo* but that is still controversial as of the writing of this book.) That does not leave much time, in evolutionary terms, for genetic mutations to separate us more than 0.1%.

As a result, each of us shares about 99.9 per cent of our DNA with other humans. If you were to take the DNA of two people from any two parts of the world, you would discover that they differ only by about one nucleotide letter (A, T, C, or G) in every 1,000-2,000 in their genetic code. This may not seem like much. But considering that each of these individuals has about 3.2 billion letters making up their complete genetic sequence this means there will be about 1.6-3.2 million places where genetic codes differ.

The bottom line is that thousands upon thousands of significant genetic differences exist between individuals. These differences are compounded by the fact that over 90 percent of human genes exist in more than one form in the human population. Some genes are known to exist in as many as 60 different forms or polymorphisms. That is why the Human Genome Diversity Project (HGDP) offers such a tremendous opportunity for learning more about these genetic variations, yielding far more accurate and relevant knowledge than one could ever hope for in animal models. The HGDP, which could be completed much quicker than the HGP, would explore the diversity that exists within the human genome. This would help scientists to determine which genes and single nucleotide polymorphisms (SNPs) make one person susceptible to the side effects of a certain drug while another is not.

SNPs (pronounced "snips") are places in DNA where one nucleotide is replaced by another—a G for a T, for example (see figure 3.3). All humans have SNPs. In "single-gene" diseases such as sickle cell anemia or cystic fibrosis, a SNP is responsible for the disease. The HGP revealed that if you look at an arbitrary strand of the DNA from two humans, 999 out of 1000 nucleotides would be identical. That 1 in 1,000 difference is what makes for about 80-90 percent of the differences between humans. SNPs can serve as markers for susceptibility to disease, responsivity to medications, or indicators of side effects to medication.

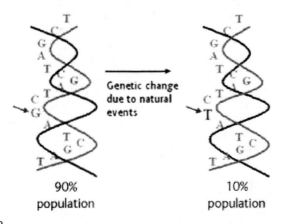

Figure 3.3

One of the unexpected findings of the Human Genome Project was that variations in the genetic makeup of people were much greater than expected. Scientists with Genaissance Pharmaceuticals Inc. of New Haven, Connecticut, studied 313 genes and found large variations between 82 unrelated people, primarily from four racial backgrounds—White, Black, Asian, and Hispanic. They found, on average, 14 different versions of each gene. Gerald Vovis, Genaissance chief technology officer and senior vice president stated, "The most surprising finding that came out of here was the fact that we found an enormous amount of variation within these genes which had not been known before." These genetic differences may help explain why people respond differently to various medications, and why one person contracts a disease while another does not. Francis Collins (of the Human Genome Project) stated about this discovery, "We have been talking a lot about how similar all of our genomes are, that we're 99.9 percent the same. That might tend to create an impression that it's a very static situation. But that 0.1 percent is still an awful lot of nucleotides (genetic building blocks)."

Genaissance researcher J. Claiborne Stephens stated that, if these finding are accurate then "the functional complement of the human genome is going to be a repertoire of something like 400,000 to 500,000 gene versions."[77] According to Dr. Gualberto Ruano, CEO of Genaissance, "These results will cause the scientific and medical communities to rethink the definition of the human genome. By being able to define gene versions, we can now determine those versions that predict drug response and...change the current drug paradigm that one drug fits all individuals."

This enormous genetic variety explains why there exist such differences in patient responses to drugs, said Dr. Stephens. "The safety and side effect profile of a drug in any particular individual depends largely on the versions of genes that each person has inherited" from his or her parents. "When you consider all of the SNPs out there in the human genome, the sheer number of them is overwhelming," Stephens told Reuters Health. "We think that an important question is how these SNPs are organized. This discovery will help reduce the complexity so that you can do these clinical trials—in terms of drug efficacy, adverse reactions, or even looking for disease genes—that's the way of really harnessing the variations that occur naturally in each gene."[78]

Many diseases are multifactorial - that is, environment and lifestyle factors as well as genes contribute to the manifestation of the disease. Finding the numerous genes involved in multifactorial diseases is much more difficult than finding the mutations responsible for single-gene disorders. In 2001, the gene NOD2 was found to contribute a 15 percent increase risk for Crohn's disease. With advances in technology, we should soon accumulate more knowledge about which genes are involved in which multifactorial diseases.

Dr. Mark A. Rubin, from the University of Michigan Medical School, Ann Arbor, used DNA microarray analysis to identify regulatory genes and candidate biomarkers in prostate cancer and found that alpha-methylacyl coenzyme A racemase (AMACR) is overexpressed in prostate cancer. It can be tested for and when combined with prostate-specific antigen (PSA), may become a new diagnostic tool for prostate cancer. AMACR is also overexpressed in colon cancer, so it may be beneficial in diagnosing colon cancer too.[79] Almost 30,000 men die each year from prostate cancer that has metastasized to other organs of the body. AMACR can be detected only in malignant cells, so screening for it may improve the chance of finding prostate cancer.[80] [81]

Of course, screening is not a cure but it does enable doctors to predict whether a patient's disease is likely to spread and design a treatment regimen based on that knowledge.[82]

Researchers are also finding ways to use a patient's particular genetic makeup to choose therapies that not only will work best but also cause the fewest side effects. A study conducted by Arul M. Chinnaiyan of the University of Michigan Medical School, along with his team of researchers, used DNA microarrays to assess the activity of genes in both localized and metastatic prostate cancer. They found 55 genes that exhibited greater activity in the metastatic samples than in the localized cases. This information may eventually allow doctors to use genetic testing to predict whether an individual patient's disease is likely to spread and design a treatment regimen based on that knowledge.[83]

In another study, appearing in *Journal of the American Medical Association (JAMA)*, Seattle scientists reported that people with high blood pressure who have a particular gene variant were 50 percent less likely to have a heart attack or stroke if they took an older medication known as a diuretic than if they took other blood pressure lowering drugs. And in yet another study in the same journal, University of Washington pharmacologists reported that people with particular genetic variants in enzymes that break down the drug warfarin are more likely to suffer serious, even life-threatening bleeding, if they take the medication. Warfarin, often sold as Coumadin, is given to prevent blood clots. "So what's happening is that patients with a variant in these genes break down the drug in the body too rapidly, allowing too much to get into the bloodstream, where it causes excessive bleeding."

Gene tests are already available for retinoblastoma, Wilms' tumor, familial adenomatous polyposis, hereditary nonpolyposis colon cancer (HNPCC), and the *BRCA1* gene mutation, which predisposes a person to hereditary breast cancer and ovarian cancer. In the near future, even more tests will be available, probably for cancers such as melanoma, leukemia, thyroid, and renal cell cancer. If a person is tested and the results are negative, he'll not only experience a great sense of relief relative to certain disease risk, but also the relief of being able to skip certain lab tests and uncomfortable procedures that he would otherwise have had to undergo every year. If a person tests positive, he and his physician can be more vigilant in taking measures to prevent the cancer and/or to catch the cancer early, when in all likelihood it will be treatable. Detecting mutated genes that are shed in urine, stool or saliva, will also aid in catching cancers earlier.

According to Professor William Bigbee, head of the Molecular Biomarkers Group in the cancer epidemiology program of the University of Pittsburgh Cancer Institute: "What we're starting to see is molecular or gene-based medicine moving on several fronts—diagnostic, therapeutic, and detection—at a level of sophistication that has not been seen before."[84] One example of this is Trugene, a gene-sequencing test that can detect potential resistance in patients suffering from AIDS. Dean Winslow, MD, head of clinical and regulatory affairs at Visible Genetics, the company that developed the test, stated, "This test is the first of many such gene sequencing tests that will change the way physicians make diagnoses and treat illness and disease."[85] Trugene allows physicians to detect whether HIV is growing resistant to drug therapy. AIDS patients' lives can be extended through combination drug cocktails, including the protease inhibitors. Unfortunately though, HIV can become resistant to these medications, and perhaps 60 percent of patients have a form of the virus that is resistant to at least one drug. Now, with Trugene, computer analysis of a blood sample could enable the physician to determine which drugs to prescribe.

It should come as no surprise that the study of humans has resulted in the great advances of linking genes to disease, as shown in the following studies. By studying tissue from 635 lung cancer patients, Dr. Christopher I. Amos, from M. D. Anderson Cancer Center in Houston, and colleagues found that people with polymorphisms in the gene for p53, a tumor suppressor protein, are at increased risk for lung cancer and the rate of these mutations differs by ethnicity. Polymorphisms were most common among African-Americans, with nearly 30 percent demonstrating a variant allele, while only 14.2 percent of Caucasians and 12.2 percent of Mexican-Americans demonstrated polymorphisms.[86]

While Herceptin is an excellent drug for some with breast cancer, in others it can do more harm than good. An assay has been developed that can be used to predict which patients are the best candidates for the drug.[87] Researchers were able to identify a faulty gene (*CHK2*), which can increase the risk of breast cancer by a factor of two, by studying more than 1,000 breast cancer patients who had a family history of the disease but who had not inherited *BRCA1* or *BRCA2* and then comparing their genes with healthy individuals.[88] Researchers at Shiga University in Japan have found that primary breast cancers often involve mutations in the *RB1CC1* gene, and combined with previous findings, indicate that *RB1CC1* may be a tumor-suppressor gene for breast cancer.[89]

By studying the breast tumors from 117 patients, scientists were able to determine that the ways genes are expressed as seen on DNA microarrays can be used to predict which breast cancers that are likely to metastasize. They found that analysis of 70 genes was adequate to allow prediction. Based on gene expression patterns, only about 20-30 percent women are at risk for metastatic disease, yet most are treated with chemotherapy or hormonal therapy in addition to surgery, Dr. van Veer, the author of the study stated: "Therefore we are overtreating 70 to 80 percent of breast cancer patients." This is a significant step in individualizing breast cancer therapy.[90]

By studying several thousand women with breast cancer, scientists were able to determine that over 50 percent of breast cancer cases are likely to occur in just 12 percent of women at high genetic risk. This means that women could soon be given screening tests to determine whether they carry these genes. These tests could also change the face of cancer prevention by allowing physicians to tailor treatment to needs instead of using a one-size-fits-all strategy.[91]

Japanese researchers are studying humans with cancer in order to map genetic differences that make certain drugs work for some patients but not others. They plan to analyze about 23,000 of the 30,000-plus genes in each of a thousand cancer patients. Since each anticancer drug is normally only effective for only 20 to 40 percent of patients, the devastating side effects so common with chemotherapeutics can be minimized. Not only can unnecessary side effects be avoided but also prognosis should be improved by starting the patient more efficiently on the drugs that are most appropriate for her.

Researchers will study the effects of about 10 drugs in treating seven types of cancer common among Japanese - including leukemia, stomach, lung, colon, and breast cancer. A key member of the team, Takashi Tsuruo, head of the Institute of Molecular and Cellular Biosciences at the University of Tokyo, said: "If we can exclude from a patient's treatment programme drugs whose effectiveness is doubtful for that particular person and choose the exact medication that is suitable, this will drastically change cancer treatments."[92]

By studying 16 families, scientists were able to learn that even very young children can develop medullary thyroid carcinoma when they bear the *RET* proto-oncogene mutation, which causes multiple endocrine neoplasia type 2 (MEN 2). The detection of this mutation could lead to life-saving thyroidectomy surgery.[93]

By studying patients affected with acute lymphoblastic leukemia (ALL), scientists were able to determine that polymorphisms in the genes for three enzymes, *NQO1*, *MPO*, and *CYP2E1*, involved in biotransformation of potential carcinogens increase the risk of childhood ALL. These genes regulate the biotransformation of a variety of xenobiotics and protect cells from the damage associated with free radicals. "There is a genetic contribution to the etiology of childhood leukemia. The underlying genetic susceptibility will be expressed when the child or the fetus is exposed to given chemicals. Several susceptibility genes as well as protective genes will be identified over the next years. Only then will we start to have a better picture of the genetic susceptibility to childhood cancer. The gene-gene and gene-environment interactions are other aspects that will need to be addressed in the near future. Our work is oriented towards preventive medicine, i.e., prevention at the level of the population by identifying risk factors"[94]

People vary from individual to individual as well as one population to another. By studying both normal and HIV-infected individuals in India, scientists were able to determine that Indians have lower CD4 T lymphocyte counts than Caucasians. This may lead to changes in when antiretroviral drugs are started in the Indian population. Currently, the Centers for Disease Control and Prevention (CDC) uses CD4 counts as an indicator of when to begin such therapy and to monitor the progress of HIV infection. However, since Indians may have naturally lower CD4 values they may not need antiretroviral treatment as early as their Caucasian counterparts.[95]

Ovarian cancer is the fifth leading cause of death from cancer among American women. Because it is so difficult to detect, most women have advanced disease at the time of diagnosis, making their prognosis grim. The five-year survival rate is 28 percent. If the cancer is detected while it is still confined to the ovaries, however, the five-year survival is around 90 percent. Hence there is a great need to detect this cancer early. Using transcriptional profiling, an *in vitro* research tool associated with mapping the genome, scientists were able to discover that ovarian cancer cells contain higher amounts of prostatsin, creatine kinase B, and osteopontin than normal ovarian tissue. This may allow early detection and hence a better chance of survival.[96] The tissue used in this study was obtained from women with ovarian cancer.

Dr. Michael Marmor, of New York University School of Medicine, and colleagues conducted genotyping for nearly 3,000 HIV-seronegative individuals from seven U.S. cities who were considered to be at high risk for HIV infection based on sexual behavior or injection drug use. They found that a mutation in the gene for the CCR5 receptor, called delta-32 mutation, provided significant protection against infection with HIV. This has implications for a vaccine and treatments. They found that even if people had only one gene that had this mutation, they were protected from HIV. This suggests that treatments or a vaccine do not need to result in complete blockade of all CCR5 receptor sites in order to be effective.[97] Gene analysis also revealed that the delta32 mutation of the *CCR5* receptor gene is associated with protection against HIV infection, even if the gene is in heterozygous form. It had already revealed that the homozygous mutation *CCR5-delta32/delta32* conferred strong resistance to infection by most strains of HIV-1. This was accomplished by studying the *CCR5* genotypes of 1892 men who have sex with men (MSM), 474 male injection drug users (IDUs), 347 women at heterosexual risk, and 283 female IDUs, all of whom were negative for HIV but at high risk for HIV infection. This discovery has implications for a vaccine, as it suggests that the protection against HIV infection could result from the diminished availability of CCR5 receptor sites in heterozygous (and homozygous) individuals compared with individuals without the mutation.[98]

Using high throughput microarray genotyping to sift through some 50,000 genes, Dr. Eric J. Topol of the Cleveland Clinic Foundation and associates discovered that multiple novel variants in the thrombospondin gene family appear to be associated with familial premature coronary artery disease. They studied 352 patients who had experienced either a myocardial infarction (heart attack), coronary revascularization, or been diagnosed with a significant coronary lesion before the age of 45 in men and 50 in women and who had at least one sibling likewise affected. The study included 400 families at 15 medical centers across the United States. The researchers compared the genotypes of the patients with those of 418 control subjects. They found that variants in three related members of the thrombospondin protein family were associated with premature coronary artery disease (CAD), primarily myocardial infarction."[99]

Researchers have identified two genetic mutations that work together to increase the risk of heart failure in Blacks by studying 159 patients with heart failure and 189 controls. According to a report published in *JAMA*, both of the mutations involve genes that code for adrenergic receptors. The alpha-2C-adrenergic receptor resides on cardiac nerves that release norepinephrine. When a certain amount of norepinephrine is released, the receptor is stimulated and stops further release. A specific mutation in the alpha-2C gene, known as *Del322-325*, prevents the receptor from shutting off norepinephrine release. Beta-1 adrenergic receptors, which are found on cardiac muscle cells, respond to norepinephrine by causing the muscle to contract. A mutation in the beta-1 gene, known as *Arg389*, produces a receptor that is overly sensitive to norepinephrine.[100]

Scientists are also using genomics to identify new diseases. For example, a team led by University of California San Francisco (UCSF) researchers has discovered a new disorder that can cause severely elevated blood cholesterol levels by searching a genetic database of about 12,000 patients and identifying a number of people who had mutations in a known gene. Then, they studied the family of one patient and found that carriers of mutations in the gene had elevated cholesterol. John Kane, MD, PhD, UCSF professor of medicine and senior author of a report on the findings, which appeared in *The Journal of Clinical Investigation*, said: "Our finding adds to the roster of genes that can cause a disorder of cholesterol in the blood and increase the risk of heart disease and stroke. By understanding the mechanism—how this gene affects cholesterol regulation—we can diagnose those at risk earlier and choose better treatments for them."[101]

Genomics is providing enlightenment to human behavior as well. Scientists have discovered that people who carry a particular genetic variant of a metabolizing enzyme appear to have more difficulty quitting the cigarette smoking habit than others. The study involved 426 White subjects who smoked at least 10 cigarettes a day and were trying to quit. "Once validated, this genetic variant could be used to identify smokers who are more prone to relapse and might benefit more from treatment," reported Dr. Caryn Lerman, from the University of Pennsylvania in Philadelphia, whose team discovered that people with *CYP2B6* variant experienced greater cravings for cigarettes when they tried to stop smoking.[102]

Genomics is not limited to humans. By studying the genomes of viruses, scientists can develop drugs and vaccines to treat viral infections. This has already occurred with viruses such as HIV, hepatitis, and influenza. After decoding the viral genome, scientists use computer programs to compare its sequence with that of other viruses. By doing this, scientists can locate genes and proteins that are susceptible to attack by a medication. By finding a gene or protein present in many viruses, and that hopefully is not present in humans, scientists can design antivirals that will be effective against many viruses. By feeding the gene into bacteria, millions of copies of the protein the gene codes for can be made. The protein can be isolated and purified and then used to see if new drug candidates bind to the protein.

Additionally, scientists can analyze the three-dimensional structure of the protein and design a drug to interfere with it. Respiratory syncytial virus, variola virus (the virus that causes smallpox), Ebola virus, hepatitis A, B, and C viruses and others have already been sequenced.

Examining the DNA of the organism is a new way to rapidly identify the presence of an infection. The World Health Organization estimates there may be about 50 million cases of dengue infection worldwide each year. Current laboratory tests check for antibodies to the virus, which takes 7 to 10 days. The Dengue Diagnostic Kit tests for the presence of dengue DNA in a blood sample and within hours will indicate which one of four types of the virus is present This may facilitate earlier detection of the mosquito-borne disease. Separate tests have to be carried out to determine the type of dengue.[103]

At the University of California, San Diego (UCSD), bioengineers have succeeded in developing a computer model that relates specific genetic mutations to exact variations of disease by using genetic information from patients who have an enzyme deficiency that causes hemolytic anemia. This feat represents the first model-based system for predicting phenotype based on genotype and actually defines the mechanism by which a genetic defect causes a disease—a mathematical calculation made by building a computer model based on the well-known metabolism in the human red blood cell. The team was able to predict which mutations would result in chronic hemolytic anemia and which would cause a less severe form of the disease by inserting specific DNA sequences into the computer model. Up until this breakthrough, most approaches have depended upon statistical correlations between reported mutations and occurrences of disease variants. Bernhard Palsson, Professor, Bioengineering at UCSD's Jacobs School of Engineering and leader of the team, predicts that there will eventually be a databank of specific genetic mutations that cause precise disease variants, which will be incredibly useful for drug development and will aid physicians in creating effective treatment plans for individuals.[104]

In fact, gene banks are already a reality in central Wisconsin, with the formation of the first large-scale gene bank in the United States—the Marshfield Clinic's Personalized Medicine Research Project. The Marshfield Project, which is being funded by a combination of federal and state grants and clinic contributions, is designed to bring the Human Genome Project from the laboratory to the patient's bedside, will collect DNA from 80,000 people and match the genetic profiles with medical histories and other information in a statistical database.[105] The project's leaders envision the gene bank as the first step toward the day when a person's individual genetic profile will be the ultimate medical record, providing a way to select medicines based on genes. First, the project's scientists are creating a database of genes, using a sophisticated computerized record-keeping system that captures key information on patients, such as laboratory data, x-rays, and diagnoses. Then, the scientists will search out subtle differences in the genetic characteristics of each of the people who have contributed to the database. Association studies, which will match the polymorphisms with patient records, will then be conducted, followed by comparison of the gene studies to disease. The hope is to reveal gene abnormalities that may be responsible for an individual's risk of developing disease.[106]

This is the research that will change lives and that should be funded instead of animal experiments. (For more examples of what the field of genomics is providing see www.curedisease.com.)

Genes and the Next Generation: Charting a Course for the Future

The plethora of discoveries linking specific genes to disease begs the question: what can we do with this information to ease human suffering and improve human health? Can these revelations help us prevent, treat, and cure disease? The answer is yes, and we are just beginning to discover the possibilities. Gene therapy involves transfection, or the introduction of new genetic information into cells for therapeutic purposes. Since genetic disease results when a gene is defective or missing, gene therapy makes it possible to correct such defects in the function of cells. Currently, gene therapy involves only somatic cells (body cells) of a patient, rather than the reproductive cells. Scientists believe that many genetic illnesses can be cured by supplying a functional gene to a sufficient number of cells.

Ex vivo gene therapy involves the transfection of cells outside the body. In this approach, scientists remove a small amount of tissue from the patient—typically, blood or bone marrow. The cells within that tissue are placed into culture and allowed to replicate. The cells are genetically modified and returned back to the patient, usually through blood transfusion or direct engraftment. *In vivo* gene therapy involves the introduction of genetic information directly into the patient's cells. This can be done in several ways. Genes can be transfused into the blood stream. They can be injected at the desired site, and they can even be topically applied to the skin and then transferred into the cells of the epidermis through a process known as electroporation. Electroporation opens temporary pores in the cell's outer membrane by using pulsed, rotating electric fields. This allows safe and efficient entrance of the genes into the interior of the cell.[107]

At the present time, single-gene recessive genetic disorders are the most practical candidates for gene therapy. For example, a team of Israeli and Italian researchers has developed a protocol for the treatment of children born with severe combined immunodeficiency (SCID), commonly known as "bubble babies". These babies are born without immune systems.[108] The condition is caused by the lack of an essential enzyme, adenosine draminase (ADA). The researchers completely cured a child of ADA-SCID using genetically altered stem cells. Doctors first began using gene therapy as a treatment for ADA-SCID in the early 1990s. The therapy involved inserting a normal human ADA gene into immune cells taken from the patient's body in the form of bone marrow. Then, they returned the treated cells to the body through a transfusion. The inserted gene instructed the cells to make normal amounts of the missing enzyme, and the patient's defective immune system began to recover.[109]

Unfortunately, doctors found that ultimately the patients still required conventional ADA replacement therapy (which is extremely expensive and lasts only one or two days at a time) because only a minute fraction of the genetically abnormal bone marrow products were repaired. Recently, however, an added step in the process called non-myeloablative conditioning, has resulted in long-term cures. Non-myeloablative conditioning involves giving patients a mild treatment to suppress abnormal stem cells, which provides a biological advantage to the genetically corrected multi-potent stem cells and their products.

Dr. Todd Rosengart, head of cardiothoracic surgery at Evanston Northwestern Healthcare is in the midst of testing a cardiac gene therapy technique known as a biologic bypass, which may redefine cardiac surgery for people suffering from coronary artery disease. His goal: to inject a gene directly into the heart that will switch on the growth of blood vessels, thus triggering the body into stimulating self-repair of damaged hearts. The technique, currently in Phase I clinical trials, is an example of the breakthroughs coming from the field of angiogenesis—the creation of new blood vessels.[110]

Gene therapy may even be used to improve cancer cure rates, according to medical physicists at Virginia Commonwealth University (VCU). They are using an innovative combination of two medical procedures, gene therapy and radiation therapy, to potentially increase cancer cure rates by up to 70 percent over present therapies that rely exclusively on radiation therapy. In this technique, known as genetic radiotherapy, cancer cells are infected with a virus that makes tumor cells more sensitive to—and more easily destroyed by—radiation such as x-rays.[111]

Through genetic engineering, scientists may even be able to resurrect anti-cancer agents that once showed poor results in clinical trials due to unacceptably high levels of toxicity. A team of chemists at the University of Washington and in Germany have developed ways to modify the genes that create maytansinoids, agents that were first discovered in the 1970s, so that they can be less toxic to humans, more effective against cancer, and bond more easily with delivery agents. With this new knowledge, scientists are exploring the possibility of combining maytansinoids with antibodies that target tumors. The antibodies would search out specific cancer antigens and attach only to cancer cells. The maytansinoids can then enter the cancer cells and destroy them without damaging surrounding healthy tissue.[112]

Researchers at Jefferson Medical College have shown that it may be possible to use small pieces of genetic material called short interfering RNAs (siRNAs) to inhibit HIV from replicating. The process, called RNA interference (RNAi), is so new that scientists are only beginning to understand its potential to treat disease. "What's so exciting for HIV therapy is that it may be a potent way of specifically inhibiting the virus," says Roger J. Pomerantz, MD, professor of medicine, biochemistry, and molecular pharmacology and chief of the division of infectious diseases at Jefferson Medical College of Thomas Jefferson University in Philadelphia.[113]

Channeling resources to these cutting edge techniques will increase the odds that the future of medicine will look something like this, as predicted by Dr. Francis Collins:[114]

By 2010
- Genetic testing will be available for 25 common conditions, such as colon cancer.
- Interventions will be available to decrease a person's risk of most of these genetic diseases. For example, patients found to be at high risk for colon cancer will be encouraged to undergo regular colonoscopies beginning at age 25.
- Gene therapy will prove successful for several conditions.
- Most doctors will begin practicing genetic medicine.
- Pre-implantation genetic diagnosis will be widely available.

By 2020
- Gene-based designer drugs will be available for common conditions, such as diabetes and high blood pressure.
- Cancer therapy will be targeted to the molecular fingerprint of the tumor.
- Pharmacogenetic applications will be standard practice for the diagnosis and treatment of many diseases.
- Genetic diagnosis and treatment of mental illness will be available.
- Geneticists will learn how to perform germ-line gene therapy, which would introduce genes into a patient's reproductive cells, without affecting other genes, and hence human germ-line therapy will be declared safe and ethical.

By 2030
- Genes involved in aging will be fully catalogued.
- Clinical trials will be underway to extend maximum human lifespan.
- Use of a full computer model of human cells will replace laboratory experiments.
- The complete genomic sequencing of an individual will be routine and cost less than $1,000.

By 2040
- Complete genome-based health care will be the norm.
- Individualized preventive medicine will be available and largely effective.
- Illness will be detected earlier, before symptoms develop, by molecular surveillance.
- Gene therapy and gene-based drug therapy will be available for most diseases and the average lifespan will reach 90 years.

Chapter *4*

Animal Tissue, Human Tissue and In Vitro *Technology*

"There was a wise man in the East whose constant prayer was that he might see today with the eyes of tomorrow."
Alfred Mercier (1816-1894)

In 1928, Alexander Fleming, a British bacteriologist at St. Mary's Hospital at the University of London, was busy studying staphylococci, which are bacteria that cause wounds to become septic. It had been more than ten years since, as a young research assistant, he had accompanied Sir Almroth Wright, the man who had discovered an anti-typhoid vaccine, to the battlefields of France during World War I. Yet he remained haunted by images of wounded soldiers who died there because there was no effective way of treating infections. One day he was working in his laboratory when, by pure chance, he happened to notice that there were less bacteria on one of the culture dishes in the area where mold was growing. Intrigued, Fleming then grew more of the mold, only this time in a broth, or liquid, and observed that the broth prevented bacteria from growing in test tubes. In that single glass dish, Fleming had discovered what was to become the first antibiotic used successfully in the treatment of serious diseases in human beings: penicillin. Clearly one of the most significant events in the history of medicine, the discovery of penicillin illustrates the profound role that *in vitro*, or test tube research has had in the advancement of scientific discovery.

In Vitro Research: A Historical Perspective – The Nobel Prizes

Latin for "in glass," *in vitro* research occurs in a controlled environment, such as Fleming's culture dish, a flask, or test tube. *In vitro* research is different than *in vivo* research, which occurs in a living organism or natural setting. It is the kind of research conducted in a laboratory using equipment one normally thinks of as being in a lab; scientists working *in vitro* utilize both human-derived and nonhuman-derived tissue.

Using *in vitro* methods, scientists strive to understand illness and therapies better by observing a given specimen and the effects of various chemicals on it. *In vitro* research has led to countless discoveries of great importance, in addition to Fleming's historic discovery. Most of what we now know about disease and drug actions on the molecular level comes from *in vitro* research. Today, state-of-the-art *in vitro* technology continues to refine and streamline the medical research process through precise tooling and miniaturization.

The impact of *in vitro* research is illustrated by a review of Nobel prizes. *In vitro*-based research has won the lion's share of recent Nobel Prizes in Medicine or Physiology. The following are examples of the Nobel Prizes since 1980 that were won, in part or in whole by performing *in vitro* research.[115] (Another discussion of Nobel Prizes, physics and chemistry, will be in Chapter 8.) Supporters of animal experimentation often report that most Nobel Laureates have at some point done some animal-based research. This is undoubtedly true. It is equally true that most of these individuals took elementary English courses. Neither of these statements have a bearing on the work which was actually recognized by the Nobel committee. The same apologists for the animal experiment industry are quick to point out that at times the tissue used as raw material was of animal origin. This is rather like crediting the brand of beakers that the scientist used and is ultimately immaterial.   Unfortunately, expense and government regulations generally favor the use of animal tissues, even though human tissue is more likely to provide better information.

1980 Baruj Benacerraf, Jean Dausset and George Snell

These scientists were honored for their contributions to the study of histocompatibility antigens. The body's ability to reject foreign invaders such as bacteria and viruses is essential for life. However, that same ability must be overcome if transplanted organs are to be functional for an extended period of time. Histocompatability antigens (HCAs) are involved in both resisting illness and rejecting transplanted organs. HCAs are similar to the ABO typing of blood. Each determines in part what happens if foreign tissue enters the body.

In this instance, mouse research and human research were conducted simultaneously but independently. It is not uncommon for one group of researchers to be working feverishly on a mouse model while other researchers were actually analyzing human data. Snell studied mice for years, learning about how mice accept and reject tissue. But it was not until Dausset studied human blood that he was able to determine which HLA types were relevant for human tissue rejection. As is often the case, the discrepancies between human data and mouse data confused the issue. As we have said before, animals and humans are alike and different. The differences can lead to life or death when treating disease.[116]

1982 Sune Bergström, Bengt Samuelsson and John Vane

Using *in vitro* research and technical instrumentation such as mass spectrometry and gas chromatography, these three scientists developed chemicals to elucidate the molecular structure and function of prostaglandins.[117] Prostaglandins contribute to the control of inflammation, body temperature, muscle contraction, and many other bodily functions. They have numerous and sometimes opposite effects. For example, some dilate blood vessels, while others constrict blood vessels.

Most of us are familiar with prostaglandins as a cause of pain. When we take aspirin and ibuprofen-type medications, we are decreasing the amount of those prostaglandins that activate pain. Each particular prostaglandin has a different chemical structure that determines what it does and how it does it. To develop and administer medications that enhance or interfere with prostaglandin productions, scientists must first determine the sequence of chemical reactions, which lead to production of a specific prostaglandin. Although these three scientists made use of animal tissue in their research of these chemical pathways, human tissue would have led to the same results. Unfortunately, regulation currently makes it less cumbersome for researchers to use animal tissue.

1983 Barbara McClintock

Barbara McClintock received the Nobel Prize for developing "techniques for visualizing, identifying, and characterizing maize [corn] chromosomes." Her recognition was long overdue. In the 1940s, McClintock had discovered that in corn, genes move around the genome. Because no one believed her, her career suffered. Not until Watson and Crick provided an explanation for genetic molecular structure was she properly credited. Ultimately, her experiments on corn rewrote the genetics textbooks. [118] This was classic *in vitro* and genetics research.

1984 Cesar Milstein, George J. F. Köhler and Niels K. Jerne

These scientists were awarded the Prize for demonstrating how to synthesize monoclonal antibodies, a development that revolutionized the field of immunology. Prior to this technique, scientists manufactured antibodies within animals or *in vivo*. This method was fraught with obstacles. Contamination was common. The antisera (fluids containing antibodies) was not consistent within the same animal, much less in separate animals. Further, cells, which secreted antibodies, could be grown in a cell culture, but had a very short life span.

The assumption that a single antibody responded to a specific antigen only after contact with the antigen predicated this science. Then, Jerne broke new ground in immunology. He proposed that a host has the ability to respond prior to encountering the antigen. This and others of his theories were the basis upon which Milstein and Kohler were able to synthesize monoclonal antibodies. They fused antibody-producing cells with "immortal" cancer cells (some cancer cells will grow indefinitely, assuming proper nutrition, and thus are considered immortal). This resulted in contaminant-free, antibody-producing cells with a very long life span. Scientists could mass-produce these monoclonal antibodies, which led to a surge in immunology research and knowledge.

All three probably conducted animal experiments at some point in their careers. But it was not the animal-based research that won them the Nobel Prize; it was the *in vitro* research conducted in a laboratory with test tubes, beakers, and cultures. The original cancer cells used were from a mouse.

Human cancer cells would have worked as well or better. The origin of the cancer was not the important factor in this discovery; it was *in vitro* research that led to the development of the monoclonal antibodies.

1985, Michael Brown and Joseph Goldstein
Brown and Goldstein determined the basic defect, a failed receptor for LDL (low density lipoprotein), in familial *hypercholesterolemia* (high cholesterol that is inherited) by studying humans and human tissue *in vitro*. The dominant gene occurs in one out of every 500 people. However, only one in one million people, who have both parents as carriers of the gene, suffer from the disease.

Goldstein studied inherited forms of hyperlipidemia in people in the early 1970s in Seattle. In 1972 Goldstein joined Brown in studying the mechanism of hypercholesterolemia. The biochemistry involved culturing fibroblasts (a type of cell in connective tissue) from affected human patients, then examining them for chemical variations. Goldstein and Brown found that affected patients had 40-60 times more HMG-CoA reductase activity than people without the disease (HMG-CoA controls the rate of cholesterol production), hence, more cholesterol. They further determined that LDL failed to bind at the site, which would turn off the HMG-CoA. This discovery eventually led to the discovery of the LDL receptor. The LDL receptor discovery revolutionized our understanding of cholesterol biochemistry. The process referred to today as *receptor-mediated endocytosis* was demonstrated in the LDL receptor. This rapidly accelerated our investigation of cholesterol biochemistry. Receptor-mediated endocytosis has since been shown to be responsible for the way cells take up molecules such as insulin, immune complexes, and many other biochemical functions. One of the clinical results of this research are the anti-cholesterol medications that today are prescribed to millions of people.[119]

1986 Rita Levi-Montalcini and Stanley Cohen
These two researchers discovered protein factors that control cell and nerve cell growth. Levi-Montalcini elucidated the nerve growth factor (NGF), which is responsible for the growth, development, and continual maintenance of nerves. Cohen contributed to this research and also identified a second protein, epidermal growth factor (EGF), which regulates the growth of other cells. Their research led to the discovery of many such proteins that serve as growth or regulatory factors for cells.

The actual biochemical identification of the proteins involved tedious yet invaluable test tube research. It began in 1954 and was not completed until 1970. Cohen continued the work started on NGF and found EGF years later.[120] Both scientists employed animal tissue; however, human tissue would have yielded the same results.

1987 Susumu Tonegawa
Tonegawa was credited for determining how our bodies create antibodies against specific invaders. Over a lifetime, we may produce millions of antibodies in response to foreign agents. For several decades, the means of production had been the pre-eminent immunological quandary. The methodology that resulted in this Nobel Prize took place over many years and required extremely complex *in vitro* research. Tonegawa required DNA from a tumor and an embryo. He could have used human tumors and human embryo tissue, but opted for mouse tissue because of its easy availability. Tonegawa examined the DNA of the two tissues and found that the immune-building process involved the splicing together of different sequences of DNA, to enable the cell to design each antibody to fit the invader.[121]

1988 Gertrude B. Elion, George H. Hitchings and James W. Black
In elegant biochemical research these scientists designed medications for major diseases. Their research concentrated on the cell and how disease affected it. Based on this knowledge, they created medications that disrupted the diseases' progress at the cellular level, and thus "killed" them. Interestingly, Elion chose her field based on her decision to avoid dissecting animals.[122] She and Hitchings created medications to subvert cancer and malaria, and many other diseases, and laid the groundwork for others to do the same with AIDS and herpes. Black did the same with ulcer medications and beta-blockers (for high blood pressure). [123]

1989 J. Michael Bishop and Harold Varmus
Bishop and Varmus received the 1989 prize for research that illustrated the role of *viral oncogenes* in cancer. All of us have genes that, if activated, can lead to unchecked cell multiplication, also known as cancer. Viral oncogenes (genes which are activated by a virus and which then lead to cancer) had been demonstrated in animals, but researchers did not know if they existed in humans. These scientists, using human cell cultures, showed that the same process could occur in humans.[124]

1991 Erwin Neher and Bert Sakmann
Neher and Sakmann won the 1991 Nobel Prize for adapting a very small version of a piece of laboratory equipment called a pipette to measuring the chemical changes in a cell. This technique, now referred to as a "patch clamp," was revolutionary. The problem of measuring microscopic volumes was not entirely solved with mini-pipettes, however. The "clamp" leaked. One day while Neher was conducting his experiments he noticed that the leaks had disappeared. He realized why and stated afterward that, it was a case of "chance favoring a prepared mind." He had sealed the leak by using fire-polished pipettes.

The patch clamp enabled the proof that ion channels actually existed, a technological accomplishment of epic proportions. Ion channels, ion currents, and the molecules that participate in them are the basis of the activity of the cell. The cells Neher and Sakmann investigated could have come from any organism with muscle tissue. The patch-clamp may be one of the greatest discoveries of all time.[125]

1992 Edwin Krebs and Edmond Fischer

Krebs and Fischer received the prize for clarifying phosphorylation, an aspect of metabolism (part of the citric acid cycle, discovered earlier in the century by Hans Krebs, no relation). The body stores energy in the form of glycogen, and when energy is needed the glycogen is broken down to glucose. This is a very efficient process for turning food stored in the cell into usable energy.

The researchers revealed that an enzyme could be turned off and on by the addition or removal of a phosphate group to the protein molecule. Therefore, phosphorylation reactions are vital to the cellular functioning and control hundreds of enzymes, important to metabolism in both plants and animals. Krebs began working with a plant version of the reaction in 1953.[126]

1993 Phillip Sharp and Richard Roberts

The belief that genes were uninterrupted protein-coding molecules was central to scientific dogma until 1977, when Sharp and Roberts found that genes are not one continuous meaningful strand. They noticed that genes were often interrupted by parts that did not appear to code for proteins at all. These regions are referred to as *introns;* the coding parts as *exons.* James Darnell of Rockefeller University stated that their research was, "the single most surprising and illuminating experiment that has ever been done in biology." *In vitro* research, electron microscopy, and other high tech modalities allowed this research to take place. They performed their research on viral DNA.[127]

1994 Alfred Gilman and Martin Rodbell

One of the most impenetrable secrets of cellular communication was the way chemicals such as hormones signal to the interior of the cell. Gilman and Rodbell received the Nobel Prize for determining the role of "G proteins" in these types of cellular communications. A hormone or other chemical arrives at the outer portion of the cell, the cell membrane, with a message to relay into the interior. Hormones are either too large to gain entrance into the cell or are not allowed access for other reasons. Therefore, they only contact the cell on the surface. When they bind with the cell membrane, it triggers a "second messenger," cyclic AMP (adenosine monophosphate), which relays the message to the inside of the cell. G proteins activate the cyclic AMP. Without G proteins, the entire process would not work.

We now know that G proteins are involved in over 33 percent of the communications between cells and chemicals. They play a role in glucose metabolism, stress response, muscle movement, fat metabolism, light sensing, odor sensing, and hormone response. Most of the medications used to treat disease probably act via G proteins. If G proteins malfunction, disease ensues. Gilman and Rodbell's research was basic *in vitro* research performed in laboratories with sophisticated technology. [128] The origin of the cells they used is not clear and again did not contribute to the discovery. The technology and test tube research did.

1995 Edward B Lewis, Christiane Nüsslein-Volhard and Eric Wieschaus
These three scientists showed that specific genes are responsible for certain expressed traits. The Human Genome Project and its spin-offs will reveal which genes match which traits in their entirety. Lewis, Nusslein-Volhard and Wieschaus used fruit flies, the convenient *Drosophila melanogaster*. Further research showed that the same coding occurs in plants and vertebrates.[129]

1996 Peter Doherty and Rolf Zinkernagel
Doherty and Zinkernagel were honored for discovering the function of the Major Histocompatability Complex (MHC). Its existence was already recognized as a barrier to organ transplantation, yet its usefulness was undetermined. When initial experiments involving mice failed to produce meaningful results, researchers turned to test tube experimentation, for which they won the Nobel Prize. Simply put, the function of the MHC is to determine what is "self" and what is "other." When viruses invade, our T-cells (a type of white blood cell) subject the invader to an assessment based on MHC criteria. A well-functioning MHC recognizes invading organisms and mobilizes our immune system to destroy them. Doherty and Zinkernagel had actually made this discovery in 1974; however, they were not honored until 1996.[130] [131]

1997 Stanley Prusiner
Prusiner expanded on the work of Gajdusek, who had won the Nobel in 1976 for identifying cannibalism as a source of Transmissible Spongiform Encephalopathies (TSEs). Prior to Gajdusek discovery, science knew that bacteria and viruses produce infectious disease. Gajdusek's findings suggested other agents might exist. Prusiner further explained the concept by identifying *prions*, infectious protein particles which can also cause fatal diseases such as scrapie, Creutzfeldt-Jacob Disease, and other transmissible spongiform encephalopathies like Gajdusek's *kuru*. Prions are non-viral and non-bacterial. Whether these proteins act alone or in combination with some still unknown agent remains to be proven. The idea that proteins can cause infectious diseases without using nucleic acids contradicted basic tenets in biology. Hence, Prusiner's discovery was extraordinary and in some ways apocryphal.

TSEs affect both humans and animals. How TSEs jumped the species barrier confused scientists for years, and the mystery intensified with the outbreak of "mad cow disease" (bovine spongiform encephalopathy or BSE) in England in 1996. The prion concept seems to have, at least in part, explained the transmission, but it also aggravated the many industries that use animal by-products and therefore potentially transmit prions to humans. The 1997 Prize was awarded for research involving diseases that affect both animals and humans, but the knowledge of how those diseases affect humans came from research on humans and from research in test tubes.[132]

1998, Robert Furchgott, Louis Ignarro, Ferid Murad
These three Americans shared the Nobel Prize for discovering that the body uses nitric oxide gas to make blood vessels relax and expand. Nitric oxide (as distinguished from nitrous oxide, or laughing gas) is a signaling substance found in our bodies. It directs blood vessels to dilate which in turn lowers blood pressure. The finding has already led to high blood pressure treatments and the sexual performance enhancement drug Viagra. The researchers used porcine (pig) tissue only because it was readily available. Human tissue would have been the ideal. In any event, the source of the tissue was not responsible for the breakthrough; rather, it was the *in vitro* research on the tissue.

The Nobel Committee stated the prize was being awarded for the first discovery that a gas could act as a signal molecule. In fact, in 1934, R. Gane had discovered that ethylene gas acted a signal molecule in plants.

1999, Günter Blobel
Various compartments of the cell perform specific functions. They perform these functions by interacting with proteins that are made outside the compartment in the cell's cytoplasm. The compartments are separated from the cytoplasm by a lipid (fatty) barrier that does not normally allow proteins to pass through. The 1999 Prize went to Dr. Blobel, of Rockefeller University in New York for his discovery of "zip codes" in the cell. Blobel answered the question as to how the proteins pass through the lipid barrier and arrive at the correct destination. He found that the proteins contain genetically coded signals that allow them to cross the appropriate lipid barrier. Blobel discovered that the proteins carry molecular signals, or "zip codes," that direct them from the ribosomes, where they are made, to the cytoplasm and then into other cellular organelles, such as the nucleus.

The discovery of the "signal hypothesis," as it is called, was vital for several reasons. First, mutations in the signal mechanisms were shown to cause numerous inherited diseases, including cystic fibrosis and hyperoxaluria. And second, the characterization of specific "address tags" that facilitate the transport of proteins into cellular compartments led to our current efficiency of using cell culture systems for drug synthesis. Much of what we know today about intracellular transport came from Blobel's classic *in vitro* work. It has been shown that all human, animal, and plant cells do this the same way.

2000, Arvid Carlsson, Eric R. Kandel, and Paul Greengard
The 2000 Prize went to three scientists who studied the brain and how it works on the molecular level: Dr. Arvid Carlsson of the University of Gothenberg in

Sweden, Dr. Eric R. Kandel of Columbia University and Dr. Paul Greengard of Rockefeller University. Dr. Carlsson studied dopamine in signal transmission, Dr. Kandel studied the biology of memory in sea slugs, and Dr. Greengard studied the cascade of events that occurs inside a neuron (nerve cell) after a signal is received. All made a contribution to understanding how the brain works at the molecular level—specifically, what happens inside the neuron after it receives a signal from another neuron.

2001, Leland H. Hartwell, R. Timothy Hunt, and Paul M. Nurse
These pioneers in cancer cell research were awarded the Prize for research that revealed, "...key regulators of the cell cycle." Much of this research was conducted on yeast, a single-celled organism. Each of us starts out as a single cell. The cell divides and divides, and the result is a baby. Babies need to grow. Some cells die, while others need to continue to divide. In order to divide, a cell must grow, replicate its DNA, and separate its DNA into two exact parts for each daughter cell. The cell must control all these processes.

Drs. Hartwell, Hunt and Nurse performed *in vitro* research that facilitated breakthroughs in understanding how normal cells and cancer cells divide, an essential step in cancer pathogenesis. Hartwell, of the Fred Hutchinson Cancer Research Center in Seattle, was awarded for his discoveries of a class of genes that control the cell cycle. One of these genes, called "start" was found to have a central role in controlling the first step of each cell cycle. Hartwell studied yeast cells and identified more than 100 genes that controlled their growth. He also used radiation to study how cells successfully inhibit the development of cancer. Hunt conducted research on special molecules that drive cell division.

Paul Nurse started with a different kind of yeast and, in 1987, identified the human gene for a protein called CDK, a building block for cell division. Tim Hunt investigated growth in cells from sea urchin oocytes (eggs). He discovered another class of proteins called cyclins that control how fast CDK operates.

2002 Sydney Brenner, Sir John E. Sulston, and H. Robert Horvitz
The 2002 Nobel Prize for Physiology or Medicine was awarded to Sydney Brenner, Sir John E. Sulston, and H. Robert Horvitz for their work with *Caenorhabditis elegans*, the nematode worm. They received the Prize "for their discoveries concerning genetic regulation of organ development and programmed cell death." Understanding the process of programmed cell death, known as apoptosis, may lead to improved treatment for conditions in which either excessive numbers of cells die (such as heart attacks and strokes) or in which cells fail to die when they should (for example, cancer).

2003 C. Lauterbur and Briton Sir Peter Mansfield (See Physics Nobel Prize 1952 in Chapter 8.)

Animal Tissue vs. Human Tissue: A Question of Relevance

As the above examples illustrate, many great discoveries have come from using animal tissue, and so no one can deny that animal tissue has given us some knowledge of human disease and physiology. Human tissue could have been used, but wasn't, generally for reasons of convenience. Tissues used have been many and varied, including rabbit aorta, dog veins, chicken rectum, cat ileum, rat stomach, duck pulmonary vein, rabbit rectum, rabbit gall bladder, cat jejunum, rat colon, and very many others. A typical research technique of many decades ago included removing tissue from an animal or human, suspending it between two points, and bathing it in an oxygenated and nutrient-rich salt water solution that kept the tissue alive. The tissue was then exposed to chemicals and measurements were made. For example, if a chemical made a blood vessel contract, the contraction was measured and compared with other chemicals that did the same.

Several fundamental properties of the body were learned using this type of technique. For example, the actions of epinephrine, norepinephrine, histamine, serotonin and others were all studied this way. Many, but not all, of these basic science discoveries were found to apply across species lines, e.g., if epinephrine made the aorta of a rat contract, it did the same to a human. Another example of this is the chemical nitric oxide. As mentioned earlier, Robert Furchgott, Louis Ignarro, and Ferid Murad shared the Nobel Prize in 1998 for discovering that the body uses nitric oxide *gas* to make blood vessels relax and expand. They used an aorta from a pig to make this discovery. Why was a pig aorta was used instead of a human aorta? Probably because obtaining human tissue is much more involved and requires much more paperwork than obtaining an animal part. In this case, the pig aorta provided the same results as a human aorta would have, but in many cases it does not.

Discovering the chemicals the body uses has been done with both animal and human tissue. The next step in studying these chemicals was to develop drugs that aided or interfered with their action. Beta-blockers, such as propranolol, interfere with receptors thus lowering heart rate and blood pressure and thus are used to treat hypertension. Beta-agonists, such as epinephrine and isoproterenol, stimulate receptors, increasing heart rate and blood pressure and as such are prescribed when a person is in heart failure.

However, while basic chemical properties were usually the same across species lines, problems arose when intact animals were then used to test the drugs developed based on the discoveries. The serotonin agonist (an agonist stimulates a receptor while an antagonist blocks it) sumatriptan is a prime example. Serotonin acts as a constrictor on blood vessels. It was thought that a drug derived from serotonin would aid in treating migraine headaches, since migraines were thought to be caused by blood vessel dilation in the head. So, the theory went, constrict the dilated blood vessels and the migraine will disappear. Based on experiments with dog saphenous veins, researchers isolated a receptor they believed was responsible for blood vessel constriction in the head and only the head. A drug that constricts blood vessels throughout the body might result in damage to the heart or other organs. So sumatriptan was developed and tested extensively on animals. No severe side effects were reported.

Humans, however, did have problems. Many people with no heart disease whatsoever took the drug for their migraine and experienced chest pain because sumatriptan was not only constricting blood vessels in their head but also the ones supplying oxygen to their hearts. Many experienced heart attacks and some died. Slight differences between species accounted for this effect. Had human tissue been used to test the drug, this problem might have been avoided. All the discoveries about serotonin could have been made using human tissue. When the drug was ready to be tested, had human tissue been used then also, the species differences would not have been missed, and the drug would have been modified to avoid coronary artery constriction. There was no reason to use either intact animals or animal tissue at any time during his process. In the long run, all it did was mislead researchers and cause human deaths.

Another example of using tissue derived from animals when human tissue or chemicals could be used is fetal bovine (cow) serum (FBS), which is used in many cell cultures. There are many problems with using FBS: 1) There is batch-to-batch variability, which is not a good thing in a culture medium since it introduces uncontrollable variables. 2) The amount and type of growth factors and growth inhibition factors varies from batch to batch. 3) The FBS may vary, depending on the sex of the fetus, species, and developmental stage. 4) FBS "can interfere with genotypic and phenotypic cell stability and can influence experimental outcomes." 5) FBS can "suppress cell spreading, cell attachment, and embryonic tissue differentiation." 6) FBS "can be contaminated with viruses, bacteria, mycoplasma, yeasts, fungi, immunoglobulins, endotoxins, and possibly, prions." 8) Many substances in FBS have not been identified, and the effect of these substances on cultured cells is unclear.[133] Since FBS introduces many known and unknown variables, its use can mislead scientists. Another serious problem with using tissue from animals is the risk of infectious disease.

The next big challenge of biomedical research is to explore the complete molecular basis of disease, drug reactions, and therapy. This can only be accomplished using human tissue, in part, because disease and drug response may involve a huge number of variables (including genes and environment), and since these factors are not independent, many interactions are possible.

The Power and Potential: In Vitro Research Using Human Tissue

Tissue is normally used not only for research but also for toxicity testing (of household products, agricultural and industrial chemicals, for example). Today, there are a number of *in vitro* techniques commonly employed in toxicity testing that use human or synthetic tissue. These include:

• Agarose Diffusion Method, which is used to determine the toxicity of plastics and other synthetic materials used in medical devices. In this test, human cells and a small amount of test material are placed in a container and separated by a thin layer of agarose, a derivative of the sea plant agar. If the test material is an irritant, a zone of killed cells appears around the substance.
• EpiDerm, which uses neonatal foreskin-derived normal skin cells, grows into three-dimensional tissue for dermal irritancy testing,
• EpiOcular, which uses an artificial tissue manufactured in a similar way to EpiDerm, but which is more similar to the cornea, the outermost covering of the eye.
• Epipack Test, which uses sheets of cloned human skin cells to estimate a human's reaction to a skin irritant.
• The Human Keratinocyte/Neutral Red Bioassay, which uses neutral red, a water-soluble dye, added to normal human epidermal keratinocyte cultures (skin cells) in a 96-well tissue culture plate. A computer measurement of the level of uptake of the dye by the cells is used to indicate relative toxicity. The cells are representative of the epithelial cells that cover the surface of the eye and skin.[134]
• Transepithelial Passage Assay uses an artificial barrier constructed of human cells to estimate the eye irritation potential of chemicals.

Bioengineered human skin is replacing animal tissue in many advanced institutions. According to the Institute of In Vitro Sciences, a non-profit organization for the advancement of alternative methods to animal testing, bioengineered human skin models incorporate several advantages over animals in the study of potential dermal toxicity:
1. The tissue constructs have stratified epidermal layers, including a **functional stratum** corneum.
2. The test materials are applied directly to the culture **surface**, which is exposed to air, allowing undiluted and/or end use dilutions to be tested directly.
3. The endpoints include cytotoxity and pro-inflammatory mediator release.[135]

Testing directly in human tissue rather than in animal models allows drug development teams to obtain vital information about what their gene of interest is doing in a human system. Because animal models are not predictive of how drugs will behave in humans, obtaining information directly from human tissues is a critical step in choosing one target from many candidates. Even after the drug development process has begun, determining where a particular gene is expressed in other, perhaps unexpected sites within the body may assist researchers in the design and interpretation of pre-clinical or clinical studies.

According to Julia Wulfkuhle, a research fellow at the Food and Drug Administration / National Cancer Institute's clinical proteomics program, the best way to get accurate information for new drug development is to use human tissue. As she has noted, proteomics in cancer research has broadened the ability to identify specific changes in a tumor and target those changes; therefore, using human tissue for protein profiles offers "a truly *in vivo* approach" and allows analysis of variation across populations.[136]

The work of J.A. Angus, of the Department of Pharmacology at the University of Melbourne, provides an example of how human-derived tissue is used in the drug discovery process. Angus and colleagues obtained heart tissue from human patients who had undergone heart transplant surgery. They studied the left and right main epicardial arteries in the tissue, and found them to have an abundance of plaque. They also obtained and studied healthy hearts that were not suitable for organ donation, as well as heart tissue from patients undergoing heart operations with cardiopulmonary bypass. (A small amount of heart tissue is removed during these operations to allow the placement of the cannulas necessary for bypassing the heart and lungs.) In doing so, Angus' group was able to compare the effects of various chemicals, such as nifedipine, sumatriptan, and potassium, on these arteries, thus shedding light on a heart condition known as variant angina. They also found that tissue from humans, rabbits, and dogs all responded differently to the chemical acetylcholine.[137] Angus stated, "This is a clear example of how coronary microvessel pharmacology varies among three species and makes extrapolation from animals to man quite hazardous."

Additional human-derived tissue that Angus' group has studied, and that has provided valuable data directly applicable to humans, include:

- Discarded internal mammary arteries, which are sometimes used to provide blood to the coronary arteries. A small portion of these arteries is usually unused and thus can be removed and studied in the lab.
- Discarded saphenous veins, which are also used to bypass occluded coronary arteries and, like internal mammary arteries, are not needed.
- Skin samples from the buttocks of human volunteers, obtained through gluteal biopsy, used to study the pharmacology of healthy and diseased small arteries.
- Small samples of forearm vein from volunteers with untreated high blood pressure as well as from people without high blood pressure, to study vascular response in hypertension.

Angus continues, "The use of human tissue in pharmacodynamic studies is becoming appreciated as we learn that experimental animal-tissue assays do not always reflect human receptor homology and tissue structure."[138]

There are many examples of human tissue being used for *in vitro* techniques that led to discoveries that would have been impossible otherwise:

In vitro research allowed scientists to develop a blood test that will help physicians identify patients with metastatic breast cancer who are likely to respond to conventional therapy and those who are not and thus would be interested in experimental therapy.[139] Bayer Diagnostics' Oncogene Science Group developed the test which measures the level of the protein Her-2/neu in the patient's blood. Her-2/neu is known to be a marker for poor prognosis if it is found in primary tumor tissue. These patients usually respond poorly to drugs such as tamoxifen. New tests can be used to monitor patients' levels of the protein instead of relying on a one-time tissue level that was taken at the time of the excision. "This test opens the gateway to individualizing therapy," Dr. Allan Lipton of Pennsylvania State University in Hershey told Reuters Health. Now oncologists can monitor the levels of Her-2/neu and make real time decisions about how effective the therapy is.

Monoclonal antibodies (MAbs) are the body's biological warheads, designed to eliminate foreign invaders from the body. MAbs are protein molecules used by the immune system to attack very specific targets. They are produced by B-lymphocytes (white blood cells) and each B-lymphocyte makes just one type of Mab, thus a B lymphocyte is specific for the invader, e.g., small cell cancer, hepatitis C, etc. In the 1980s, MAbs were purported to be a cure for all ills, including cancer, viruses, and bacteria. But they failed. One reason they failed was because of the way they were made. Originally, an antigen would be injected into a mouse and the mouse's immune system would respond by triggering the B-lymphocytes to produce antibodies against the antigen. Scientists would harvest only the B-lymphocytes that were making the antibody. They would combine the B cells with human cells, which would then be cultured to make MAbs. But the problem was that the MAbs were mouse MAbs, since they came from mice, and when injected into humans the humans rejected the MAbs as foreign. The humans also suffered a side effect known as HAMA, which stands for human anti-mouse antibodies. HAMA causes joint swelling, rashes, kidney failure, and can be life-threatening. MAbs that are fully human can now be made, via genetic engineering, thus preventing these problems. These new MAbs are now being studied and successfully used to treat cancers, immune disorders, psoriasis, and other diseases.

In vitro research is responsible for much of what we know about HIV and AIDS. Scientists have explored one idea for creating a vaccine using *in vitro* methods. To date, HIV vaccines have failed, in part, because the strain of HIV produced for live attenuated vaccines (a live virus that is very weakened and hence incapable of causing the disease but still able to produce the immune response) quickly changes to another strain that is stronger and able to produce a full blown infection, not just the immune response hoped for. Giuseppe Marzio and colleagues at the University of Amsterdam made a strain of HIV that can live only in the presence of the drug doxycycline. If doxycycline is present the virus can live but if it is not, the virus dies. The thinking is that the modified strain could be injected into humans, doxycycline given for a few days and then never given again. Thus the virus would be turned on and produce an immune response long enough for protection to be conferred but then the HIV would be turned off or in essence the patient cured from the doxycycline-dependent HIV and protected from further HIV infections. If a booster shot is needed, simply giving a few days of doxycycline will provide it. The concept has worked when tested on human cells in test tubes.[140]

Scientists discovered the structure of two cell surface receptors used by the HIV virus to infect white blood cells.[141] Two receptors, called DC-SIGN and DC-SIGNR, interact with the carbohydrate component of HIV called gp120, thus allowing HIV into the cell and possibly cross the placenta. The scientists who made the discovery stated, "DC-SIGN- and DC-SIGNR-gp120 interactions represent a potential target for anti-HIV therapy aimed at disrupting the cell-virus interaction at primary sites of infection, in order to lower the efficiency of T cell infection." *In vitro* research revealed that the density of CC chemokine receptor 5 (CCR5) on CD4 cells (the white blood cells attacked by HIV) governs the course of HIV infection in children. Determining the density of CCR5 receptors could aid in determining prognosis and in decision-making regarding treatment in children.[142]

The drug chloroquine has been used for over 50 years to combat malaria, but *in vitro* research revealed that it might also be used to combat HIV Dr. Andrea Savarino, of the University of Turin School of Medicine in Italy, and associates found that chloroquine inhibited viral antigen production and altered the structure of the gp120 glycoprotein. Chloroquine demonstrated the ability to inhibit the replication of HIV-1.[143]

HIV-1 and Ebola virus were found to infect humans through similar molecular mechanisms.[144] This study is important because it showed that 2 unrelated viruses use the same virus-host interaction, the cellular factor Tsg101. The knowledge gained from this study will be used to design drugs that prevent these and possibly other infections.

A plant derivative called prostratin, derived from the tropical plant *Homalanthus nutans,* along with HARRT (highly active antiretroviral therapy) may be useful to people suffering from AIDS. Apparently, prostratin induces latent HIV-1 to manifest thus allowing HARRT to kill it. This could help lead to an eradication of persistent viral reservoirs.

Dr. Bergeron and colleagues from Université Laval in Québec tested the microbicidal activity of sodium lauryl sulfate (SLS), a chemical that denatures proteins and a potent inactivator of a number of viruses, against HIV-1 in cultured cells.[145] They found that it might prevent transmission of HIV and other sexually transmitted disease pathogens. Dr. Michel G. Bergeron, now with the Centre Hospitalier Universitaire de Québec, told Reuters Health:

The consistent and careful use of latex condoms is an effective method to prevent the sexual transmission of HIV-1, but unfortunately, their use is not generalized. There is an urgent need to develop vaginal microbicides under the control of women to protect themselves from STDs [sexually transmitted diseases] including HIV. Taken together, these data and those of previous studies show that *in vitro* SLS demonstrates interesting inactivating potencies against HIV-1, HSV strains, and human papillomavirus. SLS could represent a potential candidate for use in vaginal microbicides to prevent the sexual transmission of enveloped and nonenveloped viruses and possibly other pathogens causing STDs. As our gel formulation acts as a double barrier—one, a physical one blocking the sexual transmission of pathogens causing STDs, and two, a chemical one destroying pathogens causing STDs—we expect that it will be effective as soon as applied and remain effective for a few hours. As there is, until now, no vaccine against HIV-1, preventive measures are the only tool that can presently reduce the transmission of this retrovirus."[146]

By using *in vitro* techniques to analyze human blood cells which were then infected with HIV, scientists at the Institute for Brain and Immune Disorders, Minneapolis Medical Research Foundation, Hennepin County Medical Center, and the University of Minnesota Medical School in Minneapolis found that Naltrexone (a drug used in the treatment of addiction disorders) may increase the effectiveness of certain anti-AIDS drugs. This could lead to a novel treatment approach for HIV, as Naltrexone appears to target only the cells infected with the virus rather than the virus itself. Current treatments target the virus itself.[147]

By using *in vitro* techniques, scientists at the French National Scientific Research Center and Johns Hopkins University discovered that sulforaphane, a compound found in broccoli and Brussels sprouts, kills the bacterium, *Helicobacter pylori* that causes stomach cancer and ulcers. Jed Fahey, a plant physiologist in the Department of Pharmacology and Molecular Sciences at the Johns Hopkins School of Medicine stated, "In some parts of Central and South America, Africa and Asia, as much as 80 to 90 percent of the population is infected with helicobacter, likely linked to poverty and conditions of poor sanitation. If future clinical studies show that a food can relieve or prevent diseases associated with this bacterium in people, it could have significant public health implications in the United States and around the world." The *in vitro* findings led the scientists to test the chemical on mice, which gave the same results as the *in vitro* studies. Even if they had not, the chemical would still undergo clinical trials.[148]

One of the greatest breakthroughs in the 20th century was recombinant DNA research, which resulted in a plethora of products. Human insulin, Hepatitis B vaccine, interferon-α 2b, Etanercept, Anakinra, and Infliximab for rheumatoid arthritis, reteplase and tenecteplase for heart attack, human growth hormone, clotting factors, erythropoietin and other drugs have resulted from this *in vitro* research.

The study of human male infertility at a leading hospital in Birmingham, U.K., is another good example of the value of human tissue in research. Scientists there were able to establish a method by which human testicular tissue obtained from biopsies could be transported and stored in a manner that maintains its cellular function. Now, they have established a tissue bank of samples, enabling vital research to take place using human tissue rather than rodent and primate tissue, which had been used before. Their research has shown for the first time in immature human sperm cells that human cells have active potassium channels but inactive calcium channels—data that is in marked contrast to that obtained by researchers working with rodents. Dr. Ian Brewis, one of the researchers on the team, stated, "We look forward to further demonstrating that human research is the way forward. Already co-workers are taking notice of our work and discussing the limitations of animal work and potential of their work becoming more human orientated."[149]

Until recently it was impossible to analyze individual subpopulations of cells in a tissue sample. However, high-throughput microdissection technology, such as that developed by Laser Capture Microdissection: Arcturus Engineering Inc. (Mountain View, CA) changed that. It is now possible to study individual cells in a tissue sample. This means that within a single tissue sample scientists can study normal epithelium, premalignant cells, and cancer cells. Different genes and proteins are found in each of the different cell lines. This is a boon for studying which proteins and genes are involved in a disease.[150]

A new tool called a Raman Spectroscope can analyse living cells. Scientists can put human cells in the Raman Spectroscope, stimulate a specific part with a laser and analyze the data to determine a cell's chemical composition. Every cell has a different "fingerprint" depending on what chemicals it contains. By injecting the tissue with a drug the scientists can analyze the changes in the data and predict what will happen when the cell, in a human, is exposed to the same drug. The speed of the Raman Spectroscope enable scientists to watch the movement of a particular amino acid in enzymes at work, or a particular base of DNA while it is being transcribed, replicated or complexed to a transcription factor.

Prostate cancer is the second leading cause of cancer death in men in the United States. Approximately 200,000 men were diagnosed in 2000 and an additional 31,500 men died from the disease. Using an *in vitro* technique called methylation-specific polymerase chain reaction to examine tissue samples from 69 patients with early-stage prostate cancer and 31 patients with benign prostate disease, scientists at Johns Hopkins University found that they could accurately discriminate between normal tissue and prostatic carcinoma, which could lead to earlier diagnosis of prostate cancer. A mutation in a gene that directs the formation of glutathione S-transferase (GSTP1) alters levels of an enzyme that detoxifies environmental carcinogens and protects against cancer.

Changes in this gene lead to hypermethylation, now known to be the most common genetic error in prostate cancer. Hypermethylation is a biochemical process that inactivates the GSTP1 gene, shutting off its cancer-preventing properties, and is most often seen in early-stage prostate cancers and rarely in normal or benign prostate disease. David Sidransky, MD, professor of otolaryngology, oncology and urology at Johns Hopkins and director of the study stated, "PSA screening has helped diagnose many men with prostate cancer and has saved countless lives, but it is far from perfect...A molecular test that can correctly identify those with cancer and exclude those with benign disease could help triage these patients early on in their evaluation for observation or treatment...A genetic marker such as GSTP1 that occurs mostly in early-stage prostate cancers may improve the way we diagnose cancer in the future and help us to catch it early."[151]

The presence of mutations in the adenomatous polyposis coli (APC) gene in fecal samples may allow early detection of colorectal cancer. Scientists analyzed stool samples from 28 patients with nonmetastatic colorectal cancers, 18 patients with adenomas, and 28 control patients without neoplastic disease. They found that 26 of the 46 patients with neoplastic disease and 17 of the 28 cancer patients had APC mutations. In contrast, no mutations were identified in any of the patients without neoplastic disease. By using this test in addition to other tests for colon cancer, physicians should be better able to diagnose colon cancer early and institute treatment.[152]

Using *in vitro* techniques, scientists have been able to reverse the painful and life-threatening symptoms of the genetic metabolic disorder Fabry's disease.[153] Fabry's is a condition that can result in severe pain, kidney disease, heart disease and premature death. It is caused when patients lack the ability to produce an essential enzyme called alpha-galactosidase A. Because they lack this enzyme, they cannot break down a naturally occurring protein in their cells. As the protein accumulates, it damages the cells found in capillaries of the skin, kidneys, heart and brain. This results in intense pain that begins in early childhood. As the patient ages the pain intensifies and infarcts start to develop. Kidney failure, strokes, and heart attacks result.

By using *in vitro* techniques, scientists were able to develop genetically engineered alpha-galactosidase A. When this was injected into 29 patients every other week for 20 weeks, 69 percent of patients on the enzyme treatment showed near complete clearing of the protein build-up in their capillaries. In the future, patients with Fabry's disease may be treated on a continuous basis with the engineered enzyme to keep the disorder in check.

Sources of Human Tissue

One reason that animal tissue, rather than human tissue, continues to be used, despite its inability to accurately predict human response, is that it is much easier to obtain than high quality human tissue. Obstacles such as consent issues, handling requirements, and the lack of availability of living sources limit the supply of human tissues. A researcher may have to fill out one form to get an animal aorta but ten to obtain a human aorta, and with a much longer wait. Moreover, many academic institutions simply do not have the resources or the technology to collect and bank human tissue. As a result, human tissue has been a squandered resource, literally and tragically ending up in the garbage. There are additional obstacles to using human-derived cells in cell-based assays: they are expensive to cultivate and difficult to propagate in automated systems. An alternative is to use *Saccharomyces cerevisiae*—otherwise known as brewer's yeast, a single-celled organism that belongs to the group of simple organisms called *fungi*. As Grabley and Thiericke write in *Drug Discovery from Nature*: "Easy handling, short generation times, ready genetic manipulation, continuous heterologous gene expression, resistance to solvents, and low cost of growing make yeast an attractive option..." [154] (Yeast, as it turns out, is a valuable tool in the laboratory. Scientists have been able to reconstitute signaling through human G-protein-coupled receptors, ion channel receptors, protein-protein interactions a, and peptide hormone receptor binding, and many other basic processes, in yeast.[155])

The National Cancer Institute (NCI) has developed the *In vitro* Cell Line Screening Project (IVCLSP), a service of the National Institutes of Health (NIH) that provides *in vitro* cell line screens that were implemented in April of 1990[156]. It was developed because of dissatisfaction with the performance of prior *in vivo* (animal-based) primary screens. The NCI states, "This project is designed to screen up to 20,000 compounds per year for potential anticancer activity. The operation of this screen utilizes 60 different human tumor cell lines, representing leukemia, melanoma and cancers of the lung, colon, brain, ovary, breast, prostate, and kidney. The aim is to prioritize for further evaluation, synthetic compounds or natural product samples showing selective growth inhibition or cell killing of particular tumor cell lines. This screen is unique in that the complexity of a 60 cell line dose response produced by a given compound results in a biological response pattern which can be utilized in pattern recognition algorithms. Using these algorithms, it is possible to assign a putative mechanism of action to a test compound, or to determine that the response pattern is unique and not similar to that of any of the standard prototype compounds included in the NCI database. In addition, following characterization of various cellular molecular targets in the 60 cell lines, it may be possible to select compounds most likely to interact with a specific molecular target."

A number of biotechnology companies have also developed human tissue banks to use in the drug discovery process. For example, the tissue bank of LifeSpan BioSciences contains over two million tissues from all areas of the human body, with all stages of disease progression and age-matched controls. Dr. Julian E. Beesley of Lifespan BioSciences stated, "Target profiling using high quality human tissue is critical, considering that animal models are not always predictive of the human condition."[157] If you are conducting research on a particular disease, LifeSpan can aid you in identifying genes or pathways activated in that disease process. If you have isolated certain genes and wish to determine if they are expressed in human tissues, when they are expressed during development, and identify the relationship between expression and the disease process LifeSpan can also aid in that process. Their tissue bank contains more than 175 types of normal tissues and over 1,500 diagnostic disease categories (see Table 4.1)[158] Their tissue bank contains more than 175 types of normal tissues and over 1,500 diagnostic disease categories

Such human tissue banks are an extremely valuable resource for researchers. For example, in contrast to the United States, Japan does not allow human organs that prove unsuitable for transplantation to be used as sources for tissue. However, in 2001, the Japan Health Sciences Foundation began asking medical institutions and university hospitals in Tokyo to donate human tissue taken from consenting surgical patients in the hopes of creating a nonprofit, public bank of tissue that can be used for medical and pharmaceutical research. The bank is expected to maintain a supply of up to 10 grams each of livers, lungs, kidneys, and other organs. The development of a human tissue bank was sparked by the failure of many drug development projects when tested on humans, even though the drugs had been used successfully on animals.

Ardais, a Massachusetts-based company, has collected almost 120,000 samples of human tissue from 10,000 cases. About 60 percent of the cases are from tumors, 30 percent from inflammatory diseases, and the rest from other diseases "with research value," according to Martin Ferguson, senior vice president of bioinformatics for the company. The samples are stored in fresh-tissue format, which can generate RNA, protein, and small molecules.[159]

BioWhittaker offers human stem cells for research as well as a number of highly purified standard cell types and custom cell isolation services.

In early 1995, during the course of reviewing data from the cancer screen, it became obvious that many agents were completely inactive under the conditions of the assay. A protocol for a 3-cell line prescreen was developed in collaboration with the Information Technology Branch (ITB, DTP). This prescreen would test for the presence of toxicity at extremely low (10^{-4}M) drug concentration and could eliminate a large proportion of the inactive agents, but preserve "active" agents for multi-dose 60 cell line testing. Computer modeling indicated that approximately 50% of drugs could be eliminated by this prescreen without a significant decrease in ability to identify active agents, and should be able to increase the throughput and efficiency of the main cancer screen with limited loss of information.

Pharmagene, in the UK, utilizes human tissues in their development of pharmaceutical and biotechnology products. They have one of the most comprehensive collections of human tissues. They do no work on animals or on embryonic or fetal tissues, and do not supply human tissue to third parties. By linking data obtained by the company's scientists from human tissue samples to the known clinical histories of the donors of those samples through a proprietary database, Pharmagene also provides a relevant human context to early stage drug discovery targets and candidates. Pharmagene believes that its pre-clinical, human tissue-based approach offers a more relevant and rational approach than animal-based research for the discovery and development of pharmaceuticals for humans. At present, considerable time and resources are invested by pharmaceutical and biotechnology companies studying candidate compounds that have been tested in recombinant or animal-based test systems that are unreliable indicators of safety and efficacy in humans.[160] (Table 4.2)

Table 4.1

Organ	Diagnoses
Bone and joint diseases	Degenerative arthritis, osteoporosis, rheumatoid arthritis, bone tumors
Breast diseases	Fibrocystic disease, fibroadenoma, infiltrating ductal carcinoma, lobular carcinoma, medullary carcinoma, colloid carcinoma, carcinomas in situ
Cardiovascular diseases	Atherosclerosis, heart failure, valvular disease, vasculitis, coarctation, Monckeberg's medial sclerosis, aneurysms
Female reproductive diseases	Ovarian cysts, ovarian cancers (all types), atrophy, cystadenoma, granulosa cell tumor, hydatidiform mole, choriocarcinoma, cervicitis, endocervical polyps, cervical carcinoma, cervical dysplasia, endometrial carcinoma, leiomyoma, adenomyosis, uterine atrophy, endometriosis, salpingo-oophoritis, fallopian tube carcinoma, endometritis, squamous cell carcinoma of vagina
Gastrointestinal diseases	Esophageal carcinoma (squamous), leiomyoma, carcinoma of stomach, Barrett's esophagus, atrophic gastritis, gastric ulcer, peptic ulcer, celiac sprue, regional enteritis (Crohn's), ulcerative colitis, adenomatous polyps, villous adenomas, polyposis coli, diverticulosis, colon cancer, appendicitis

Genitourinary diseases	Chronic cystitis, prostatitis, benign prostatic hypertrophy, transitional cell carcinoma of bladder, epidermoid carcinoma of bladder, adenocarcinoma of bladder, prostatic carcinoma (all Gleason grades), epididymitis, testicular atrophy, testicular neoplasias (all types)
Head and neck diseases	Leukoplakia, epidermoid carcinoma, giant cell granuloma, sialadenitis, dentigerous cyst, sinusitis, tonsillitis, nasopharyngeal carcinoma, parotitis, papillomas, mucoepidermoid cancer, Warthin's tumor, mixed tumor, sarcoidosis, thyroid adenoma, Grave's disease, Hashimoto's disease, goiter, thyroid carcinoma (various types), parathyroid adenoma, parathyroid hyperplasia, parathyroid carcinoma
Hepatobiliary diseases	Pancreatitis, Type I and Type II diabetes mellitus, pancreatic carcinoma, islet cell tumors, hepatitis, cirrhosis, cholangitis, cholecystitis, cholangiocarcinoma, hepatocellular carcinoma, primary biliary cirrhosis, sclerosing cholangitis
Kidney diseases	Renal cell carcinoma, systemic lupus erythematosus, glomerulonephritis (many types), transitional cell carcinoma, adenomas, atrophy, hydronephrosis, hypertension, interstitial nephritis, polycystic kidney disease, pyelonephritis, diabetes mellitus, nephrolithiasis glomerulosclerosis
Lung diseases	Asthma, emphysema, adenocarcinoma, small cell carcinoma, epidermoid carcinoma, bronchoalveolar carcinoma, bronchial carcinoid, mesothelioma, ARDS, COPD, pneumonia

Neurological diseases	Alzheimer's, Parkinson's, multiple sclerosis, astrocytoma, glioblastoma, meningioma, oligodendroglioma, acoustic neuroma, craniopharyngioma
Muscle diseases	Atrophy, myositis, rhabdomyosarcoma, myoblastoma, leiomyosarcoma
Skin and soft tissue diseases	Melanoma, nevi, basal cell carcinoma, squamous cell carcinoma, lipoma, dermatofibroma, senile elastosis, granuloma pyogenicum, giant cell tumor, hemangioma, keratoacanthoma, mesenchymoma, neurofibroma, vasculitis, seborrheic keratosis, lupus erythematosus, psoriasis, neurilemmoma, liposarcoma, hemangiosarcoma, neurogenic sarcoma, malignant fibrous histiocytoma, nodular fasciitis

Clonetics Cell Systems sells purified human cells for research. Clonetics cells are primarily derived from normal human tissue. The following human cell systems are available:

Airway Cell Systems
Keratinocytes
Melanocytes
Neural Cells
Skeletal Cells

Endothelial Cell Systems
Dendritic Cells
Smooth Muscle Cells
Prostate Cells
Stromal Cells

Fibroblast Cell Systems
Mammary Epithelial Cells
Skeletal Muscle Cells
Renal Cells
Cell Blots

Table 4.2

ORDER	BIOMATERIAL	ORGAN SYSTEM
1	HEART : LEFT ATRIA : CARDIAC MUSCLE	CARDIOVASCULAR
2	HEART : LEFT VENTRICLE : CARDIAC MUSCLE	CARDIOVASCULAR
3	BLOOD VESSEL : CORONARY : ARTERY	CARDIOVASCULAR
4	OESOPHAGUS : WHOLE	ALIMENTARY
5	STOMACH : FUNDUS : WHOLE	ALIMENTARY
6	STOMACH : BODY : WHOLE	ALIMENTARY
7	STOMACH : ANTRUM : WHOLE	ALIMENTARY
8	STOMACH : PYLORIC CANAL : WHOLE	ALIMENTARY
9	DUODENUM : WHOLE	ALIMENTARY
10	JEJUNUM : WHOLE	ALIMENTARY
11	ILEUM : WHOLE	ALIMENTARY
12	ADIPOSE : OMENTAL - ILEUM	ALIMENTARY
13	BLOOD VESSEL : MESENTERIC (COLON)	CARDIOVASCULAR
14	CAECUM : WHOLE	ALIMENTARY
15	COLON : WHOLE	ALIMENTARY
16	RECTUM : WHOLE	ALIMENTARY
17	GALLBLADDER : WHOLE	ALIMENTARY
18	PANCREAS	ALIMENTARY
19	LIVER : PARENCHYMA	ALIMENTARY
20	BRAIN : CEREBELLUM	NERVOUS
21	BRAIN : HIPPOCAMPUS	NERVOUS
22	BRAIN : LOCUS COERULEUS	NERVOUS
23	BRAIN : MEDULLA OBLONGATA	NERVOUS
24	BRAIN : AMYGDALA	NERVOUS
25	BRAIN : CAUDATE	NERVOUS
26	BRAIN : **HYPOTHALAMUS - ANTERIOR**	**NERVOUS**
27	BRAIN : HYPOTHALAMUS - **POSTERIOR**	**NERVOUS**
28	BRAIN : CORTEX : CINGULATE - ANTERIOR	NERVOUS
29	BRAIN : CORTEX : CINGULATE - POSTERIOR	NERVOUS
30	BRAIN : CORTEX : FRONTAL - LATERAL	NERVOUS
31	BRAIN : CORTEX : FRONTAL - MEDIAL	NERVOUS
32	BRAIN : CORTEX : OCCIPITAL	NERVOUS
33	BRAIN : CORTEX : PARIETAL	NERVOUS
34	BRAIN : CORTEX : TEMPORAL	NERVOUS
35	BRAIN : NUCLEUS ACCUMBENS	NERVOUS
36	BRAIN : SUBSTANTIA NIGRA	NERVOUS
37	BRAIN : DORSAL RAPHE NUCLEUS	NERVOUS
38	SPINAL CORD	NERVOUS

39	DORSAL ROOT GANGLION	NERVOUS
40	PINEAL GLAND	ENDOCRINE
41	PITUITARY GLAND	ENDOCRINE
42	BLOOD VESSEL : CHOROID PLEXUS	CARDIOVASCULAR
43	BLOOD VESSEL : CEREBRAL : MIDDLE CEREBRAL ARTERY	CARDIOVASCULAR
44	TRACHEA	RESPIRATORY
45	LUNG : PARENCHYMA	RESPIRATORY
46	LUNG : BRONCHUS : PRIMARY	RESPIRATORY
47	LUNG : BRONCHUS : TERTIARY	RESPIRATORY
48	BLOOD VESSEL : PULMONARY	CARDIOVASCULAR
49	KIDNEY : CORTEX	URINARY
50	KIDNEY : MEDULLA	URINARY
51	KIDNEY : PELVIS	URINARY
52	BLOOD VESSEL : RENAL	CARDIOVASCULAR
53	URETER	URINARY
54	BLADDER	URINARY
55	BLADDER : TRIGONE	URINARY
56	OVARY	REPRODUCTIVE
57	FALLOPIAN TUBE	REPRODUCTIVE
58	UTERUS : MYOMETRIUM	REPRODUCTIVE
59	UTERUS : CERVIX	REPRODUCTIVE
60	PROSTATE	REPRODUCTIVE
61	VAS DEFERENS	REPRODUCTIVE
62	TESTIS	REPRODUCTIVE
63	SPLEEN : PARENCHYMA	HAEMOLYMPHOID
64	BLOOD : MONONUCLEAR CELLS	HAEMOLYMPHOID
65	LYMPH GLAND : TONSIL	HAEMOLYMPHOID
66	MUSCLE : SKELETAL	MUSCLE
67	SKIN : FORESKIN	INTEGUMENTAL
68	ADRENAL GLAND	ENDOCRINE
69	THYROID GLAND	ENDOCRINE
70	UMBILICAL CORD	REPRODUCTIVE
71	PLACENTA	HAEMOCHORIAL
72	BREAST	INTEGUMENTAL

New Frontiers in *In Vitro* Technology

Stem cell research is a relatively new field of endeavor. Although mouse stem cells were discovered in 1971, it was almost another 30 years before human stem cells could be grown in culture. Stem cell research is a form of *in vitro* technology that holds great promise in several key areas: human disease treatment, drug and chemical testing, gene therapy, and toxicology. Stem cells could be used to treat patients suffering from a wide range of illnesses from Alzheimer's disease to cancer, Parkinson's disease, diabetes, stroke, heart attack, multiple sclerosis, blood, bone, and bone marrow ailments, and spinal cord injuries. Stem cells can even be used to help victims of severe burns by providing skin grafts.

What, exactly, are stem cells? There are about 220 types of specialized cells that make up the human body. Embryonic stem (ES) cells are flexible "master" cells that have the ability to develop into any of these specialized cells. You might call them a sort of "blank page" awaiting the complex set of instructions that will tell them what special tasks they will ultimately perform and what part of the body they will serve.

During development, stem cells transform into heart, muscle, brain, skin, or other tissues. This is how a one-celled organism—the human fetus, for example—becomes a fully formed baby. When the sperm fertilizes an egg, the DNA of both parents combine and form a single cell. By five days after fertilization, this cell and its daughter cells have reproduced and formed what is called a blastocyst—a hollow sphere of about 100 cells. Cells in its outer layer go on to form the placenta, while the inner cells go on to form the tissues of the body. These cells, which can develop into any of the body's tissues, are the embryonic stem cells.

ES cells have the ability to divide for indefinite periods in culture and to give rise to specialized cells. Pluripotent stem cells are cells that are capable of giving rise to most tissues of an organism, while totipotent stem cells are cells that have an unlimited capability. Totipotent cells have the capacity to specialize into any other cell.

Adult stem cells are different from ES cells. Adult stem cells are found in the bone marrow, brain, liver, and other tissues. Unlike ES cells, they do not have the ability to evolve into every kind of cell. But they can give rise to more cells of their own kind. Stem cells in the adult bone marrow can make red blood cells, white blood cells, and blood platelets.

Scientists generally agree that ES cells have greater potential for disease treatment than adult stem cells. However, ES cell research is highly controversial because of how the cells are harvested for research. ES cells can be harvested from aborted embryos, umbilical blood samples, and the placenta. Usually, however, they are harvested from embryos left over in fertility clinics after *in vitro* fertilization procedures (IVF). When a couple decides to have IVF, they create many fertilized eggs and implant them one or two at a time in hopes of becoming pregnant. Usually there are fertilized eggs left over. These are generally destroyed, since the couple no longer needs them.

How does cloning relate to stem cell research? Cloning is the process of making an identical copy of a biological entity—be it a cell, gene, or whole organisms like a frog. *Therapeutic* cloning is the process of making stem cells from the DNA of the human that the stem cells may eventually be placed in. *Reproductive* cloning is the process whereby a human cell is cloned, then implanted into a woman for gestation and birthing. Cloning, be it reproductive or therapeutic, can be accomplished by what is called somatic cell nuclear transfer. This is when the nucleus of a cell is transferred into an oocyte (egg cell) that has had its nucleus removed. The oocyte then divides and makes stem cells—and, eventually and theoretically, a person.

Animals have been cloned for years. Scientists began cloning female frogs a couple of decades ago. In 1997, Dolly the sheep became the first mammal successfully cloned from a somatic (non-egg) cell. Now people are starting to attempt to clone pets. It is interesting to note that despite the fact that several species, including mice, pigs, and cows, have been cloned, scientists still encounter new obstacles every time they set out to clone a species that has not yet been cloned. This underscores the fact that differences between species make it difficult to translate results from one species to another. This is also true of stem cells. Scientists grew stem cells from animals in culture long before they succeeded in growing human stem cells in culture. Just because scientists can do something to an animal does not mean the process will work in humans. Also interesting is the fact that it took scientists about 90 attempts to clone a cat.

Cloning stem cells or therapeutic cloning is very different from cloning a human. Cloning animals will likely continue, but the process will have little effect on improving human health. Apparently, it does not have as much value as a means of reproducing a favorite pet either, since cloned animals suffer a variety of health problems the original did not. In fact, Ian Wilmut, one of the scientists at the Roslin Research Centre in Scotland who helped produce Dolly, has gone on record as saying that every cloned animal is genetically and physically defective. Dolly suffered from arthritis at a far younger age than is normal for sheep and was eventually euthanized because of this. Other studies involving pigs, sheep, and cows have also shown premature development of arthritis as well as oversized offspring, premature aging, sterility, kidney and liver dysfunction, malignant tumors, and structural changes to their hearts, spleens, and salivary glands.

Dartmouth neuroscientist Michael Gazzaniga stated at an ethics meeting in Washington DC: "It is a truism that the blastocyst has the potential to be a human being. Yet, at that stage of development it is simply a clump of cells.... An analogy might be what ones sees when walking into a Home Depot. There are the parts and potential for 30 homes. But if there is a fire at Home Depot, the headline isn't 30 homes burn down. It's Home Depot burns down."[161]

Despite the controversy surrounding ES cell research, the field, though still in its relative infancy, is advancing and helping scientists make great strides in helping patients. In 2002, scientists at the National University of Singapore (NUS) succeeded in growing ES cells with only human cells and absolutely no animal input—a world first that eliminates the risk of transmitting animal diseases to people.[162] All 78 embryonic cell lines approved for research in the U.S. were grown on mouse feeder layers—the base layer on which the cells are grown—with nutrients from cows and pigs. (A cell line replicates the original 30-40 cells taken from a blastocyst to produce large quantities for research and clinical use.) The NUS team has since developed feeders using human muscle, skin, and fallopian tubes.[163]

Stem cells have already been used to restore sight. Mike May was three years old when he was blinded in an accident. His right eye was operated on and corneal stem cells placed around the cornea. This resulted in scar tissue being replaced and regeneration of the ocular surface, thus allowing a cornea transplant to be performed. Today, May can see with the eye but not well. He still cannot interpret what he sees well enough to walk unassisted because his brain is not *wired* for it (In order for a person to interpret what he *sees* his brain must develop as vision develops.)[164] Nevertheless, the technique offers hope for millions. By using fMRI scanning, scientists are studying why the brain acts this way. Stem cells are being used to repair damaged corneas, offering new hope to many patients, including those who have had their sight impaired by chemical burns or severe microbial infections. The procedure takes the patient's own stem cells harvested from the undamaged eye and places them onto a substrate where they grow. The corneal sheets that are grown are then grafted onto the damaged eye.[165]

Stem cell transplants have been shown to help patients suffering from severe, progressive multiple sclerosis (MS) that is refractory to conventional treatment. MS creates lesions in neural tissue. Stem cells have been shown to decrease the number of lesions. During the three months pre-transplantation, between 1 and 38 lesions were detected per month per patient. The number of lesions dropped to zero in eight patients in the month following conditioning therapy.[166] This type of research offers the best hope MS patients have ever had. Studying 26 patients with severe multiple sclerosis who had undergone stem-cell transplantation following high-dose immunosuppression revealed stabilization of disease in patients.[167] Approximately 80% of patients in the study either stabilized or improved after treatment. Before treatment, all were exhibiting rapid deterioration.

As long as eight years after fetal cell transplant, embryonic dopamine cells continue to mature in the brains of patients with Parkinson's disease and to exert therapeutic effects.[168] Rejection, as occurs in organ transplants, has not been a problem because the cells are embryonic and the brain lacks a strong rejection response. Many stories came out of the September 11 attack on the World Trade Centers, but one involved stem cells. One of the survivors was a man who worked as electrician on the 34th floor. He walked down the 33 flights of stairs, ran five blocks, then walked three miles to Penn station and took a train home. What makes the story interesting is the fact that he suffered from Parkinson's disease, and several years earlier, had participated in a study where fetal neurons were implanted in his brain.[169]

Stem cells from bone marrow have been used to grow new bone in porous hydroxyapatite, which is then placed in patients who need bone grafts. The bone grafts can be taken from the pelvis, but this has been associated with persistent pelvic pain.[170] These bone marrow stem cells, called hematopoietic stem cells, are also being used today to treat lymphomas and leukemias. They are obtained from the blood or bone marrow and can generate cells found in the bone marrow or blood.

Some blood banks now offer parents the opportunity to store their baby's umbilical cord blood for possible later use. The blood needs to be collected either during delivery of immediately thereafter. Public and private blood banks now exist that will hold the blood. If the family consents the blood may be made available for anyone needing such stem cells.[171]

Current estimates are that a child born today will have only 1 chance in 2700 of needing to use this blood.[172] But if needed, it could be life saving and advocates of the practice point out that the use for umbilical cord cells could increase as scientists learn more. Hematopoietic stem cells, which are also found in umbilical cord blood, can be used for treating cancers, inborn errors of metabolism, congenital immunodeficiency syndromes, hemoglobinopathies and some autoimmune diseases. Stem cells from umbilical cord blood offer a better option than bone marrow transplant for some diseases. Further, some of the stem cells found in umbilical cord blood can differentiate into non-blood cells thus widening the options available.[173]

Human ES cells have been used to produce human blood cells. This breakthrough could lead to an unlimited supply of blood cells for transfusion. It was accomplished using *in vitro* research that resulted in exposing early stage stem cells to bone marrow and other cells as well substances that encourage growth.

Heart attack patients are also seeing the benefits of stem cell therapy. A German man had stem cells from his pelvis injected into the area of his heart damaged by the infarction. They turned into viable heart muscle cells and began to beat. Professor Bodo Eckehard Strauer, who carried out the operation, stated, "Ten weeks after the transplantation, the size of the damage has reduced by nearly a third and the capacity of the heart itself has clearly improved. Stem cell therapy could be more successful than all other previous treatments put together. Even patients with the most seriously damaged hearts can be treated with their own stem cells instead of waiting and hoping on a transplant."[174]

Currently, an estimated 4,000 to 6,000 Americans die each year while awaiting a bone marrow match. Only about 60 percent of White Americans now find a suitable donor, and the rates for ethnic minorities range from just 20 percent to 50 percent. Physicians have more difficulty finding a kidney or bone marrow match for Blacks than Whites because Blacks have more antigen combinations on their cell's surface and some of the antigens are very rare in non-Black populations. Stem cells may change that. Stem cells from umbilical cord blood can be used instead of bone marrow for both children and adults. "This field will explode" and may even replace bone marrow and other sources of stem cells, according to Dr. Andrew L. Pecora, director of the blood and marrow stem cell center at Hackensack University Medical Center in New Jersey. "Cord blood transplantation holds the promise of making it so everyone has a donor."

Umbilical cord-derived stem cells can develop into any type of blood cell: oxygen-carrying red blood cells, clotting platelets, or infection-fighting white blood cells. After destroying the cancer-ridden bone marrow with radiation, physicians can transfuse stem cells, which will grow into new bone marrow. There is no need for immunosuppressive therapy as the stem cells are immunologically *naïve* unlike cells from adults, and the cells from newborns are less likely to contain viruses that are dangerous to transplant patients. Further, cord blood stem cells can be located within weeks, rather than the months it usually takes to arrange a bone marrow transplant.

The benefits of stem cells are myriad. Stem cell research could revolutionize the development and testing of pharmaceutical drugs. By using stem cells, scientists say, they could more effectively eliminate potentially harmful drugs before they reach the point where they are tested on humans in clinical trials. Children with sickle cell anemia, immunodeficiency syndromes and inherited enzyme deficiencies can also benefit from transplantation of stem cells. Patients suffering from a broad range of cell-based diseases like juvenile onset diabetes mellitus and Parkinson's disease can also benefit. Replacing faulty cells with healthy ones offers hope for treatment and possibly cures. Likewise, injecting healthy cells to replace damaged or diseased cells could in theory, rejuvenate failing organs. Already people with autoimmune diseases – multiple sclerosis, scleroderma, juvenile arthritis, systemic lupus erythematosus and vasculitis/cryoglobulinemia – have been successfully treated using stem cell therapy. Around two-thirds stabilize or improve. Stem cell transplantation has been particularly successful in treatment of persistent systemic lupus erythematosus when combined with chemotherapy.

Scientists have also used stem cells from mice to study genetic defects. They removed a gene from a mouse at the ES cell stage and see what happened to the adult mouse as a result. This method was fraught with problems, however, as exemplified by the disease known as Lesch-Nyhan syndrome, a rare type of mental retardation in boys caused by a single-gene defect. Lesch-Nyhan manifests as self-mutilating behavior such as lip and finger biting and head banging. When mice were engineered to lack the gene that causes the disease in humans, they suffered no ill effects. Now that scientists can alter the genes in human stem cells, they can study defects such as Lesch-Nyhan on the molecular level in the species of interest: humans.

It is only very recently that scientists have been able to manipulate the genes in human ES cells. Since scientists have been doing this to mouse stem cells for years (in order to generate knockout mice) why have they been unsuccessful in doing the same to human ES cells? According to the report in *Nature Biotechnology:* Significant differences between mouse and human ES cells have hampered the development of homologous recombination in human ES cells. Thomas P. Zwaka and James A, Thomson, the authors of the study stated, "Indeed, homologous recombination is one of the essential techniques necessary for human ES cells to fulfill their promise as a basic research tool and has important implications for ES cell-based transplantation and gene therapies." Because of this discovery stem cells may now be more easily and successfully directed into becoming specific cells such as neurons, heart cells, blood cells or any other kind of cell that can be used to treat cell-based diseases like Parkinson's, diabetes, or heart disease. Zwaka went on to say, "This is a big benefit for the human ES cell field. It means we can simulate all kinds of gene-based diseases in the lab - almost all of them."[175]

Scientists learned how to perform homologous recombination in mice but that success did not translate to humans. They had to find new ways that would work in humans. This once again, illustrates what we have been saying: humans are not funny looking mice. They are different even in how their stem cells act in culture medium. Stem cell therapy may offer cures to diseases that today we are far from understanding. Research on stem cells will benefit humans if and only if we study stem cells from humans as the above quote illustrates.

In vitro technology continues to advance in other new and remarkable ways, taking maximum advantage of automation and computerized systems to accelerate and refine the collection and analysis of data. For example, in Houston, Rice University scientists have designed the first fully automatic, computerized system that can track the movement of individual cancer cells growing in a three-dimensional culture of living tissue. The system can be used to categorize the metastatic patterns of different cancers. It can also help test the effectiveness of therapeutics that prevent cancer or slow cancer growth. Two types of cancer cells were used in the experiments that led to this breakthrough—a strain of breast cancer and a variant of skin cancer. "Studying tumor cell invasion in live cultures in real time is a significant advance," said study co-author Larry McIntire, chair of Rice's Institute of Biosciences and Bioengineering. The system not only enhances knowledge about how cancer invades tissues, it dramatically alters the methodology by which scientists study the movement of cancer cells in living tissue. It is only through these *in vitro* studies of 3-D cell migration that scientists are able to gather data on critical factors that influence metastasis.[176]

These and other important discoveries discussed earlier demonstrate that *in vitro* technology is the cornerstone of medical research. Even the federal government acknowledges this: "There is virtually no field of biomedical research that has not been affected by *in vitro* technology."[177] As human tissue becomes more accessible to researchers, *in vitro* technology utilizing human tissue will no doubt lead to even more stunning breakthroughs. As Martin Ferguson of Ardais (a company using human tissue) stated, if scientists begin using human tissue, they "are going to find some very low-hanging fruit for druggable targets."[178]

In other words, in the race to ease human suffering, scientists involved in *in vitro* technology using human tissue have the opportunity to speed along the superhighway to finding the cures and treatments that will improve human health. Yet all too many are still trudging along the unpaved road marked "animal model"—with all its wrong turns and potholes—to the great disservice of patients and taxpayers.

A study published in 2001 revealed the fact that the same protocol looking for carcinogens, performed repeatedly on rats yielded different results each time it was performed. These tests were being performed to ascertain cancer risk in humans but revealed that when the study was repeated the results were the same only 57% of the time. Clearly animal tests for carcinogens do not work.[179] Similarly, in a study published in *Science* in 2001, researchers found that institutional animal care and use committees (IACUCs) cannot even agree among themselves whether a study in animals is worth doing. Scott Plous and Harold Herzog showed that the probability that one institution will approve the same animal experiments conducted at a second institution was about the same as a coin toss.[180] *In vitro* research using human tissue is simply not fraught with such inconsistencies. (See www.curedisease.com for more examples of breakthroughs due to *in vitro* and human-based research.)

Chapter 5

The Past, Present, and Future of Human-Based Research

We know what we are, but know not what we may be.
William Shakespeare *Hamlet* Act IV, Sc. 5

A picturesque town of winding streets dotted with lovely Cape Cod homes, Framingham, Massachusetts is typical of the suburbs that surround the city of Boston. What is not so typical, however, is the stunning role Framingham and its residents have had in the history of American medicine, for no other town in America can lay claim to be the catalyst for some of the most remarkable advances ever made in heart disease research. Thanks to 5,209 Framingham residents who, in 1948, stepped forward to become part of a long-term epidemiological study on cardiovascular disease, researchers have been able to identify the major risk factors associated with heart disease, stroke, and other diseases. Every two years, these volunteers submitted to extensive medical examinations, including medical histories, and blood tests, as well as bone scans, eye exams, and echocardiograms. In doing so, they made history.

Today, the influence of cholesterol and the typical American lifestyle on cardiovascular health is well known and accepted. However, prior to the Framingham Heart Study, doctors were convinced that atherosclerosis was an inevitable part of the aging process. They even thought that blood pressure was supposed to increase with age, so that the heart could pump blood through an elderly person's narrowed arteries. Few doctors thought that modifying certain behaviors could enable their patients to prevent or reverse heart and vascular disease. It is no exaggeration to say that the Framingham Heart Study, the longest epidemiological study in the history of medicine, has revolutionized the way scientists view, treat, and prevent cardiovascular disease. Through this study, researchers learned that dietary fat can increase the risk of heart disease, that there is a link between cholesterol levels in the blood and an individual's risk for developing heart disease, in addition to the beneficial role of high-density lipoprotein (HDL) cholesterol and the negative consequences of low-density lipoprotein (LDL) cholesterol.

The Framingham Heart Study was the first to identify key elements of the American lifestyle that contributed to the high rates of disease and disability. Before Framingham, cigarette smoking was not viewed as a risk factor in developing heart disease. However, the study quickly demonstrated that smokers were at increased risks of having a myocardial infarction or experiencing a sudden death. The study was even able to show that the risk was associated with the number of cigarettes smoked each day, and that people who quit smoking cut their risk in half when compared to those who continued to smoke. Other lifestyle factors, such as a fat-rich diet, sedentary living, and being overweight were also found to increase risk factors. It was through the Framingham Heart Study that we now know the protective effect on the heart from even low levels of exercise.

Less well known is the extensive and highly significant data generated through the Framingham Heart Study on a variety of other diseases. In addition to the invaluable insights into the epidemiology of heart failure, peripheral arterial disease, stroke, and arrhythmia, Framingham has taught researchers much about the prevalence and genesis of dementia, cancer, arthritis, osteoporosis, and hearing and eye disorders.

The Framingham Heart Study continues today. In 1971, 5,124 children (and their spouses) of the original group started participating in the Offspring Study. In addition, 500 members of Framingham's minority community have been enrolled in the Omni Study, which is designed to determine how closely the risk factors associated with disease for these individuals mirror what researchers have seen in other Framingham study groups. Researchers have also amassed a DNA library of blood samples from over 5,000 (and two generations) of study participants. The library will help researchers investigate the hereditary factors of disease and identify the genes responsible for a wide range of illnesses. The data from that study, which has spawned more than 1,000 scientific papers, remains a crowning achievement in the field of epidemiology.

Epidemiology is the field of research that involves the study of the distribution of diseases in populations and the factors that influence the occurrence of disease. It is part of the much larger field of clinical research, which also includes autopsies, clinical trials, ethical research with humans, and human observation. (The division of research into fields like epidemiology, *in vitro* research, clinical research, genomics, and so forth is a rather artifical separation in that all these disciplines interact. Nevertheless, we will separate research into these areas for ease of explanation and in order to distinguish research that is patient-based versus research that is laboratory-based, which involves chemicals and instrumentation.)

Clinical research is a vast field and, when all its various components are taken together, it is responsible for shedding light on every disease and every drug. In fact, all knowledge of medical practice is, in the end, essentially human observation. Clinical research such as human trials of new medications, chance observations of unanticipated effects of medications, studying large groups of humans to evaluate the effects of life style on disease, and conducting autopsies are all historically viable ways of finding new treatments for human disease and are the only reliable way of saying with certainty whether a new treatment or medical theory is effective or correct. The Framingham Heart Study is an outstanding example of the power and potential of studying humans for the purpose of better understanding human disease. There are countless others, some of which are described in the following pages.

Human-based Research: A Historical Perspective

Clinical research has a long and illustrious history, beginning with Hippocrates in the fourth century BCE. Hippocrates, now known as the Father of Medicine, was the first to understand that by observing enough cases, physicians could predict the course of a disease, both in terms of its likely effect and vulnerable populations. Since ancient times, human-based research has been the cornerstone of medical progress. It has stood the test of time and will continue to be the driving force behind the great medical developments in the future by providing researchers with the information they need to advance our understanding of human disease.

Many consider Louis Pasteur's germ theory of disease—that disease was communicable because of small organisms spread from person to person—to be the greatest single contribution ever to the world of medicine. Pasteur developed his theory based on observation and thought. In the 1870s, German scientist Robert Koch used samples from human tissue to isolate the causative agent for tuberculosis. In 1895, Dr. Robert T. Morris demonstrated ovarian function in a surgical procedure on women. Human-based research thrived during this time and contributed much to our knowledge of disease.

Clinical research is the mainstay of research conducted by physicians and is what determines how you are treated and with what therapeutic modality; medication, surgery, watchful waiting and so forth. The journals that are most widely used by practicing doctors are filled with clinical research. Pick up any medical journal, for example *The New England Journal of Medicine* or the *Journal of the American Medical Association,* and you find almost every article is about what happened when physicians compared one treatment with another or looked at human tissue under a microscope, what a new disease of the respiratory system, say SARS, looks like on a chest x-ray and what its presenting symptoms are, or what happened when they tried a new surgery on a patient who was dying.

There are countless examples of clinical observation and research contributing to the advancement of medical knowledge. While animal experimentation is commonly credited by its own industry as responsible for nearly every discovery, time and again animal studies have merely mimicked what was originally observed in humans. When challenged with the notion that animals are not necessary to medical progress, defenders of animal research often insist that we must use animals in research because we cannot ethically use humans. This line of thinking flies in the face of reality, since ethically conducted research on humans, from epidemiological studies to clinical trials of new medications to experimental imaging studies, is a widespread and well-established practice.

Yet the explicit claim that if we took animals away from scientists they would have to resort to using humans preys upon the public's often negative perception of what is really meant by "human experimentation." All too often, these words conjure up nightmarish images of Nazi experiments on concentration camp prisoners, preying on some of society's worst fears. As *New York Times* medical writer, Lawrence K. Altman, MD notes in his book *Who Goes First?*: "Significant advances were made more often in the twentieth century than in all of history, and underlying these advances is a cardinal fact: they were achieved only through experiments on humans. This uncomfortable truth makes many people squeamish."[181] It is a fact that there have been incidences in history of dangerous and harmful experiments performed on *non*-consenting patients. These experiments have often been performed on captive people in an institution, especially when those people are considered undesirable or to have less value to society. The Holocaust experiments by Nazi doctors are perhaps the most notorious, but there are numerous other examples as well. But a vast majority of human-based research has been of the highest ethical standard.

The Tuskegee Syphilis Study is a well-known example of unethical human experimentation performed in the United States. In this study, which was carried out in Macon County, Alabama from 1932 to 1972 by the U.S. Public Health Service, researchers withheld adequate treatment from a group of poor Black men who had syphilis, even when penicillin became the drug of choice for syphilis in 1947. Between 1944 and 1975, 60,000 American GIs were subjects of a series of chemical weapons experiments; at least 4,000 were used in gas chamber experiments during which they were exposed to poisonous gasses used in chemical weapons. Between 1960 and 1972, researchers at the University of Cincinnati subjected 88 cancer patients, most of them low-income Blacks, to high levels of whole body irradiation without obtaining informed consent. For several decades in the 1900s, the Atomic Energy Commission (the predecessor to today's Department of Energy) and the Department of Defense sponsored research in which hospital patients, prisoners, mentally disabled children, and military service personnel were exposed to radiation or injected with radioactive substances without their knowledge.

These and other incidents spawned the NIH Policies for the Protection of Human Subjects in 1966, which later became formal federal regulations in 1974. In 1991, the Federal Policy for the Protection of Human Subjects, which is designed to make the human subjects protection system uniform, was adopted. The fundamental requirements for the ethical conduct of research involving humans include: respect for people, minimizing risks while maximizing benefits, and assurance that subjects are fairly selected.

Experimenting on humans without their knowledge and consent is unethical, and therefore unacceptable. But the tragic incidents that took place in the early and mid-1900s do not reflect the manner in which the vast majority of clinical research is conducted today in the United States. Lawrence Altman:

The deficiency [of ethical experimentation on humans] has helped foster many misconceptions and myths about the way research is carried out and has led many people to the mistaken impression that all experiments can be—and are—done on animals. Ultimately, however, humans must become test subjects, and the leap from experimenting on animals to experimenting on humans is always a huge one. [182]

For example, clinical trials—research studies designed to answer specific questions about the safety and effectiveness of a pharmaceutical drug or other therapy—are conducted under strict ethical guidelines to protect the rights of the human volunteers involved. These volunteers may either be healthy individuals or people who have the disease for which the study drug or treatment has been developed. But the first time any of us takes a drug is in essence an experiment.

Today, all entities that conduct and sponsor clinical trials—government agencies (such as the National Institutes of Health, the Department of Defense, and the Department of Veteran's Affairs), pharmaceutical companies and health care institutions, must abide by these guidelines. Every clinical trial must be approved and monitored by an Institutional Review Board (IRB) to ensure that the risks are as minimal as possible, and are worth any potential benefits. IRBs are mandated by the FDA, which oversees industry-sponsored clinical trials and by the U.S. Department of Health and Human Services, which oversees government-sponsored trials. They are made up of physicians, scientists, and community advocates, and are responsible for formulating criteria and trial procedures and monitoring trial implementation and review. IRBs are empowered to immediately stop a clinical trial in progress if the established protocols are not being followed, or if significant adverse reactions are occurring.

All prospective volunteers for a clinical trial may choose whether or not to participate. This decision is called *informed consent*. Individuals who are considering entering a clinical trial receive informed consent documents that outline why the research is being done, what the researchers hope to accomplish, what will be done during the trial, how long the trial will last, the potential risks and potential benefits, and what other treatments are available. All participants have the right to leave a clinical trial at any time.

In 2002, more than 8 million Americans participated in upwards of 80,000 clinical trials. Some of these studies involved little more than weekly trips for a blood draw for a period of year, while others may last 10 years or more. There are several types of clinical trials:

- Treatment trials test new treatments, new combinations of drugs, or new approaches to surgery or radiation therapy.
- Prevention trials look for better ways to prevent disease in people who have never had the disease or to prevent a disease from returning. These

approaches may include medicines, vitamins, vaccines, minerals, or lifestyle changes.

* Screening trials test the best way to detect certain diseases or health conditions.
* Quality of Life trials (or Supportive Care trials) explore ways to improve comfort and the quality of life for individuals with a chronic illness or old age related condition.

Despite the widespread and accepted use of clinical trials to test potential drugs, defenders of animal-modeled research often assert that drug testing comes down to "your dog or your child." Somehow, in all the rhetoric, they seem to have forgotten that drugs *are* tested on children. For example, the cholesterol-lowering drug Lipitor has been approved for use in children 10 to 17 years of age for the treatment of familial hypercholesterolemia (FHC) after a clinical study in adolescent boys and girls with FHC showed that patients treated with Lipitor revealed that they did not experience any more adverse events than those treated with placebo. Infants six to 23 months old were given the allergy drug Zyrtec in clinical studies, and the drug was also tested in children two to 11 years old.[183] Clinical trials have a critically important role in the vast field of human-based research, since they represent the most efficient and effective, and indeed the only sane way to test experimental drugs, treatments and procedures.

In addition to clinical trials, the vast field of human-based research includes several disciplines, some of which study the living, and some of which study the deceased to gain new understandings of the disease process.

Studying the Living: Epidemiology and Clinical Research

As stated above, epidemiology is a field of research that involves the study of the distribution of diseases in populations and the factors that influence the occurrence of disease. It is based on the premise that most diseases do not occur randomly, but are related to environmental and personal characteristics that vary by place, time, and subgroup of the population. Epidemiologists study *epidemics*, which are outbreaks of disease involving large numbers of people at about the same time. They also study *endemic* diseases, which are diseases that exist permanently in a particular region or among a particular population. In addition to conducting observational studies, epidemiologists also conduct experimental studies by altering the behavior, exposure, or treatment of people to determine how these alterations impact on disease occurrence.

Epidemiological studies, both observational and experimental, can increase scientists' understanding of disease by:

* Determining who is most likely to develop a particular disease.
* When the disease is most likely to occur.

- The pattern of disease occurrence over time.
- What type of exposure (such as exposure to an industrial chemical) the victims of a disease have in common.
- How much exposure increases the rate of disease occurrence.
- How many cases of the disease eliminating the exposure could prevent.

As mentioned earlier, the Framingham study linked cholesterol to heart disease, but epidemiological studies have also made a number of other significant contributions to medical science. Epidemiology was in part or in whole responsible for:

- Discovering the ill effects of using diethylene glycol in early antibiotic preparation.
- Linking drugs to the side effects that resulted in their being relabeled or recalled.
- Discovering the cause of scurvy.
- Stopping the practice of bloodletting.
- Discovering the link between folic acid deficiency and spina bifida.
- Revealing the cause and effect relationship between smoking and cancer.
- Linking heart disease and cholesterol.
- Linking high blood pressure and stroke.
- Linking high blood pressure and heart disease.
- Linking repetitive motion and carpal tunnel syndrome.
- Linking smoking and heart disease.
- Linking glass fibers and cancer.
- Linking dietary fat and cancers of the colon and prostate.
- Linking laundry and dry cleaning industries with cancers, and so on.
- Linking environmental poisons produced by industrial chemicals with occupational diseases e.g., coal dust and black lung disease, cotton dust and byssinosis, phosphorous poisoning in munitions workers, silicosis in sandblasters, mercury poisoning in felt workers, and carbon monoxide poisoning in steel workers.
- Finding the cause of building-related illnesses such as Legionnaires' disease and Pontiac fever.
- Finding the association between diet and cancer.
- Linking obesity to cancer of the stomach and esophagus.
- Revealing that a diet high in fiber and vegetables is protective against colon cancer.
- Showing that women who do not smoke, but who live with men who do smoke, have a 50 percent greater incidence of lung cancer than women who live with non-smokers.

- Identifying the cause and mode of transmission of AIDS.
- Revealing that a sexually transmitted virus probably causes some anal cancers and that using a condom could prevent them.
- Revealing that cumulative exposure to sunlight and vitamin C deficiency could lead to cataracts.
- Demonstrating that obese women have a two-to-fourfold increased risk of having a stillborn baby.
- Revealing an increased risk of death and birth defects in fetuses whose mothers lived on or near farms where such pesticides as phosphates, pyrethroids, halogenated hydrocarbons, carbamates, and endocrine disruptors were sprayed.
- Confirming that exposure to cigarette smoke increases the incidence of middle ear disease, asthma, bronchitis and wheezing illnesses in children, as well as umbilical cord blood mutations.
- Revealing that babies born to women who smoke, or to women exposed to passive cigarette smoke, can have carcinogens in their body at birth and gene mutations that may lead to leukemias and lymphomas.
- Proving that smoking decreased uptake of vitamin C.
- Showing that women who gain weight after reaching adulthood are at an increased risk for breast cancer.
- Finding a high incidence of acute myelogenous leukemia in jet pilots, perhaps due to exposure to cosmic radiation.
- Revealing that men who are exposed to high levels of lead are at increased risk of fathering pre-term infants.
- Revealing that mercury produces birth defects including developmental delays and mental retardation.
- Linking low birth weights of babies to cerebral palsy, retinopathy of prematurity, respiratory distress, autism, epilepsy, and other conditions.
- Linking maternal rubella and birth defects.
- **Linking most the known** causes of birth defects **to the condition.**
- **Linking many genes to** the illness associated **with them.**
- Revealing how most infectious diseases are transmitted.
- In a population-based, matched case-control study, researchers in Stockholm discovered that the risk of early spontaneous abortion is significantly increased in women with low plasma folate levels.[184]
- By studying the DNA of 61 pairs of siblings who had had heart attacks, scientists found three clusters of genes linked to heart attacks.[185]
- By studying 718 families with more cases of breast cancer than would be expected just by chance, scientists were able to locate a mutation in the *CHEK2* gene associated with an increase for the risk of breast cancer in both women and men.[186]

- Researchers conducting a meta-analysis of studies in the UK, Denmark, France, and other countries on the association between polymorphisms and type II diabetes found that a single nucleotide polymorphism predisposes to type II diabetes.[187]

Epidemiology is used to identify increases and decreases in the incidence of disease. For example, a study of data from 3,050 pediatric head and neck cancers that were reported to the U.S. National Cancer Registry between 1973 and 1996 revealed that the incidence of these cancers among children younger than 15 years old rose 35 percent from 1973 to 1975 and from 1994 to 1996.[188]

Epidemiology continues to shed light on factors that increase risk of disease. One study revealed that toxic chemicals pose an elevated cancer risk in two-thirds of Americans. By studying 32 toxic chemicals, including those emitted from automobiles, power plants, and other industries, scientists discovered that the chemicals cause 10 additional cancers for every one million people.[189]

Researchers used data from 898,835 women enrolled in a randomized controlled trial of screening for breast cancer to examine the association between smoking and breast cancer risk. It was found that long duration, high-intensity smoking is a breast cancer risk, and that those who smoked for at least 40 years and at least 20 cigarettes per day had the highest risk for breast cancer.[190]

DDT (dichlorodiphenyl trichloroethane), the poison brought to the attention of the general public by the environmentalist Rachel Carson, was once thought to cause breast cancer, based in part on studies in animals. But epidemiological studies have failed to confirm this.[191] However, findings from a study conducted by geographers and epidemiologists at the University of Buffalo have shown that women who developed breast cancer were more likely to have lived closer together at birth and at menarche, a concept called clustering, than women who didn't develop breast cancer. The findings indicate that there may be something in the environment close to these clusters that influences a woman's breast cancer risk, according to Joe Freudenheim, Ph.D., professor in the Department of Social and Preventive Medicine in the University of Buffalo School of Medicine and Biomedical Sciences and senior author of the study.[192]

These studies, and many others cited in Chapter 4 as well as those that are described later, demonstrate how often research methodologies overlap, since these studies incorporated both epidemiology and *in vitro* technology.

Epidemiology has also revealed factors that reduce the incidence of disease. For example, the largest epidemiological study ever conducted in North America of a childhood nervous system cancer known as neuroblastoma suggests that women who take multivitamins during pregnancy can cut their children's risk of the tumor by 30 percent to 40 percent.[193] In another classic epidemiological study,[194] scientists analyzed data from the parents of 72 infants with nonsyndromic omphalocele (a birth defect where the infant is born with a hernia at the navel) and compared data from the parents of 3,029 infants without birth defects born in Atlanta between 1968 and 1980. The researchers discovered that maternal use of a multivitamin was linked with a lower omphalocele risk. This means that women who use multivitamins around the time of conception may be less likely to have an infant with omphalocele than women who do not use them.

An epidemiological study of 209 men with prostate cancer and 228 control subjects revealed that men with high levels of lycopene (a nutrient found in tomatoes) in their blood appear to be at a lower risk for prostate cancer than men with low levels.[195]

Epidemiology has also led scientists to more effective treatments for disease. By studying the records of 212 children who were diagnosed and treated for Hodgkin's disease between 1970-1994, scientists in India found that use of cyclophosphamide instead of nitrogen mustard in chemotherapy regimens resulted in a low incidence of second malignancies. In fact, no cases of secondary hematologic malignancies were seen in a 25-year follow-up of these children.[196]

By studying 538 patients infected with HIV subtype A to those of 507 patients infected with HIV subtype D, scientists discovered that HIV subtype D is linked to faster disease progression than A in Uganda.[197] The scientists told Reuters News, "If the envelope region [of the virus] plays a major role in pathogenicity, this information may be important in vaccine research and therapeutic interventions."

By studying the genetic make-up of a family in which 8 of the 20 members demonstrated high bone density, a thickened mandible, and other bones, scientists were able to determine that the gene for the LDL receptor-related protein 5 *(LRP5)* appears to result in high bone density. This could have important implications for the treatment of osteoporosis. *In vitro* studies were then conducted that showed that the *LRP5* mutation allowed the unopposed activation of a key bone formation pathway.[198]

Epidemiology continues to make significant contributions to our understanding of the aging of our mental ability. In a population-based study, researchers from the University of Edinburgh collected data on 466 surviving subjects, without signs of dementia, from the Scottish Mental Survey of 1932. They found that individuals with the apolipoprotein *(APOE) epsilon4* gene fare worse in cognitive testing at 80 years of age compared with similar subjects who do not have the gene.[199]

Epidemiology has always been a very sound gauge for determining the sources of disease. Not surprisingly, many of the causes are work-related. A fairly recent hazard is flock, which is the dust from short nylon fibers. Flock workers glue fibers onto fabric to produce a velour look. Injured lung tissue and inflammatory reaction characterize the ensuing disease, known as "flock worker's lung."

These, and other cases we cite, are examples of epidemiology. However, some would classify them as clinical research, which demonstrates that human-based research crosses into many areas. Epidemiology is closely related to clinical research. As Lawrence K. Altman, MD, medical correspondent for *The New York Times,* professor at the New York University Medical School, a Master of the American College of Physicians, the American College of Epidemiology and the New York Academy of Medicine, and a member of the Institute of Medicine of the National Academy of Sciences explains: "If those goals—curing AIDS, cancer and other diseases—are to be realized, human experimentation will continue to be mandatory since medical progress hinges on learning how humans respond to cutting edge therapies."[200] Further, he asserts, "More people will come to recognize that ultimately the right animal in experiments designed to advance our knowledge of human diseases must be human. And they will realize the obvious fact that someone must be the first volunteer."[201]

MC Reade and JD Young wrote in the *British Journal of Anaesthesia:*

> As a result, the bulk of the literature investigating the pathogenesis of septic shock uses rodent models, or isolated or cultured cells. Therapeutic advances based on this research may well promise new hope for owners of rats requiring intensive care, but there is increasing evidence that human sepsis may be a fundamentally different disease. Conclusions based on animal models may not be applicable to humans. While accepting that there are ethical and practical limitations on the scope of human studies, to not do this runs the risk of developing excellent treatments for rat sepsis that are of no use to humans at all.[202]

As for the value of using animal-modeled research versus human-based research, Irwin D. Bross, Ph.D., former Director of Biostatistics at the Roswell Park Memorial Institute for Cancer Research had this to say:

> In my cancer research days, I never saw a valid claim that animal research provided results that had any real benefit for human cancer patients. The only major advances in cancer treatment or prevention that can be clearly traced to scientific research all came from clinical studies that predated the animal research "discoveries."
>
> For some minor advances, there is some ambiguity. Animal studies on drugs, for example, gave positive results for one model system and negative results for others—which is the usual result in animal studies. Hence, until there were strong *clinical* results, there was no good reason to go ahead with the drug.
>
> With so many pre-clinical systems that are much more reliable than animal research now available, the only reason I can see to use animal experiments is this: there is no need to think when doing such experiments.

Killing animals is so much more congenial than thinking for some "scientists" that animal research remains popular.

Human-based research continues to provide clues about cancer. In 2002, for example, a team of researchers achieved an extraordinary breakthrough in cancer immunotherapy research by exploiting the action of the body's principal soldiers of cellular immunity, the T cells. They extracted T cells from patients with metastatic melanoma, isolated and grew the cells that were particularly effective in killing the cancer cells *in vitro,* and then reinfused the cells into patients whose native immune cells had been destroyed by chemotherapy, thereby allowing the new, potent T cells to preferentially repopulate the immune system. Of 13 volunteer patients; six showed at least 50 percent tumor reduction and four others showed shrinkage to a lesser degree.[203]

A wealth of clinical and epidemiological studies have illuminated factors that contribute to a higher or lower risk of developing cancer. In a population-based, case-control study among South Asian women, researchers from the London School of Hygiene and Tropical Medicine examined the role of lifelong vegetarianism on the risk of breast cancer. (A case-control study is an investigation that uses a group of people with a particular condition, rather than a randomly selected population. These cases are compared with a control group of people who do not have the condition.) The researchers evaluated 240 breast cancer patients between 1995 and 1999 from two cancer registries, as well as 477 randomly selected, age-matched South Asian controls. They found that lifelong vegetarianism slightly reduced the odds of developing breast cancer relative to lifelong meat-eaters, and that the reduced risk may be associated with an increased consumption of vegetables, rather than the absence of meat in the diet.[204]

In a hospital-based study of Singapore Chinese women, researchers collected demographic and dietary data on 303 cases of lung cancer and 765 age-matched controls. Of these, 176 cases and 633 controls were lifetime nonsmokers. They found that intake of dietary soy food and a longer menopausal cycle protect against lung cancer in nonsmoking women, suggesting an involvement of estrogen-related pathways in lung cancer among nonsmoking women.[205] A study by William B. Grant, Ph.D., who specializes in dietary and environmental links to disease, explored the association of diet and sun exposure with breast cancer by studying women in 35 countries. His study demonstrated that while dietary fat was found to be an imporatnt predictor of dying from breast cancer, the amount of calories consumed from animal products is actually the key factor. He found that the more calories derived from vegetable products, the lower the risk of cancer. His study also found that exposure to UV-B light lowers the chance of dying from breast cancer.[206] Through a case-control study of breast cancer among Chinese, Japanese, and Filipino women in Los Angeles County, researchers at the Keck School of

Medicine of USC found that eating soy foods on a regular basis, especially during adolescence, might lower the risk of breast cancer.[207]

Many, many studies have linked poor diet and lifestyle to heart disease and strokes. Even secondhand smoke increases the risk.[208] A recent example at the University of Boston found that a healthy lifestyle reduced the risk of myocardial infarction, congestive heart failure, and stroke by 82 percent. Participants demonstrating the lowest risk were those who did not smoke, were not overweight, averaged about half a drink of alcohol per day, exercised moderately or vigorously for a half-hour or more a day; were in the top 40 percent of the group for six dietary variables: intake of cereal fiber, omega-3 fatty acids, folates, sugar, and carbohydrates; and had an optimal ratio of polyunsaturated to saturated fat. With lower fat intake and more fresh produce, the risk could decrease further, according to the leader of the study.[209] Whoever discovered a way to cure 82 percent of heart disease would win a Nobel Prize the same day. But even non-Nobel candidates have the power to *prevent* heart disease.

Other studies have explored the specificity of dietary impacts. High intake of fruits and vegetables (particularly cruciferous and green leafy vegetables and citrus fruits), for instance, has been shown to protect against stroke. Findings support the recommendation for at least five servings of produce a day.[210] Other research indicated that fiber consumption positively affects insulin levels and cardiovascular risk even more strongly than total or saturated fat intake. The American Heart Association's dietary recommendation is that individuals should get twenty-five to thirty grams of fiber a day from food, not supplements."[211]

Studies suggest that too much iron increases the risk of heart disease. Iron overload in the body can damage the inner lining of the blood vessels (the endothelium). Iron may generate chemicals (free radicals) that can interfere with the process of letting blood flow freely. This endothelial dysfunction precedes and promotes atherosclerosis.

Many believe that artery problems crop up along with middle age, but this may be just because that is when physicians start looking for them. It turns out that Americans in particular get an early start on cardiovascular disease. Intravascular ultrasound of donor hearts from teenagers showed "unequivocal evidence of arteriosclerosis" in one out of six donors. This is perhaps not so surprising when one considers the high cholesterol levels and sedentary lifestyles in today's young people. The physician in charge of the study, Dr. E. Murat Tuzcu advised, "Children need to change their eating habits, they need exercise, weight control, and [they need to] stop smoking."[212]

Epidemiology and clinical observation deepen our understanding of the incidence of premature (coronary artery disease) CAD within families.[213] That awareness, combined with *in vitro* gene analysis broadens the view of CAD susceptibility. Carriers of the hemochromatosis gene, which includes anywhere from ten to thirty percent of the population, are twice as susceptible to CAD.[214] Mutations in another gene, the *lamin A/C*, cause dilated cardiomyopathy and conduction-system disease. Investigators examined genes in eleven families with the condition and confirmed the reasons for the predisposition.[215] And it is not just hearts that suffer. Risk factors such as these can also lead to atherosclerosis in arteries in the legs and neck, according to human examinations.[216] Cardiovascular disease has been a growing problem, and studies like Dr. Tuzcu's augur a monumental need for public education.

Clinical research revealed that high levels of triglycerides were not only dangerous for the heart but predisposed to stroke as well.[217] The physicians who conducted the research followed more than 11,000 patients ranging in age from 40 to 74, with coronary heart disease but no history of stroke for 6-8 years. By studying a large group of men and women between the ages of 30 and 88, scientists found that a mutation in the gene coding for endothelial-leucocyte adhesion molecule 1 (E-selectin) allows development of coronary artery disease. The mutation, called *S128R* causes more white blood cells to stick to the walls of the coronary arteries thus allowing the buildup of plaque. The discovery may allow people to be screened for this gene and hence have therapy instituted earlier.[218]

High levels of apolipoprotein B (apoB) and low levels of apolipoprotein A-I (apoA-I) were found to be highly predictive of fatal myocardial infarction (MI), regardless of what the patients' cholesterol levels were. Scientists studied 175,553 men and women and measured levels of total cholesterol, apoB, apoA-I, and triglycerides. They found that apoB concentrations and the apoB/apoA-I ratio correlated with an increased risk of fatal MI. Dr. Walldius and colleagues who conducted the study wrote, "Although LDL-cholesterol and HDL-cholesterol are known risk factors, we suggest that apoB, apoB/apoA-I, and apoA-I should also be regarded as highly predictive in evaluation of cardiac risk. Although increased throughout the range of values of LDL-cholesterol, apoB and apoA-I might be of greatest value in diagnosis and treatment in men and women who have common lipid abnormalities, but have normal or low concentrations of LDL-cholesterol."[219] This may change the way people are screened for heart disease risk.

Stroke is the third leading cause of death in the United States and the most common cause of disability. It swallows up to ten percent of US healthcare costs. By studying data from 530 patients who suffered a stroke, scientists developed simple models using only six variables that are effective in predicting 1- and 6-month outcome after the stroke. The six variables were age, living alone, independence in activities of daily living before the stroke, the verbal component of the Glasgow Coma Scale, arm power, and ability to walk.[220] On the treatment side, scientists are perfecting a technique to rectify brain damages resultant from stroke using magnetic stimulation. This technology, perfected on human stroke patients, is naturally regarded as a major step in rehabilitation.

Clinical research involving more than 1,500 colon cancer patients between the ages of 30 and 79 years, and over 2,400 people without colon cancer revealed that individuals who consumed an average of 7.5 ounces of wine, 35 ounces of beer or 3.75 ounces of hard liquor per week over a 20-year period were 60% more likely to develop a colon tumor from a gene defect known as microsatellite instability (MSI).[221] This study suggests that lifestyle factors such as alcohol may damage DNA, thus triggering a gene and contributing to cancer.

An independent analysis of more than 50 medical studies by 29 experts from 12 countries concluded that billions of people around the world who are exposed to involuntary (second-hand) smoking have an increased risk of developing lung cancer. The scientists also found evidence that in addition to causing 90 percent of lung cancer cases, smoking contributes to cancers of the stomach, liver, kidney, uterus, cervix, and to myeloid leukemia. Through these and other studies, scientists are also beginning to see just how damaging cigarette smoking is when a generation begins to smoke at an early age and continues to smoke through their adult lives.[222]

Even with the number of clinical and epidemiological studies that have been conducted and are currently being undertaken, much more could and should be done in the way of human-based research into the cause and treatment of cancer, as Rampton and Stauber write in *Trust Us, We're Experts!*[223]:

> Rather than efforts to identify environmental causes affecting cancer-rates, however, much of the scientific research and public discussion has focused on treatments—the so-called "race for the cure." On paper, about a third of the U.S. National Cancer Institute's $2 billion annual budget is dedicated to prevention research, but those are "rubber numbers," according to longtime cancer researcher John. C. Bailar III of McGill University. Most of what the institute calls "prevention" is actually basic research into the cellular mechanisms of cancer development rather than epidemiological studies and prevention trials. Research into cellular mechanisms and molecular biology has yet to accomplish much by way of saving lives, but it is politically safe research because it doesn't rock many boats. A researcher who studies cell biology doesn't have to risk getting hammered by the tobacco industry, agribusiness, or chemical manufacturers. "The prevention of cancer on a big scale is going to require that we change our habits, change our life styles, clean up the workplace, clean up the environment, change the consumer products that contain hazardous materials," says Bailar. "It's going to mean a whole new approach to everyday living."

The story with breast cancer research is much the same as the story with research into other types of cancer. Instead of prevention, researchers focus on the basic cellular research or on various treatments for women who already have the disease. The major treatments are surgery, chemotherapy, and radiation – termed "slash, poison, and burn" techniques by Dr. Susan Love, a breast surgeon at the University of California at Los Angeles and author of *Dr.*

Susan Love's Breast Book. Prior to the 1980s, no major studies on preventing breast cancer had ever been approved by the National Institutes of Health, the clearinghouse that awards the bulk of U.S. government medical research grants. NIH officials note that funding for breast cancer [prevention] research has increased consistently since that time, but even in recent years, several promising studies have been rejected, postponed, or abandoned.

Diabetes is the sixth leading cause of death by disease in the United States where it affects more than sixteen million people. When the body is ineffective at producing and/or using insulin, high blood sugar levels and diabetes ensue. Diabetes can generate severely debilitating or fatal complications, such as blindness, kidney disease, heart disease, and severe nonhealing infections or ischemia of the limbs resulting in amputations. *Experimental Models of Diabetes* lists thirty species as noninsulin-dependent diabetes (NIDDM) animal models. It goes on to qualify human criteria:

> It has been established through numerous epidemiological, adoption and twin studies [all human studies] that dietary and environmental triggers and genetic susceptibility determinants are important etiologic factors for human NIDDM... Human studies have revealed mutations in a number of candidate NIDDM genes including those for insulin, the insulin receptor...Impaired insulin-stimulated glucose disposal is a major characteristic of NIDDM. The offspring of two NIDDM parents from populations of Pima Indians, San Antonio Hispanics, and Utah Caucasians (sic) were found to be insulin resistant several years before the development of NIDDM. This observation led to the conclusion that insulin resistance is inherited autosomally and that a single gene may be involved. [224]

In other words, human studies suggest that some people are born insulin-resistant and therefore predisposed to becoming diabetic. The first gene believed to be associated with an increased risk of Type II diabetes was identified by studying certain high-risk groups such as Mexican Americans. The gene itself does not cause diabetes, but seems to increase the risk of developing diabetes, along with other risk factors like obesity and lack of exercise. Most need not necessarily manifest the disease unless poor diet and environment take their toll. Fiber consumption, as an example, affects insulin levels positively, influencing the glycemic response to carbohydrates, and therefore, the insulinemic response as well.[225] A high muscle content in the body also helps ward off diabetes. Once again, diet and exercise are the key to disease prevention.

In late 1999, Myriad Genetics Inc. announced the discovery of a human gene involved in the susceptibility to insulin-dependent diabetes. Their finding was based on analysis of families with the disease. Myriad said that it is investigating the therapeutic potential of this gene.[226] Also working in tandem with epidemiologists, other researchers have located two regions of chromosome number 20 that seem to create susceptibility to non-insulin dependent diabetes. Precise genes will be identified within the next few years.[227] By studying blood samples from two families with five boys who were diagnosed with XLAAD (a rare disorder known as X-linked autoimmunity-allergic dysregulation syndrome) and IDDM (Type I diabetes), scientists were able to identify the gene called *JM2*. This gene defect is only one of many involved in Type I diabetes, but it advances the knowledge of how diabetes occurs.[228]

Islets of Langerhans cells are found in the pancreas. In March 1999, a team at the University of Alberta at Edmonton transplanted live Isle of Langerhans cells from recently deceased people into patients suffering from diabetes. The surgery was attempted in animals for decades, but this time the team was successful because they removed a medication normally used by transplant patients, steroids, from the post-transplant patients' regime. Using *in vitro* technology, scientists developed the first human beta cell line to respond to glucose stimulation by secreting insulin. Scientists hope to refine this method. It could overcome the formerly insurmountable hurdle of the organ donor shortage.[229] They found the same effect when they transplanted the cell line into lab animals, but this was unnecessary and irrelevant.

Clinical research has enabled researchers to make groundbreaking discoveries and great strides toward understanding a host of other human diseases and conditions. If more emphasis, with more funding, were placed on clinical research today, we would see more breakthroughs in diseases like AIDS, heart disease, and cancer. (See www.curedisease.com for more examples of breakthroughs due to human-based research.)

Studying the Deceased: Post-Mortem Examinations

The living have much to learn from those who are no longer living. Post-mortem examinations, also called autopsies, have always been an invaluable source of knowledge for scientists. Indeed every disease has been either discovered at autopsy or we have learned more about it because of autopsy. Performed by specially trained physicians called pathologists, they are performed in rooms that resemble operating rooms. Information learned from autopsies has contributed greatly to our understanding of a host of diseases, from diabetes to hepatitis, appendicitis, rheumatic fever, typhoid fever, ulcerative colitis, congenital heart disease, and hyperparathyroidism.[230] Autopsies have also revealed the mechanism of shaken baby syndrome, sudden infant death syndrome, and head injuries suffered during car accidents.[231] Autopsies allow diagnosis of disorders that could not have been diagnosed otherwise, such as kidney and lung abnormalities and congenital heart disease.[232]

Post-mortem examinations have been responsible for actually discovering the causes of some illnesses *in toto* or completing the picture in others. By identifying clinical problems for which there may be no other method of analysis, autopsies remain a valuable investigatory tool for physicians who treat critically ill patients. Autopsies represent such a vitally important opportunity for learning that it is unfortunate how dramatically the rate of autopsies has declined in recent years. In years past, almost every patient was autopsied, which is why so many important discoveries were made. However, the rate of autopsies has dropped to less than one-quarter of what it was in the 1950s. If errors in diagnosis and disease management are not actively sought, improvements in knowledge and future patient care may not occur.

And errors in diagnosis do occur—not due to incompetence, but because arriving at causes of death clinically is an inherently imperfect process. Scientists at the University of Miami School of Medicine in Florida, a Level 1 Trauma Center, reviewed autopsy reports and medical records of 153 trauma and burn patients who survived initial resuscitation but subsequently died in the surgical ICU. They found that major diagnoses were missed in four patients—a large number, considering the skill and expertise of intensivists at a Level 1 Trauma Center. The missed diagnoses might have led to a change in treatment and better outcome if they had been recognized sooner. Twenty-four patients had missed diagnoses that probably would not have changed the course of their recovery if they had been found early. This included 11 cases of pneumonia and three cases of pulmonary embolism/infarction. There were also cases of thoracic spine fracture with epidural hemorrhage, hemoperitoneum, hemorrhagic gastritis, cervical subluxation, and adrenal hemorrhage. Many of these patients had nonsurvivable head injury; nonetheless, the conditions were missed. Autopsies need to be done in order to continue the education process all physicians engage in throughout their careers.[233]

There are several reasons for the decline in autopsies, despite their unquestionable value to medical progress. One of them—perhaps not surprisingly—is money. Quite simply, no one will pay for them. Pathologists do not routinely perform autopsies unless insurance companies reimburse them. But that usually does not happen. Few universities perform autopsies, because the NIH funds few research projects that utilize them. Another problem is cultural. Western society in general does not deal well emotionally with death. The decision for the next of kin to authorize an autopsy on a deceased loved one is an excruciatingly difficult one. It can be even more difficult when dealing with the death of a baby, but the information these examinations yield can be invaluable for other parents and children. For example, Dr. Malcolm Brodlie and colleagues in Edinburgh measured the rate of post-mortems conducted in newborns over a 10-year period from 1990 to 1999, at a neonatal center in Scotland. They found autopsies were performed in two-thirds of neonatal deaths, and new information was obtained in 26 percent of cases. In 3 percent of cases, the information was beneficial for the parents considering having another baby.[234]

Direct examination of the brain after death is particularly valuable, and opens the door to many of the brain's mysteries. Often, such an examination is the only way to confirm a diagnosis, such as Alzheimer's disease. Dementia in the elderly, for example, can be caused by a number of conditions in addition to Alzheimer's disease, such as stroke, Parkinson's disease, and alcoholism. The fact that these conditions may occur alone or in combination makes clinical diagnosis even more difficult. It is also very important to study the brains of healthy persons, to see how brains change as they age. Direct examination of healthy brains can help scientists learn which changes in the brain are caused by disease, and which are caused by aging.

In addition to autopsies, there are a number of ways that scientists use the deceased to advance medical knowledge. Cadavers are used in Advanced Trauma Life Support (ATLS) courses and other medical teaching courses. Cadavers of people who donate their bodies to science are used to help researchers in their quest to reduce the number of crash-related deaths in the United States. Once a month, for example, at the University of Virginia's Automobile Safety Laboratory, a cadaver is placed in the driver's seat of an automobile for a crash test. This enables scientists to study the resulting injuries using CAT scan and MRI data. Such data helps automobile companies design safer cars. The U.S. Army uses cadavers to test protective gear for soldiers. For example, one Army study explored how a certain type of anti-landmine boot could protect against landmine explosions. And many people are familiar with the Forensic Anthropology Center at the University of Tennessee in Knoxville, known as The Body Farm. Here, bodies donated to science are left to decay outdoors, so that scientists can study the different rates at which bodies decompose in different environmental conditions. This kind of information is extremely helpful to law enforcement authorities and forensic experts because it helps them pinpoint the time of death of crime victims.

Not only do many people donate their bodies to science, some are even donating their bodies, brain-dead yet heart-alive so that physicians may conduct otherwise ethically impossible research. This type of research is being done by Renata Pasqualini and Wadih Arap, a husband and wife team at M.D. Anderson Cancer Center in Houston. There, Drs. Pasqualini and Arap have given brain-dead humans medications designed to treat cancer, and they have been able to determine where in the body the drugs traveled and what they did there. The results of one such research project yielded results that were published in the February 2002 issue of *Nature Medicine*. Other institutions are following M.D. Anderson's lead and approving such protocols.[235] Only time will tell whether society accepts this form of biomedical research. We hope society will. But clearly, there is a world of difference between what Drs. Pasqualini and Arap are doing, and what happened in Nazi Germany and Tuskegee, Alabama.

Studying the living, dead, and heart-alive but brain-dead—in an ethical manner that preserves the dignity, respect, and rights of all individuals—is the best way humans can learn about the human body and unlock its mysteries for the improvement of human health. Hippocrates knew this centuries ago, and it remains as true today as in ancient times.

Modern-day Human-based Research: Evidence-based Medicine

A somewhat recent development in medicine is what is called evidence-based medicine or EBM. One definition is:

> Evidence-based medicine is the conscientious, explicit and judicious use of current best evidence in making decisions about the care of individual patients. The practice of evidence-based medicine means integrating individual clinical expertise with the best available external clinical evidence from systematic research. Because the randomized trial, and especially the systematic review of several randomized trials, is so much more likely to inform us and so much less likely to mislead us, it has become the "gold standard" for judging whether a treatment does more good than harm.

Some say that good doctors have been using EBM for ages but as a formal method of study it is new.

Medical evidence has historically been ranked in order of reliability as follows:

1.   Evidence obtained from at least one properly randomized controlled trial.

2.   Evidence obtained from well-designed controlled trials without randomization.

3.   Evidence obtained from well-designed cohort or case-control analytic studies, preferably from more than one center or research group.

4.   Evidence obtained from multiple time series with or without intervention. Dramatic results in uncontrolled experiments (such as the results of the introduction of penicillin treatment in the 1940s) could also be regarded as this type of evidence.

5.   Opinions of respected authorities, based on clinical experience, descriptive studies or reports of expert committees.[236]

The following is from the Oxford Centre for Evidence-Based Medicine:[237]

> In selecting treatments for patients, until recently it had been considered sufficient to understand the pathophysiological process in a disorder and to prescribe drugs or other treatments that had been shown to interrupt or modify this process.

> For example, the observation that patients with ventricular ectopic beats following myocardial infarction were at high risk of sudden death. However, subsequent randomised controlled trials examined hard clinical outcomes, not physiologic processes, and showed that several of these drugs increase,

rather than decrease, the risk of death in such patients, and their routine use is now strongly discouraged.

Other randomised trials (their total number now between 250,000 and 1,000,000!) have confirmed the efficacy of many treatments and confirmed the uselessness or harmfulness of many others. And a still more recent methodology, the systematic review or overview (when it uses specific sorts of statistics it's called a meta-analysis) has permitted us to draw even firmer conclusions by combining all the proper randomised trials on an issue in health care.

Equally powerful methods have been developed and applied to determine the validity and usefulness of the clinical history and physical examination, diagnostic tests, and prognostic markers. For example, there are more than 30 bits of the history and physical examination that we could pursue (and often are taught to do so!) in deciding whether a patient had chronic airflow limitation. But when these bits are subjected to rigorous evaluation for their precision and accuracy, the emerging evidence reveals that most of them either bear no relation to simultaneous physiological measurements (such as peak flows or FEV1) or can't be confirmed on repeat examination, even by the same clinician! The bottom line is that there are some specific items of the history and physical exam that are very precise and accurate in the bedside diagnosis of chronic airflow limitation, and clinicians who know them and can integrate them with their other knowledge and judgement will be better, faster clinicians than their peers.

There are many questions in medicine to which we have no answer because the research needed to answer the question has not been performed or there are conflicting studies. EBM seeks to point out what we don't know, what we do know and how confident we should be in that knowledge. Systematic reviews are providing us with data when we have conflicting studies or no consensus on the issue. If patients are to receive the best that medical care has to offer then EBM must be incorporated into every physician's routine and it must be expanded. Studies must be done to determine what the best options are and this will be a very large undertaking. But this is the kind of research that must be done if medicine is to advance.

As this chapter has shown, knowledge about human health and illness always comes from the study of humans. The new field of EBM suggests we need to make sure medical decisions are based on careful analysis of human medicine and human-based research. (Please see www.curedisease.com and www.cbem.net for a fuller description of EBM.)

Chapter 6

The Search for Better, More Effective Medications

Where there is no vision, the people perish.

Proverbs XXIX. 18

On a bleak morning in 1775, British physician William Withering braced himself to deliver the worst possible news to one of his patients who was suffering from a severe heart condition. Sadly, he told the man, there was nothing more that he could do for him. But the patient would not accept the devastating news and refused to simply go home and die. He sought out a local gypsy known for her herbal remedies. After drinking the gypsy's herbal teas, the man's condition improved dramatically.[238] When Dr. Withering heard about his patient's remarkable recovery, he himself sought out the gypsy woman. After much bargaining between the two, the gypsy woman agreed to share her herbal tea recipe, which included the leaves of the plant *Digitalis purpurea*, the purple foxglove.

Around the same time Dr. Withering made his observation, an herbalist in the village of Shropshire was successfully treating people suffering from "dropsy"—a condition in which fluids accumulate in the lower extremities as a result of cardiac incapacity—with a special tea. Once again, Dr. Withering, who had a particular interest in botany, tracked down the herbalist and discovered that the active ingredient in her tea turned out to be none other than purple foxglove leaves. Intrigued, Dr. Withering set about drying foxglove leaves to study how their potency changed over the course of the growing season. After some study, he conducted experiments on 163 dropsy patients, two-thirds of whom showed improvement.[239] Today, Dr. Withering is credited with being the first person to document the medicinal value of the purple foxglove; digoxin, the botanical extract from the purple foxglove, today remains the most effective treatment for congestive heart failure. This story of the "discovery" of the medicinal properties of digitalis is echoed again and again in the annals of medicine.

Aspirin is an example of how sheer luck played a significant role in the early days of drug discovery. An English vicar named Edward Stone believed that God had placed natural remedies close by so people who needed them could find them. Observing that people who lived in swampy areas seemed to be more prone to fevers, and concluding that God must have put an anti-fever plant nearby so His children could treat their affliction, he went in search of a plant common to swampy areas. He found the willow tree, pulverized its bark, and administered it to people with fevers. And it worked. In 1859, a German chemist synthesized the active ingredient in the willow bark—salicylic acid. In 1897, German researchers discovered salicylic acid's acetyl derivative, which reduced the side effect of gastric disorders, and less than two years later, it was introduced into the market under the trade name Aspirin. Today, aspirin is the most commonly used medication in the world.

We've come a long way from the days when physicians searched out gypsy women for potions, and literally beat the bushes for ways to save their patients' lives. Today, the world of drug discovery and development is ruled by big business, state-of-the-art technology, and an explosion of biological information. The stakes are astonishingly high—with the risks and rewards measured in billions of dollars, not to mention the lives at stake. It is no surprise then that this area of biomedical research boasts some of the most sophisticated technology, and some of the most innovative minds, in all of the life sciences.

As we shall see, the process of drug development remains a long and difficult process—but for many different reasons. Moreover, it is far more expensive than Dr. Withering could ever have dreamed—on average, it costs $802 million (in 2000 dollars) to bring a new drug to the end of Phase III clinical trials. In another way of calculating costs: it costs $403 million "out of pocket" for each successful drug of which $282 million (70%) is expended in clinical trials.[240] A recent example is the new AIDS drug Fuzeon. According to *Nature Biotechnology*: "It cost $565 million to develop Fuzeon with 50% of the cost associated with clinical trials and 1% with research."[241]

Drug Discovery and Development—A Historical Perspective

Nature provided humans with their first medications. Prior to the 1900s, virtually all medications were derived from plants, and were discovered as a result of careful observation or pure serendipity. For example, around 800 CE the monks of the Benedictine order, learned the value of using plant extracts for medicinal purposes. They used the poppy plant *Papaver somniferum*, whose active ingredient is morphine, as an anesthetic and pain remedy.

There are a host of other examples. In the 1600s, Spanish conquistadors and missionaries brought the bark of the Peruvian *Cinchona* tree back to Europe, after observing Indians of the region using it to reduce the fever of malaria. In 1820, the active ingredient in the Cinchona tree—quinine—was isolated.[242] It was observed that quinine decreased fevers, so it was given to people suffering from malaria. Before the cause of malaria was known, quinine was administered to relieve this symptoms. By chance, the drug cured the people, instead of merely masking the symptoms, because quinine actually kills the protozoa responsible for the fevers of malaria.

Drugs for mental illness were not an exception. Dr. J. M. Davis stated in *Comprehensive Textbook of Psychiatry*:

Many of the psychotropic drugs were discovered by chance when they were administered for one indication and observed to be helpful for an entirely different condition. The history of the development of both the major antidepressants and the antipsychotic drugs points up the fact that major scientific discoveries can evolve as a consequence of clinical investigation, rather than deductions from basic animal research.[243]

The drug discovery process in the early days of medicine was one in which scientists would attempt to find the active ingredient in a plant or other organism and test it for activity in humans and/or animals. For example, Francois Magendie used dogs to prove that the seizures induced by *nux vomica* (a strychnine-containing drug) originated in the spinal cord. Claude Bernard used animals to prove that curare, used in poison arrows, worked at the neuromuscular junction, interrupting the stimulation of the muscle by the nerve impulses. In the early 1900s, Paul Ehrlich, considered to be the father of chemotherapy, used rats and mice to search for substances that acted against selected parasites.[244] And John Jacob Abel, one of the first scientists in the U.S. to study pharmacology as a career, most likely used animal tissue to isolate epinephrine from adrenal gland extracts, and histamine from pituitary gland extracts.

Of course, there were a few early drug researchers who didn't use animals. One was Friedrich Serturner, who isolated the first chemical from opium in 1805 and then proceeded to administer a very large dose (100 mg) to himself and some friends. All experienced days of excessive sleepiness. The chemical was therefore named morphine, for Morpheus, the Greek god of sleep.

Identifying and synthesizing active compounds from natural products and then studying how these ingredients acted in animals was a long and painstaking process, and due to the inability of animal models to adequately predict human response, it was also fraught with wrong turns and blind alleys. Flawed as it was, practitioners of the process were still able to ignore aberrant animal data and managed, by the mid 20th century, to produce a wealth of medications that have successfully served humanity.[245] In addition to morphine, digitalis and aspirin a few more notable examples of drugs derived from plants include atropine (used to relax the muscles of the eye during eye examinations and to speed up the heart), reserpine (formerly used to treat mild hypertension), and the anticancer drugs vincristine and paclitaxel (commonly known as Taxol). One of the most recent examples of a medication derived from nature is Reminyl (galanthamine hydrobromide), a treatment for Alzheimer's disease that is derived from daffodil bulbs.

Our reliance on nature to provide us with vital medications remains, and will likely remain, a driving force in the drug discovery process. Of all drugs approved by the FDA between 1983 and 1994, 40 percent were natural compounds or derivatives thereof.[246] Between 1989 and 1995, 60 percent of the approved drugs and the pre-new drug application candidates (excluding biologics) for anticancer and anti-infective treatment were of natural origin. Even now, researchers sponsored by corporate entities and research institutions are regularly sent into remote areas, such as the Amazon rainforests, to track down herbal remedies used by indigenous people, which can be brought back to the laboratory for study.

High Stakes: The Risks and Rewards of Bringing a New Drug to Market

Today we no longer rely exclusively on finding new drugs in nature then testing them on humans and animals to study their effects. Remarkable advances in molecular biology, medicinal chemistry, information technology, genetics, and pharmacology have ushered in a new paradigm for drug discovery, in which pharmaceutical companies are increasingly using an integrated, multidisciplinary approach to bring a new level of speed, efficiency, and of course, profit, to the process. But before we delve into the high-tech world of drug discovery, it is important to understand exactly what we mean by "drugs." For purposes of our discussion, we will use the terms "drug" and "medication" interchangeably to mean any chemical compound that may be used on or administered to humans or animals as an aid in the diagnosis, treatment, or prevention of a disease or other abnormal condition, for the relief of pain or suffering, or to control or improve any physiologic or pathologic condition.

While drugs had only a marginal role in the practice of medicine in earlier times, over the past 100 years they have become a cornerstone in the practice of medicine, and it is difficult to imagine what health care would be like today without them. Not only are drugs administered to patients as a way to treat and cure disease, they make possible other therapeutic techniques. Without anesthetic drugs, modern surgery would be impossible, and without immunosuppressive drugs, there would be no successful organ transplants.[247] The need for new medications is staggering. Less than 10,000 of the 30,000 diseases that have been described can be treated symptomatically—that is, treating just the symptoms, not what causes the symptoms—and only a very few can be cured.[248]

Given the importance of drugs in saving lives, prolonging lives, relieving suffering, and supporting other therapeutic techniques, it is not surprising that the pharmaceutical industry, often referred to simply as *Pharma*, has grown to be what it is today. Worldwide, Pharma is a trillion dollar industry, employing millions of people. And with the potential revenues of a blockbuster drug bringing billions of dollars to a pharmaceutical company, the profit motive involved in the pursuit of newer and more effective medications cannot be underestimated. The stakes are high, and the competition is fierce. The large pharmaceutical firms, known as Big Pharma, as well as the hundreds of biotechnology firms that have sprung up in the past decade, have much to gain in the successful marketing of a blockbuster drug (a blockbuster drug being one that is marketed successfully to the general population, such as Prozac). Profit motivates these companies to utilize the best of what science and technology can deliver, which is why these companies stand at the forefront of innovation in biomedical research and why some of the most remarkable advancements in the cure and treatment of disease are occurring in their laboratories.

A wide range of highly educated professionals, including pharmacologists, microbiologists, biochemists, and geneticists are bringing their challenge of newfound knowledge of molecules, how cells grow, reproduce, and die, and how genes are involved in the disease process to bear on the finding new drugs. New developments in technology and automation are giving them the tools they need to speed up the process and maximize effectiveness. The process of discovery itself represents only the first link in a long and complex chain of events which involves testing, production, distribution, and marketing—and which ultimately leads to that bottle of pain reliever in your medicine cabinet. Along the way, business issues, legal issues, and regulatory issues have a profound impact on the process. It is no wonder then, that an experimental pharmaceutical drug takes an average of 12 to 15 years—at an average cost of $802 million—to make it from the laboratory to a patient's medicine cabinet. According to the Pharmaceutical Manufacturers Association, only five in 5,000 chemical compounds that enter preclinical testing make it to human testing. And only one of those five tested in people is approved.

As we explore the coming together of some of the greatest minds in science today with powerful, sophisticated technology to meet the challenge presented by human disease, it may seem as if we're describing a laboratory from the beginning of the 22nd century, not the 21st. All this knowledge we have about what happens in the human body at the microscopic level, and all the technology we have at our disposal to process that data and make ever more advanced discoveries, only underscores the foolishness of continuing to expend resources on the animal model. Our *Star Trek* science does not need the foot-powered contrivances of *The Flintstones*.

New discoveries about the diversity of molecules, a better understanding of disease at the molecular level, and the sequencing of the human genome have all sparked dramatic shifts in the drug discovery process, shifts that promise a shorter and more efficient path to new medications. Until the mid-1900s, most drugs were discovered and developed one at a time in the laboratory, where organic chemists would make a new chemical compound or isolate (separate) an active ingredient from a natural source such as plants, molds, bacteria, animals, or minerals. Using this procedure, a scientist could manually synthesize, or create, between 50 and 100 compounds a year. However, the chemists did not have a great deal of understanding of the ideal compound desired, making it a rather hit or miss proposition. Chemists had a compound, and then went about the long and laborious search for the effect that compound would have in a living organism. These compounds were tested on entire organisms—animals—without any specific endpoint. If a drug made an animal sleepy, maybe it would do the same to a human. Douglas A. Livingston, the director of chemistry at the Genomics Institute of the Novartis Research Foundation, La Jolla, California describes the process:

> When I first started in this business, you went and made a compound. You gave it to a biologist, and he fed it to an animal. The animal did one of three things: It got better, it stayed the same, or it died. You got the results and went back and made another compound.

All that has changed. Today we know that almost all drugs create their effects by altering cell activity. They enter the bloodstream and travel throughout the body, passing from the blood into the cells of the tissues where the drug action occurs. The *receptor theory* explains how a drug alters cellular activity. According to this theory, a drug acts on a cell by altering one or more of the chemical reactions that control the cell's activities. Each controlling reaction causes a particular cell activity to begin, to speed up, or to slow down. A drug alters this action by attaching to *receptor* molecules in the cell. Working together, chemists and biologists study the physiologic pathways of disease on a molecular level and isolate the tissues involved. Then, they locate the receptor molecules that are likely to interfere with the disease. The drug is then designed around the structure of the receptor. This process, in which scientists design new drugs that will interact with cellular components to effect a desired action, is called *rational drug design*. Before, chemists would ask, "What behavior does this compound I've just created have on an animal?" Today, they ask, "How can I find a drug that will interact with this receptor?"

A classic example of rational drug design is Captopril, an angiotensin converting enzyme (ACE) inhibitor used in the treatment of high blood pressure. Other examples include the protease inhibitors used to treat AIDS.

Drug development is the process of turning a newly discovered molecule into the most effective medicine possible. The first stage of drug development is known as drug discovery, in which chemical compounds are identified and evaluated for biological activity against a targeted disease. Drug discovery uses *in vitro*, or test tube research in which cultured human or animal-derived cells are placed in test tubes (or another type of controlled environment), and then a compound is applied to them and tested for biological activity. A *first hit* is a chemical found to possibly be active for a certain receptor type or molecule. *Lead compounds* are first hits that pass the second stage, which involves tests based on bioactivity, metabolism, toxicity, applicability, biostability, bioavailability, cell penetration properties, tissue selectivity, specificity of bioactivity, and distribution. This stage, which assesses the safety of the drug as well as efficacy, involves animal testing. These initial stages are called preclinical testing, and they take an average of three and a half years for each lead compound.

When a lead compound completes preclinical testing with favorable results, a pharmaceutical company files an Investigational New Drug Application (IND) with the U.S. Food and Drug Administration, which allows them to test the drug on people, in a process known as clinical trials. Each IND, which is reviewed and approved by the Institutional Review Board where the studies will be conducted, contains detailed information about the proposed drug, including results of previous experiments, how, where, and by whom the new studies will be conducted, the chemical structure of the compound and how it is thought to work in the body, any toxic effect found in animal studies, and how the compound is manufactured. The IND becomes effective if the FDA does not disapprove it within 30 days. The proposed drug then proceeds to clinical trials.

Clinical trials—ethical human experimentation—have always been vital for medical progress; clinical trials are where most drugs are found to be wanting. Clinical trials for new medications are conducted in four phases:

In Phase I clinical trials, a new drug or treatment is tested on a small group (20-100) of healthy volunteers for the first time to evaluate its safety, determine a safe dosage, and possibly identify side effects by determining what happens to the drug in the human body: how it is absorbed, metabolized, and excreted. Phase I is primarily concerned with determining the maximum safe dose of a drug. Healthy volunteers, usually male college students, are paid to take very small single doses of the drug; incremental dosage increases are made until the study participants develop side effects. (Drugs thought to be dangerous are not given to healthy volunteers; rather, they are given to people who are very ill with the disease the drug is thought to ameliorate, and thus have relatively little to lose by taking it.) Next, multiple doses are tested, and the participants' blood is analyzed to learn about how the drug affects humans. Phase 1 of a clinical trial takes one to two years to complete, and the average cost is about $10 million.

Phase II involves 100-500 people and takes about two to three years. In Phase II clinical trials, the study drug or treatment is theoretically given to evaluate its effectiveness. Most Phase II trials are randomized studies, where one group of patients receives the experimental drug, and another group receives a standard treatment or placebo. These studies are often blinded, meaning that neither the patients nor the researchers know who is getting the experimental drug.

In Phase III clinical trials, the study drug is given to large groups of people (thousands) to gather a wide range of information, such as confirming the drug's effectiveness, monitoring any side effects, and comparing its performance to commonly used treatments. Most Phase III trials are randomized and blinded and last several years. In Phase III clinical trials, clinical investigators hope to establish which patient populations the drug helps, and how long it should be administered. Tens of millions of dollars are spent during Phase III clinical trials. In fact, half the money and half the time involved in bringing a lead compound to market are spent on Phase II and III clinical trials.

In Phase IV clinical trials, the drug continues to be monitored after it is marketed to the general public (although in reality this rarely happens). Pharmaceutical companies use post-marketing studies to compare a drug with others in the market, to monitor its long-term effectiveness and impact on a patient's quality of life, and to determine the cost-effectiveness of a particular drug therapy relative to other traditional and new therapies.

When the first three phases of the clinical trials have been completed, the pharmaceutical company analyzes all of the data that have been generated through each phase. If the drug successfully demonstrates safety and effectiveness, the company files a New Drug Application (NDA) with the FDA. The NDA, which must contain all the scientific data the company has gathered (although not all the animal data), can run to 100,000 pages or more. Once the FDA approves the NDA—which takes an average of about two and a half year— the new medicine becomes available for physicians to prescribe. The pharmaceutical company is required to submit periodic reports to the FDA, including any cases of adverse reactions and appropriate quality-control records.

Today's High-Tech World of Drug Development: An Integrated, Multi-Disciplinary Approach

Some of the most exciting developments in biomedical research today can be seen in the laboratories focused on the earliest stages of the drug discovery process, where researchers are applying the concept of rational drug design— and harnessing the power of remarkable new enabling technologies—to develop new lead compounds that interfere with disease processes. Recent discoveries in cellular physiology, as well as the sequencing of the human genome, have provided scientists with a vast amount of new data about the genetic and molecular basis of disease. As Thomas F. Bumol and August M. Watanabe explain:

> This explosion of biologic information about the proteins and pathways relevant to cellular physiology and disease has stimulated biotechnology and pharmaceutical researchers to assign top priority to identification and validation of key targets (known or novel) to develop therapies for...diseases. Hypothesis-based biological research is now supplemented with multidisciplinary approaches to systems and circuit-based biology that integrate bioinformatics, genomic databases, and cellular and molecular biology with the traditional drug discovery disciplines of physiological biochemistry, pharmacology, and medicinal chemistry.[249]

Virtually all the drugs on the market today, except for those treating infections, affect less than 500 different targets in the body. (A biological "target" is a receptor molecule or protein in a physiologic pathway. A target is considered pharmaceutically accessible, or "druggable," when an organic molecule, such as a peptide, protein, or monoclonal antibody can modulate the target's function.) The predominant target of current research is the G protein coupled-receptor family of molecules.[250] Receptors involving enzymes, ion channels, and hormones are increasingly being utilized as targets.

We now know that the human genome contains around 30,000 genes. We also know that the 100 or so diseases that represent medically and commercially viable targets for drug research are caused by a mix of genetic and environmental factors. Geneticists have estimated that there are probably no more than ten genes substantially involved in a disease such as hypertension, which means that about 1,000 genes in the human genome are involved in all the 100 or so common multifactorial diseases. Each of those "disease" genes may correspond to three to five proteins that represent suitable target molecules, which would yield between 3,000 and 5,000 potential target molecules for new medicines—roughly ten times the number of biochemical targets influenced by the drugs available today.[251] It is estimated that at least half of the drug targets being pursued today are genomics derived.[252]

Assays are techniques for measuring a biological response. By definition, an assay is the determination of the amount of a particular constituent of a mixture, or of the biological or pharmacological potency of a drug. This is accomplished *in vitro*—by placing target cells or cell components in small testing wells and then adding a chemical compound to the cells. The target cells can be human cells, which are obtained from tissue removed during surgery, biopsies, or postmortems. These cells can be grown outside the body in the test tube. The cells are carefully cultured inside special flasks or dishes, and bathed in a nutrient fluid. The fluid is a complex mixture of all the substances essential for the cells' continued survival and contains nutrients, enzymes, hormones, and growth factors. Cell and tissue preservation technology is now so advanced that many different types of cells can be kept alive almost indefinitely. By culturing complex mixtures and layers of cells, scientists can create more realistic models of parts of the body, such as skin and capillary vessels, which enhances our insight into how they function. Advanced Tissue Sciences, Inc., for example, has developed a technology in which organ-specific human cells are "seeded" onto a three-dimensional mesh framework in a proprietary, closed bioreactor system that simulates the environment of the body. These cells form completely functional human tissue by attaching, dividing, and secreting extracellular matrix proteins and growth factors using the mesh as scaffolding.

In vitro techniques have a long and illustrious history, even changing the course of drug discovery with Sir Alexander Fleming's discovery of penicillin in 1928. Fleming's discovery of penicillin opened the door to the discovery, through classic *in vitro* research of almost all the classes of antibiotics we have today—the tetracyclines, the polyethers, mycins, macrolides, and aminoglycosides. The same kind of agar plate Fleming saw growing penicillin was used to develop the agar diffusion assays that found these new classes of antibiotics. (Agar is a mucilaginous complex sulfated polymer of galactose units, *Gelidium cartilagineum, Gracilria confervoides*, and related red algae.)

Advances in this technique paved the way for the discovery of other chemicals that led to drugs such as cyclosporin (used to prevent organ rejection), the avermectins (used against parasites), and the statins (cholesterol lowering drugs). In the 1960s, Taxol was discovered at the National Cancer Institute (NCI) in the United States through *in vitro* assays on human cells.[253] Subsequent *in vitro* studies demonstrated the mechanism of action and revealed that it was effective against some cancers. Testing the drugs on isolated systems using *in vitro* techniques allows scientists to manipulate the chemicals in ways that are not possible in intact organisms. Both animal-derived tissue and human-derived tissue are used in this process; however, human-derived tissue is superior because it allows scientists to achieve a much better approximation of what the chemical will do in the human body.

While the sequencing of the human genome has given us a wealth of new molecular targets, it is combinatorial chemistry that is delivering, in large part, the new wealth of compounds available for screening. Combinatorial chemistry, or *combichem* as it is often called, is the process whereby large libraries of chemicals are generated by making a few changes in the structure of the molecule. Because the structure of a chemical determines its function, even a small change in the structure can alter function. Subtle differences in the way carbon, hydrogen, nitrogen, oxygen, and other atoms are put together mean one drug may cure cancer and another meningitis. By adding a carbon atom here or a nitrogen atom there, scientists can change the structure of a drug a little, but alter its chemical interactions with other molecules markedly.

For example, the structure of the chemical dopamine (DA) is shown in Figure 6.1. Because DA is diminished in the brains of patients suffering from Parkinson's disease, it would seem logical to administer DA to such patients. However, DA cannot get past the blood-brain barrier. (The blood-brain barrier safeguards brain tissues from the damage that could result from contact with certain large molecules carried in the bloodstream.) By changing the structure of DA slightly (see Figure 6.2), we now have a drug that is able to cross the blood-brain barrier and also is converted to DA after it crosses.

Figure 6.1

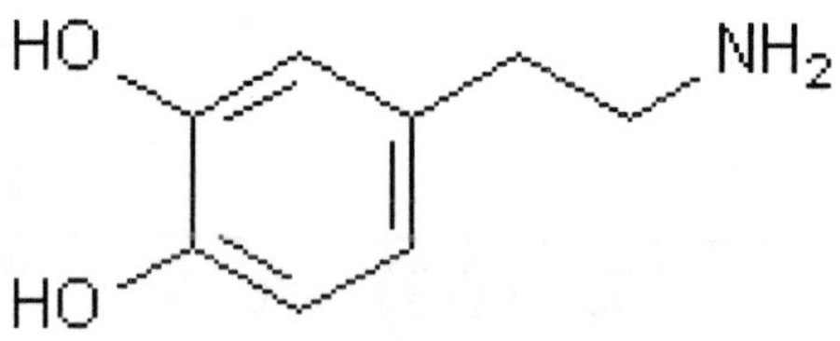

dopamine

Figure 6.2

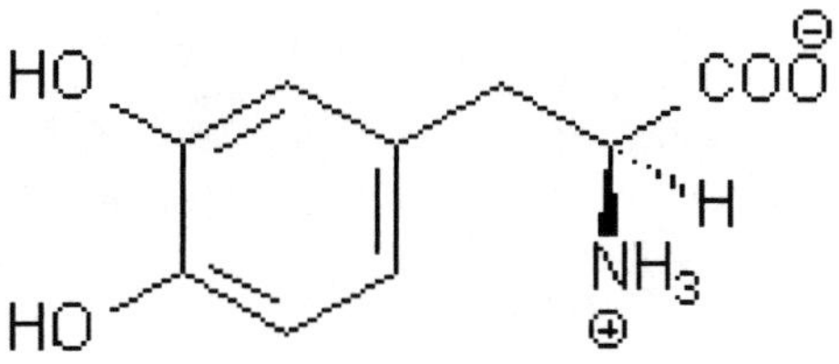

L-dopa

In this sense, combichem is an adult version of playing with building blocks, where different chemicals are added together in different ways, and the results are analyzed. This is accomplished by treating chemical A with chemical a, b, c, d, e, and so forth, thus yielding compounds, Ab, Ac, Ad, Ae, and so on. Chemical B is then treated with the same chemicals, yielding compounds Ba, Bb, Bc, Bd, Be, and so on. This is repeated until thousands of different chemicals have been generated. These compounds are then analyzed for their physicochemical properties and logged in a library where they can be accessed when a scientist is looking for a chemical with those properties. These libraries, which contain hundreds of thousands of chemicals, are based on the controlled and sequential modification of the chemical starting blocks.

One very successful use of these chemical databases occurred when scientists at Sweden's Gothenburg University discovered how hereditary tyrosinemia type 1, or HT-1, a rare genetic metabolic disorder causing progressive liver failure and liver cancer in young children, could be treated. The scientists searched chemical databases for compounds that might block the disastrous action. They found a failed herbicide that had been created by Zeneca, Inc., and the company eventually donated the chemical for medical use. The drug, Orfadin, works by blocking formation of the liver-destroying toxins.[254]

The analysis of the physicochemical properties of the compounds is based on the three-dimensional structure of a molecule and the active sites, or receptors that exist within it. Combichem allows chemists to make molecules that will fit into the protein receptor, thus changing the protein, such as turning an enzyme on or off. After thousands of molecules have been generated using combichem, high throughput screening (HTS) is used to isolate which ones are probably shaped in ways that will generate the desired action on a biological target and identify a lead compound. HTS involves using automated robotic systems. When coupled with high-throughput screening, combichem greatly speeds up the identification—the hit rate—of lead compounds. Achievements in miniaturization, robotics, and computer systems have enhanced the ability of scientists to manipulate many thousands of samples and reactions in the time and space where previously only a few could be performed. As University of Pittsburgh chemist Peter Wipf explains:

> As our first-line therapeutic defenses against infectious diseases and cancer fall victim to biological resistance, there is a rapidly increasing need for fundamentally new agents with new modes of action. Combinatorial chemistry in combination with high-throughput, high-content, biological screening is an ideal driving force for innovation in the drug discovery process.[255]

High-throughput screening is the "next generation" of screening technologies that began with thin-layer chromatography (TLC). In the field of drug discovery, chromatography is used to separate and identify products of chemical reactions. In TLC, chemists place a drop of a mixture on one end of a plate—a thin, flat sheet of glass or other material coated with an adsorbent film, such as silica gel—and stand the plate on end with its lower edge in solvent. As the solvent rises by capillary action through the adsorbent, the components of the sample are carried along at different rates and can be visualized as a row of spots after the plate is dried and stained or viewed under ultraviolet light.

DNA chips or microarrays enable researchers to screen a large number of compounds for biological activity against a target in a single experimental run. Using this technology, scientists spot very small samples onto a microscopic slide or other solid surface (also called "chips") and subject them to target molecules and see which spots have biological relevance. DNA microarray technology enables scientists to monitor the whole human genome (or a large portion of it) on a single chip, providing a "snapshot" of the interactions among thousands of genes simultaneously. The technology is primarily used for measuring differential expression in genes—that is, comparing the relative levels of gene expression between two populations of cells.

For example, Biologic Inc. of Hayward, California manufactures a technology called Phenotype MicroArrays™ (PMs) that can monitor most aspects of cell function, including cell-surface binding, transport functions, catabolic and biosynthetic pathways, energy production, cellular architecture, cellular respiration, stress and repair function, and other cellular properties within a 96-well microtiter plate. The microtiter plate is the workhorse of screening. Each of these 96-well plates contains a chemical designed to test a different cellular pathway or property. Researchers then add a cell suspension to the wells, and the system monitors, records, and interprets the response in the cells of each well. This system enables scientists to analyze thousands of cellular properties simultaneously. A high-throughput automation system known as OmniLog™ automatically incubates, monitors, records, and analyzes the results.

Miniaturization of the simpler types of assay has now made possible a 384-well plate, which has become the standard for the simpler assays. 96-well plates continue to be used in more complicated assays. Amersham Biosciences is producing the next generation of robust screening platforms, its LEADseeker being a primary example. LEADseeker is designed for decentralized primary screening, and it uses imaging technology based on a charge-coupled device that detects fluorescence and luminescence, and allows a whole 96-, 384- or even 1,536-well plate to be read at one time.[256]

Most screens use assays designed to test the effects of compounds on a particular protein target. CombinatoRx, a company based in Cambridge, Massachusetts, instead screens binary combinations of existing drugs to see whether drugs that have known effects when acting singly might have different—and unexpected—effects when used in combination. Based on the premise that most drugs interact with a number of targets at a variety of potencies, rather than targeting single proteins, the data generated by CombinatoRx's screens are built into "interaction spaces" to illustrate the dose-response relationships of the two drugs in combination. With a screening library of 12.5 million binary combinations of molecules that have already been approved by the FDA, the company believes that it will be possible to rapidly develop any hits for further testing.[257]

Combinatorial chemistry is being aided by computational chemistry and molecular modeling (also known as computer-aided molecular design, or CAMD), both of which are made possible by the tremendous speed of today's computers. Molecular modeling uses sophisticated computer programs to determine the structures and properties of molecules of interest and then intelligently analyze the data to predict the structure of an ideal drug candidate. This represents yet another step away from traditional laboratory research to "virtual" research *in silico*. Molecular modeling programs that predict and design molecules can save both time and money in the drug discovery process by eliminating the need to screen a huge library of compounds for activity against a target.

At first glance, it may seem incongruous for a non-living system like a computer to be able to generate biological data, but in fact a computer can be programmed to combine and mutate "virtual" molecules. Not only can molecular modeling programs create new molecules from various combinations of existing molecules, they can also use evolutionary techniques to test the data and eliminate the poor performers, just as in nature we see the application of the "survival of the fittest" principle. In this way, virtual evolutionary techniques can help scientists design more potent and precise drugs. In order to build molecules with the desired properties, scientists need to know the structure-activity relationship, and this is done in two stages. The first stage is known as the structure-to-property stage, which is determining the properties of a molecule based on its structure. The second stage, known as the property-to-structure stage, involves building a structure based on desired properties. Scientists use genetic algorithms to produce mutations, and thus new species of data, and the fitness function to test the data and eliminate the poor performers. In this way, only the best data are randomly exchanged and mutated until a new generation of data is produced. In the case of computer modeling, the genetic material is not strings of real DNA molecules, but other linear strings of symbols. As Michael J. Fulton, staff editor of *Modern Drug Discovery* explains:

> The key advantage of genetic algorithms is that they not only use the computer as a tool for modeling and understanding properties, but also enable the computer to develop new structures and determine whether those structures serve a specific purpose. This allows discoveries of a random, almost accidental nature. Accidents made by humans have led to some of the greatest scientific discoveries of all time.[258]

The importance of determining the three-dimensional structure of a molecule is illustrated by the success in 2001 of a team of researchers, including scientists at the pharmaceutical firm Glaxo SmithKline, in determining the three-dimensional structure of pregnane X receptor (PXR), a liver enzyme that plays a key role in breaking down more than half of all drugs. "Unraveling the structural basis of how PXR recognizes an array of different...compounds is critical to our understanding of how harmful compounds are cleared from the body and may also improve our ability to predict and avoid dangerous drug-drug interactions," writes Dr. Matthew R. Redinbo, of the University of North Carolina in Chapel Hill, and his colleagues.[259]

Currently, protein structures are determined by x-ray crystallography or nuclear magnetic resonance (NMR) spectroscopy. X-ray crystallography is the study of how crystals diffract, or spread out, x-rays. Scientists use x-rays to study the structure and composition of many complex chemical substances, such as enzymes and proteins. NMR is an advanced spectroscopic technique. Spectroscopic analysis involves using the radiation and absorption of energy from different regions of the electromagnetic spectrum. In spectroscopy, electrons and nuclei in different atoms are "excited" selectively. Because the molecules and atoms of any single substance give the same characteristic pattern for the absorption of electromagnetic radiation, these spectra can be used as "fingerprints" to identify unknown substances. NMR produces a spectrum of a series of absorption peaks corresponding to energy changes of the nuclei of one element in a chemical compound. Because the various elements in different chemical groups absorb at different magnetic fields, scientists can identify compounds from the spectral patterns produced. Sophisticated as these techniques are, x-ray crystallography and NMR spectroscopy may soon be eclipsed by computer programs developed by sciences that can analyze a sequence and apply patterns and rules to it in order to predict a structure. For example, Andrej Sali and colleagues at Rockefeller University in New York created MODELLER, a program that generates three-dimensional structures using spatial restraints.[260]

Antisense (see figure 6.3 "Antisense") drug design is based on the fact that most diseases are caused by proteins—either a cellular excess of protein or an incorrect production of the protein. (Antisense DNA is the DNA that is complementary to the sense strand. The sense strand has the same sequence as the mRNA transcript. The antisense strand is the template for mRNA synthesis. Synthetic antisense DNAs are used to hybridize to complementary sequences in target RNAs or DNAs to effect the functioning of specific genes for investigative or therapeutic purposes.) Since proteins are made, or coded for, by genes and since genes do this by first making mRNA, antisense drug design seeks to interfere with the gene to mRNA process or the mRNA to protein process. Antisense drugs are chains of nucleotides, called oligonucleotides that are complementary (and thus "sticky") to the mRNA of interest. Thus the drug binds to the mRNA, which disables it from telling the cell to make the protein. Vitravene, manufactured by Isis for the treatment of AIDS-related CMD-induced retinitis is one such drug. Antisense medications offer the promise of a high degree of specificity, since they should interfere only with the manufacture of the protein in question. Thus more effective drugs with fewer side effects. Using antisense technology, scientists performed a comprehensive genomic analysis of *Staphylococcus aureus* and identified new targets for antibiotic therapy. They identified 150 staphylococcal genes whose antisense ablation led to the demise of the bacteria.[261]

Structural Bioinformatics, Inc. (SBI) is involved in proteomics-driven drug discovery—the large-scale generation and use of protein structural information to accelerate the discovery and optimization processes. They seek to:

1) speed the drug discovery and optimization processes;
2) greatly increase efficiency in time and cost for both high throughput screening and virtual screening;
3) foster improved performance (e.g., selectivity, toxicity, efficacy) toward generation of "best-in-class" and "next generation" drugs; and
4) maximize the intellectual property position (e.g. composition-of-matter patent protection for multiple drug-like chemical scaffolds), and greatly increase the likelihood of ultimate technical and marketing success.

SBI has a database called Variome™, which consists of protein structures generated from the genetic sequence variants (polymorphisms) from tens of thousands of individuals. This allows potential drug developers to have an understanding of the structural variations of drug targets within the potential patient population. SBI also uses *in silico* screening technologies to generate drug leads for pharmaceutical and biotech corporate partners.

With SBI's Lead Discovery program, numerous compounds from diverse chemical classes can be computationally tested to narrow the list of appropriate and effective compounds, thereby providing a more reasonable number of

Antisense

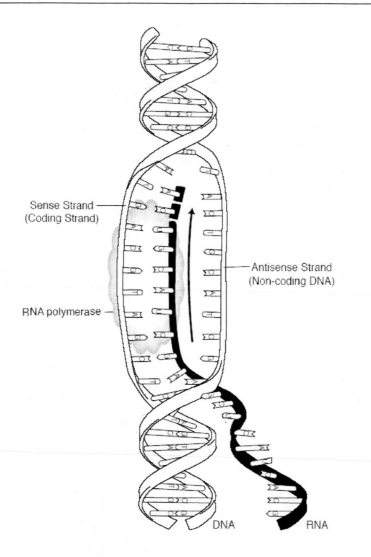

Sense Strand
(Coding Strand)

Antisense Strand
(Non-coding DNA)

RNA polymerase

DNA   RNA

National
Institutes
of Health

National Human Genome Research Institute

Division of Intramural Research

Figure 6.3

starting points for lead optimization and the foundation for broad, composition-of-matter patent coverage. The process typically yields active initial drug leads in 60-120 days, and can be validated with wet chemistry. DynaPharm® templates are virtual constructs of active sites of proteins derived from dynamic simulations of the changes in flexible protein shape (essentially "molecular movies") that predict the 3D molecular characteristics of likely drug leads. DynaPharm® templates are used to computationally screen and select active molecules from SBI's CombiLib® database (a virtual library of millions of drug-like small-molecule 3D structures) or from any other compound collection. This process yields typical "hit rates" of 10 percent.

At Duke University Medical Center, researchers have developed a method to safely turn on and off the effects of drugs. This method would create a class of drugs with the intent of creating a matching antidote that could counteract the effects of the initial drug when needed. The antidote would be useful when patients experience complications from a drug, or when a change in the course of treatment is indicated, and doctors can't wait for the effects of the drug to wear off naturally. To develop drugs and matching antidotes, researchers concentrated on a class of drugs called aptamers, which are compounds made of nucleic acid that bind directly to a target protein and inhibit the protein's activity. "We theorized we could neutralize the aptamer by using small nucleic acids that could be paired with the aptamer, much like the DNA in our cells forms paired strands. We developed an aptamer that inhibits a protein required for blood clotting to make a new anticoagulant (blood thinner)," said Chris P. Rusconi, Ph.D., director of Duke's Research Program in Combinatorial Therapeutics and lead author of the study.[262]

Combinatorial chemistry, computational chemistry, and computer-aided molecular design are all helping to meet the increasing need for new chemicals that are structurally unlike any we have now by enabling scientists to create synthetic compounds in the laboratory. Even so, nature will still remain an important element in the drug discovery process. Novel products from microorganisms, fungi, plants, and other sources containing a vast number of unique chemicals are still out there waiting to be discovered. Moreover, Mother Nature—the first combinatorial chemist, after all—can open our eyes to entirely new compounds. Nature has produced thousands of compounds using only a few chemicals—amino acids, nucleic acids, monosaccharides, and so forth. Nature has also shown us new biochemical pathways and has suggested drugs that could aid in maintaining or interfering with these pathways. While isolating the active ingredient in compounds from nature and determining their chemical structure can be difficult and time consuming, nature has provided us with insights and therapeutics we probably would never have come up with otherwise. As S. Grabley and R. Thierike state:

> Currently, natural products are passing through a phase of reduced interest in drug discovery because of the enormous efforts that are necessary to

isolate the active principles and to elucidate their structures. However, if one considers the diversity of chemical structures found in nature with the narrow spectrum of structural variation of even the largest combinatorial library, it can be expected that natural products will become even more important. Mainly actinomycetes, fungi and higher plants have been proved to biosynthesize secondary metabolites of obviously unlimited structural diversity that can further be enlarged by structure modification by applying strategies of combinatorial chemistry.[263]

Examples of nature's contribution to drug discovery abound. We have already discussed the discovery of penicillin and most people know the anticancer drug paclitaxel (Tamoxifen) came from the needle of the yew tree. Cyclosporin A was isolated from culture broths of the fungus *Tolypocladium inflatum*. And the anti-cholesterol drug lovastatin, which for many years was commercially the most successful drug from nature, was discovered as a metabolite from *Aspergillus terreus* (another mold) cultures by a target-directed screening for inhibitors of HMG-CoA-reductase, a key enzyme of cholesterol biosynthesis.[264]

New technology is helping to overcome the difficulties of synthesizing drugs from nature. Chemical screening and physico-chemical screening can be used to evaluate chemicals based on their structure. The first step in chemical or physico-chemical screening is to isolate the chemical from the complex mixture it arrives in out of nature, usually through chromatography, which separates similar chemical compounds from one another by using differences in the strength of their adsorption on an inert material. Then, the chemical is tested for its properties. All of this is basic chemistry or *in vitro* research, performed in a laboratory.

Other technologies involved in these processes include nuclear magnetic resonance, diode array detection, U/VIS absorbance spectral libraries, and infrared and mass spectrometry. Mass spectrometry, made possible by advances in electronics, is an analytical procedure based on the fact that chemical compounds lose electrons and form positively charged ions when bombarded in a vacuum with streams of electrons or highly concentrated light beams from a laser. (An ion is an atom or group of atoms that carries an electrical charge.) These positively charged ions are characteristic of the original compound and can be used for its identification. In infrared spectrometry, a device analyzes the chemical composition of a substance either by passing infrared light through a specimen and characterizing its absorption spectrum, or by measuring the amount of infrared light emitted by excited atoms or molecules in a specimen; infrared light is emitted or absorbed in a given band in proportion to the concentration of the molecule characterized by the band.[265]

With innovative thinking such as this, as well as sophisticated technology and automated techniques that we have described earlier, one would think that the process of drug discovery and development would be accelerated, and new, more effective, and lifesaving drugs would be available to patients at a much faster rate. Yet, new drugs rarely are substantial improvements on existing ones. According to the Associated Press, the NIH reviewed 1,035 drugs that FDA approved between 1989 and 2000, and found that only 153, or 15%, were really very different from currently available drugs. Most were simply variations on existing medicines. Interestingly, during the same time, consumers doubled the amount they spent on prescription drugs. This trend tends to cast doubt on Big Pharma's claims of altruism.[266] This trend increased as the decade wore on: Between 1995 and 2000, the FDA approved 304 such drugs, compared with 168 in the previous six years. Vanlev marketed by Bristol-Myers, was found to be merely equivalent, but not superior, in treating heart failure when compared to a widely used generic drug called enalapril. Vanlev was shown more effective than enalapril for treating high blood pressure, but several patients taking it had dangerous allergic reactions known as angioedema that were not seen with the other drug, thus limiting its usefulness.[267] Such is frequently the case for copycat or *me-too* drugs.

By 2001, the number of annual new drug approvals had dipped to 66. Most disturbing is the precipitous decline of new drug industry applications for "priority" new drugs, which are seen as the most likely to provide breakthrough, potentially life-saving treatments. While there were 32 priority applications in 1997, there were only six in 2001.[268] Much has been written about the reasons for the precipitous drop in the number of industry applications for innovative new drugs. But the trend means that the number of new drugs coming to the market has declined significantly, which means disappointment for patients and their families. Several theories have been put forward, including FDA's increasing scrutiny of drug applications in the wake of the alarmingly high incidence of drugs having to be withdrawn from the market as a result of serious and unexpected adverse reactions. Interestingly, the pharmaceutical companies blame the slowdown in the shift from using traditional chemistry to develop new drugs to using cutting-edge biotechnology. If this is true, we should see an explosion of new drugs in the near future.

Clearly, many of the technologies we've discussed are still in their relative infancy, and it will take time for them to deliver on their promise of new and more effective medications. Nevertheless, the discovery of the plant compound cyclopamine's ability to kill brain tumor cells, illustrates another problem that is rarely discussed. This is the fact that the use of animal models during the drug discovery and development process creates unnecessary redundancy, often resulting in confusion and delays. Cyclopamine is a chemical isolated from a weed that grows in mountain meadows in the western United States. Researchers at the Howard Hughes Medical Institute discovered that cyclopamine effectively killed cultured mouse medulloblastoma cells and tumors implanted in animals, as well as medulloblastoma cells extracted from human tumors. (Medulloblastoma is an aggressive brain cancer that affects some children, and currently there is no effective treatment.) The researchers found that the compound blocks a signaling pathway that appears to be important for the survival of this particular cancer. Since cyclopamine proved to be effective in human cells using *in vitro* technology, there was no need to use cultured mouse cells. Moreover, had the cyclopamine proved ineffective in mouse cells, the researchers either would have abandoned the hypothesis, or tested it on human cells anyway, regardless of the outcome with the mouse model. Either way, using mice was a waste of time and resources. Had the researchers stopped if the cyclopamine had failed in the mouse model, they may not ever have uncovered a possible treatment for the disease in humans. Had they continued on anyway with *in vitro* investigations using human cells, then why would they bother with a mouse model to begin with? One wonders how many prospective drugs have been abandoned after not working in animal models, when they would have proved lifesaving for humans. By the same token, using animal models to duplicate results demonstrated in human tissue wastes valuable time and resources, which underscores the urgent need to abandon the animal model in favor of the non-animal technologies that hold much greater promise for delivering safe and effective medications to patients in need.

A recent editorial in *Nature Reviews Drug Discovery* stated:

In Tamoxifen's case, a drug first developed as a potential contraceptive languished for many years before its present application was found. Furthermore, its propensity to cause liver tumours in rats, a toxicity problem that thankfully does not carry over into humans, was not detected until after the drug had been on the market for many years. If it had been found in preclinical testing, the drug would almost certainly have been withdrawn from the pipeline. With the COX2 inhibitors, Rod Flower notes that the transgenic animal models used to test the hypothesis that COX2 would make an anti-inflammatory target gave results that, if relied upon, might have killed the project. Both stories emphasize the role of the dogged researchers who kept their eyes focused on the prize while navigating around obstacles and exploiting any opportunity that came along. It might sound a bit trite, but at the very least we can say that one of the best strategies for drug discovery is to start with a group of people who really want to discover drugs.[269]

Chapter 7

Replacing the Animal Model in Drug Testing

My beloved niece was diagnosed with epilepsy as a baby and back then I got a publication called *The National Epilepsy Spokesman* to stay on top of research for her and my sister. In their Jan. 1990 issue, they reported that the medication "Vigabatrin" had been tested on animals in the U.S. and believed to cause brain damage but was tested on people in Europe and was then used as a medication on people and worked for seizures. That medication was denied to my niece BECAUSE it was tested on animals first.

Judy

(Author's note: As of the writing of this book, Vigabatrin was still not available in the US.)

Jeff Smith—successful business executive, husband and father of three children—woke up on the morning of his forty-second birthday with nagging thoughts about his own mortality. Despite his robust health, Jeff knew he was a prime candidate for heart disease. After all, his father had died of a heart attack at age 52, and his older brother, Paul, was the survivor of three heart attacks before the age of 50. So Jeff vowed to do what he had been thinking about for a long time. As soon as he arrived at his office, he made an appointment with Paul's cardiologist.

One of the top cardiologists in the city, Dr. Peter Haney didn't hesitate to put Jeff through his paces. He asked Jeff to fill out a 12-page questionnaire on his family medical history, diet, and lifestyle even before coming in for an exam. On the day of his appointment, Dr. Haney gave Jeff a complete physical examination, drew blood, and ordered a stress test. When the test results revealed that Jeff's cholesterol level was high, Dr. Haney wrote him a prescription for Baycol, a member of the class of cholesterol-lowering drugs known as *statins*.

There is no doubt that Jeff did what he was supposed to do. Given his family history of heart disease, he put himself under the care of a competent cardiologist. And Dr. Haney did what *he* was supposed to do. After diligently putting his patient through a battery of tests, he prescribed a medication that had not only been approved for release by the U.S. Food & Drug Administration (FDA), it was being used successfully by hundreds of thousands of people to reduce cholesterol levels, thus preventing heart attacks and prolonging life. Nevertheless, Jeff—a healthy man in the prime of his life—died six months later from a condition known as rhabdomyolysis, which causes the muscles in the body to disintegrate and irreversibly damages the kidneys.

What went wrong?

Jeff's tragic story reveals a stark but little publicized fact about prescription drugs in the US: they kill about 100,000 people every year, as a result of severe adverse reactions. (Adverse reactions to pharmaceutical drugs are also responsible for 15 percent of all hospital admissions.) In 1994, adverse drug reactions were the fourth leading cause of death in the U.S., killing more people than all illegal drugs combined and costing the general public over $136 billion in health care expenses.[270] In 2001, Baycol was shown to be one of those killer drugs.

Germany's Bayer AG said in January 2002 that the number of known deaths related to use of the cholesterol-lowering drug Baycol (cerivastatin), which was withdrawn from the market last year, had doubled from an earlier estimate of 52.[271] Then, a Bayer spokesman told Reuters that the group was aware of around 100 deaths linked to use of the drug but estimates run much, much higher. People who at the time were successfully taking Baycol to lower their cholesterol were advised to contact their doctors for a prescription for one of the other statins, and to discontinue use of the new medication immediately if they experienced any muscle weakness or pain.

The Baycol debacle is hardly an isolated incident. There are many such cases, and they all demonstrate the dramatic need to improve drug testing. And one of the most important ways to improve testing is to replace the animal model.

Replacing the Animal Model in Drug Testing

Forbes magazine published an article in their December 27, 1999 issue about why new inventions and discoveries don't pan out. They singled out the failure of drug companies to find drugs to treat sepsis or cancer in humans as due in large part to their reliance on animal experiments:

Each [drug company] had a drug that targeted one or another link in the supposed chain – endotoxin, the irritant spewed out by invading bacteria: tumor necrosis factor, which the body deploys against bacteria; interleukin-1, a chemical signal by which the body marshals all its weapons. All seemed to help in animal models of sepsis and Wall Street entertained high hopes. Indeed, the main question for investors was not whether the drugs would work, but which would work first. None did. In several cases the drugs were so much worse than the sugar pill given as an experimental control that the trials had to be cut short...'We don't know what went wrong,' says R Phillip Dellinger, a specialist in critical care medicine at Rush-Presbyterian-Saint Luke's Medical Center in Chicago, who headed a panel that investigated the problem.

'The animal models may have been inappropriate; we may have been treating the wrong patients...' [Speaking about the hype that accompanies discoveries] Sometimes, it's enough to just repeat yourself loudly – as, for instance, on the front page of the New York Times. Last year an article in that sensitive place informed readers that Judah Folkman and his company, Entremed, were going to cure cancer 'in two years.' Aside from that appeal to authority, the article reported nothing that had not already appeared in an understated piece the Times had run months earlier, a summary from the British journal *Nature*. No matter that no controlled trials in humans had yet been completed. No matter that encouraging results in rodents had been found in countless cancer studies that ended up failing in humans.[272]

Professor Sir Michael Rawlins, chairman of the British National Institute for Clinical Excellence, told representatives from the pharmaceutical industry, regulators, academics, and patient groups that the animal study regime, which could take up to six years, was "utterly futile" and that the industry must do more research on how to conduct efficient clinical trials.[273]

To understand how the animal model is used in drug testing—and why it has a long history of failures, one needs to know how a drug is tested before it reaches the marketplace.

A new chemical that appears to fill a niche in a pharmaceutical company's business plan is called a lead compound. Once a lead compound is discovered— that is, it has been determined to have potentially beneficial pharmacological properties, meaning that it exhibits biological activity against a target—scientists proceed to optimize it. Scientists must also learn how a potential drug will affect the body at numerous levels, from the action it has on molecules to cells to tissues to organ systems. It must be evaluated for effects on the liver, kidneys, skin, lungs, heart, nerve cells, the immune system, germline cells (cells used for reproduction), and the embryo. The scientist must also understand how the chemical will interact with epithelial cells and the small intestine.

Drug optimization involves changing the chemical properties of the compound incrementally to allow for improved target penetration or to lessen the chance of side effects. Tests on the drug's pharmacokinetic properties (what the body does to the drug), as well as its potential toxicological effects, then occur or may even occur simultaneously with the optimization process. A drug's pharmacokinetic properties are evaluated through a series of tests referred to as ADME, which stands for Absorption, Distribution, Metabolism, and Elimination. During this phase of preclinical testing, scientists seek to determine how a drug is *absorbed*, or taken into the body, how it is *distributed* through the body and reaches the site of its action, how it is *metabolized*, or broken down by the body's enzymes, and how it is *eliminated*, or passed from the body. Toxicological studies seek to determine if a chemical has any adverse effects on the body. Together, ADME and toxicological studies are known as ADMET.

Whatever may be the potentially beneficial pharmacological properties of a drug, it is useless medicinally if it cannot be taken up, metabolized, and eliminated from the body in a safe and appropriate manner. Ideally, a drug enters the body, homes in on a specific molecular target without disturbing any other cells, makes the appropriate adjustments to the target, and leaves the body without harming it. In the real world, it rarely happens as perfectly as researchers hope. The process of weeding out good chemicals from bad chemicals is extraordinarily complex, and those in the pharmaceutical industry often refer to it as "the ADMET problem." An overwhelmingly large component of the ADMET problem lies in industry's historical reliance on data generated by tests in animals. The fact that there are problems extrapolating between species should come as no surprise. Analytical chemist, Jeremy Nicholson professor of biological chemistry at Imperial College, London has said that many of the animal models are pretty useless because, as his research shows, there is significant metabolic variation even between *genetically identical* mice.[274]

According to William Bains, chief scientific officer of Amedis Pharmaceuticals (Royston, UK), deficiencies in ADMET properties cause approximately half of all drugs in development to fail to reach the market, and further, half of the drugs that do make it to market still exhibit ADMET problems.[275] Barry Selick, CEO of the ADMET modeling company Camitro (Menlo Park, CA) estimates that for every drug that is pulled from the market as a result of ADMET difficulties not revealed in clinical trials, there are ten more that remain on the market with label restrictions because of the potential for interactions between drugs.[276]

Looking just at the absorption process—the "A" in ADMET—illustrates the enormous challenges posed by the ADMET problem. The ways a drug can enter the body and the body's tissue can be complicated and varied. In order to get to the target, a drug must cross several membranes. First, it must pass from the environment to the interstitial fluid. This can be done by swallowing the drug and having it enter the interstitial fluid of the lining of the stomach or intestines. (Or it can enter via the skin, nasal mucosa, rectum, veins, arteries, vagina, or lungs.) From the interstitial fluid the chemical must cross a membrane to enter the bloodstream, and likewise, in order to exit from the blood to the target tissue it must cross another membrane. Once in the interstitial fluid of the tissue it needs to penetrate, the drug must then cross a membrane to enter the cell. Scientists must study the chemical to understand what will happen at each of these membranes.

The "T" in ADMET, *Toxicology* demonstrates the extent to which conducting ADMET studies are a complex, time-consuming process, with many twists and turns. Toxicology is the study of the adverse effects of chemicals on living organisms. Modern-day toxicology is a multidisciplinary field composed of pharmacologists, chemists, biologists, physiologists, pathologists, immunologists, public health officials, and others. According to the American Chemical Society, the ultimate goals of toxicology assessments are:

- To characterize toxicity in animal models for the purpose of identifying potential problems in short/long term clinical studies;
- To identify circumstances under which toxicity occurs;
- To evaluate the extent to which toxicity data can be extrapolated to humans;
- To recommend safe levels of exposure; and
- To contribute to the decision-making process for testing in humans.[277]

Accepted toxicological theory states, "The dose makes the poison." In other words, *all* chemicals are toxic, and the smaller the dose necessary to cause injury, the more toxic is the chemical. Chemicals are absorbed into the blood stream and distributed to various tissues. The toxicity of most chemicals is determined in large part by how they are metabolized in the body, and different genes control the metabolism of different chemicals. As a result, small differences in gene structure or regulation can mean huge differences in the way chemicals are metabolized.

When a chemical is first identified to be of potential use in combating human disease, toxicologists will screen the chemical using animal tests. If the drug continues to be considered a good candidate for development, before being given to humans, it will be tested, again on animals, for carcinogenicity (ability to cause cancer) and teratogenicity (ability to cause birth defects). While the chemical is undergoing clinical trials in humans, it will again be tested for cumulative effects in animals, and this testing will continue until the drug is approved. (Tests that are run during this time include those to determine acute toxicity, cumulative toxicity, absorption from various routes, how the drug is eliminated in animals and how long that takes, how it penetrates barriers like cell membranes and the blood-brain barrier, whether it is excreted in the milk, whether it causes birth defects, DNA mutations or cancer, and whether it causes local irritation, e.g., of the skin.)

The first phase is generally for acute toxicity, where scientists hope to discover the dosage that produces toxic effects in a single administration or with repeated administration within a twenty-four-hour period. In the recent past, the LD50 tests, which include the Oral LD50 and the Dermal LD50, and the Inhalation Toxicity (LC50) tests have been used to determine acute—single dose—toxicity levels. LD stands for lethal dosage, and the LD50 test is designed to measure the dosage that proves fatal for 50 percent of a group of experimental animals over the course of a maximum of two weeks after a one-time administration of the drug. In the Oral LD50 test, animals—usually limited to rats and mice, but occasionally also dogs—are fasted overnight and then administered the drug by mouth. In the Dermal LD50 test, albino rabbits are used, and the drug is placed on an area of the skin that has been clipped free of hair and abraded. (Skin is abraded by using adhesive tape to remove several layers of skin.) The substance being tested is kept in contact with the skin for 24 hours. The inhalation toxicity (LC50) measures the lethal concentration of an acute dosage by exposing animals to the substance in the air they are breathing for four hours.

The LD50 test has long been criticized as a way to determine acute toxicity levels. Even toxicologists have admitted that the test is flawed in many ways, particularly the difficulty in extrapolating the data to humans. In addition, many factors, such as age, gender, nutritional status, housing, vehicle, rate of administration, and diet, can affect estimates of LD50.[278] Today, many toxicologists believe that there is no valid reason to conduct LD50 tests. As Dr. Drews explains:

> More significant than the LD50 are the relationship between dosage and toxic effect, the temporal course of toxic effects, the determination of those organs or organ systems first affected, and the reversibility of toxic phenomena. In general, such acute toxicity experiments carried out on two species have only an orienting character.[279]

For an example of how species differ in the LD50 see table below:

Comparison of the LD50 in Rats and Mice

(NIOSH/Registry of Toxic Effects of Chemical Substances)

Chemical	Rat mg/kg	Mouse mg/kg	Ratio
Carbon tetrachloride	2350	8260	0.28
Dextropropoxyphene HCl	84	225	0.37
Dichloromethane	1600	873	1.80
Diphenylhydantoin	1640	150	10.90
Ethanol	7060	3450	2.00
Mercury (II) chloride	1	6	17
Nicotine	50	3	16.70
Paracetamol	2400	340	7.00
Sodium oxalate	11,200	5100	2.20
Thioridazine HCl	995	385	2.60

Acute toxicity tests also involve primary eye irritation and skin irritation tests. Typical protocols for the primary eye irritation test use rabbits, in which the test substance is placed in one eye, with the other eye serving as a control. Eye irritation is then evaluated at one, two, three, four, and seven days, then every three days thereafter until toxicity subsides. In the Primary Skin Irritation test, the skin of rabbits is clipped in two areas, with one of those areas slightly abraded. The substance is placed on the skin and covered by gauze and then plastic. The chemical remains in contact with the skin for four hours. Redness and swelling are evaluated 24 and 72 hours after application of the chemical.

Subacute and subchronic toxicity tests are designed to study the appearance and decline of toxicity levels during continuous applications of the substance over a longer period of time. Typically, subacute tests are conducted on rodents and take place over a 14-day period. In subchronic testing, two species are used—generally, dogs and rats. The animals are dosed daily (or five times a week) over 10 percent of the animal's lifespan, which is 90 days in rats and one to two years in dogs.

Chronic toxicity testing attempts to:

- Evaluate the risks associated with long-term use of a substance;
- Identify observable toxic effects;
- Determine the range of dosage in which only pharmacological effects are observed, as well as the range of dosage in which no toxic effect appears;
- Establish the maximum tolerated dose (the dosage with no side effects); and
- Determine the largest dose that can be tolerated without significantly lowering life expectancy.

As in subchronic testing, chronic testing is conducted, in accordance with the general requirements of regulatory agencies on both a rodent species (rat or mouse) and a non-rodent "second" species (usually a dog or nonhuman primate). **Chronic tests last over the lifespan, or a substantial portion of the lifespan, of the test animals (two years in rodents).** Unfortunately, all of the above have failed as predictors for humans. We will discuss the more reliable alternatives in a moment.

Carcinogenicity tests are also performed on test substances in separate experiments. Generally, these tests are conducted on rodents over their lifespan of two years. Reproduction and development studies, which are designed to provide information on the effects of a substance on breeding, fertility, parturition, neonatal development, and lactation, are conducted in three segments. The first studies are those on the effects of the chemical on the fertility and general reproductive performance. The second segment determines toxicity levels in the embryo and birth defects. During the third segment of reproduction and development studies, researchers attempt to discern the chemical's effect on late fetal development, labor and delivery, neonatal viability, growth and lactation.[280]

One cause of concern in toxicology is whether the drug will cause mutagenicity—that is, changes in DNA. This may lead to cancer or birth defects. If the DNA mutation occurs in a germ cell (egg or sperm), birth defects or genetic diseases may result. If the mutation occurs in a somatic (non-germ) cell, cancer, premature aging or other diseases may result. Mutagenesis researchers study the way DNA responds to chemicals. As we have previously described, genes are made of DNA, which codes for RNA. Replication is the process of DNA making DNA—it replicates or makes a carbon copy of itself. Transcription is when DNA makes RNA. Translation is when RNA makes amino acids or proteins. Damaged DNA can either be repaired or replicated with the mutation. Most mutations are repaired, but if the mutation is replicated and cells containing the mutation do not die, then cancer or other diseases can occur. As in the toxicity tests detailed above, the mutagenicity studies in animals have failed to be good predictors of mutagenesis in humans.

Animals are also used in toxicology studies in an effort to determine the correct dose for humans. In accordance with federal regulations, two species must be used; usually rodents, dogs or nonhuman primates but not infrequently pigs, cats, ferrets, or other animals.[281]

But this system is far from perfect. Indeed, there have been innumerable problems associated with the practice of using animals in ADMET studies (see table 7.1). To begin with, most animals are exposed to very high doses of the chemical over a short period of time, while most humans are exposed to low doses over a very long period of time. Humans tend to be exposed to medications in small doses and intermittently (e.g., every eight hours) or continuously in small doses (e.g., air pollution), while animals are exposed in large doses intermittently or in large doses continuously.

The routes of exposure can also differ between animals and humans. Animals may be exposed via their blood vessels while humans are exposed via their lungs. Humans may metabolize the chemical to a different chemical than animals will metabolize it to or to the same chemical but by a different pathway. Animals and humans may also differ in the way their organs and genes respond to the chemical. Different humans may even respond differently because of genetic differences. Acute toxicity tests are like comparing drowning in a swimming pool to drinking eight glasses of water a day.

Lois Gold, director of the Carcinogenic Potency Database Project at Lawrence Berkeley Laboratory said: "Testing for carcinogenicity in animals at near toxic doses does not give enough information to predict the excess number of cancers from low doses typically experienced by humans."[282]

The Toxicology Working Group at the House of Lords conference of the Select Committee on Animals in Scientific Procedures concluded that "the effectiveness and reliability of animal tests is unproven. It [was] recommended that the reliability and relevance of all existing animal tests should be reviewed as a matter of urgency." Also that "the scientific basis for the use of two species is questionable; tests could be conducted in any number of species and the relevance of the findings for man would be equally uncertain for all the species used...The formulaic use of two species in safety testing was not considered to be a scientifically justifiable practice, but rather an acknowledgement of the problem of species differences in extrapolating the results of animal tests to predict effects in humans.... some animal testing was done for 'administrative', rather than scientific reasons."

Subjects	Animals	Humans
Numbers	Large groups	Individuals
Age	Young adult	All ages
State of health	Healthy	Usually sick
Genetic background	Homogeneous	Heterogeneous
Dose - Magnitude	Therapeutic to toxic	Therapeutic
Dose - Schedule	Usually once daily	Optimum
Housing	Uniform/Optimal	Variable
Nutrition	Uniform/Optimal	Variable
Concomitant therapy	Never	Frequent
Verbal contact	None	Intensive
Physical exam	Limited	Extensive
Clinical lab	Limited/standardized	Individualized
Timing	Predetermined	Individualized
Autopsy	Always	Exceptional
Histopathology	Extensive	Exceptional

Table 7.1

The group unanimously agreed that the standard rodent carcinogen test falls into this category, though that is not recorded in the report.[283]

As Dr. Miles Weatherall, former director of Establishment, Wellcome Research Laboratories wrote in *Nature*:

Every species has its own metabolic pattern, and no two species are likely to metabolize a drug identically. Small differences in the rate of conversion of drug to inactive, or toxic, metabolite can have large effects on the concentration of active substances at the point of action. Most experiments to seek toxic effects in whole animals involve oral administration; differences in diet, gut physiology, rate of passage and liver enzymes raise serious questions about the relevance of findings in rats or mice to man. Compounds that are not absorbed in laboratory animals are not, with minor exceptions, ever tested in man. Nobody knows how many drugs, which would be useful in man, may have been lost in this way. Similarly compounds toxic in laboratory animals at doses near the predicted therapeutic level do not receive trial in man, so it is never revealed whether they would actually have been harmful in man. Thus we lack the evidence of the false positive element in animal toxicology studies, so it is easy to give more weight to such studies than is justifiable.

Toxicity is determined mostly by how the chemical is metabolized by the body. Many different genes influence how this. As James P. Kehrer, Ph.D., of the Division of Pharmacology and Toxicology at the University of Texas at Austin stated, "Small differences in gene structure can make large differences in function."[284] Because ADMET studies in animals are so unreliable, when a drug enters clinical trials, the company has very little idea if it will damage humans. Tom Patterson, chief scientific officer at Entelos, likens the current practice of drug testing in humans during clinical trials to making airplanes, trying to fly them, and marketing the one that does not crash.[285]

Moreover, the most common side effects of drugs cannot be predicted from animal tests. Nausea, dizziness, headache, heartburn, fatigue, tinnitus, vertigo, and other side effects cannot be judged in animals. Likewise, animal tests have often derailed good drugs because of adverse effects seen in the animal that did not occur in humans, or because of the general ineffectiveness of the animal model. Drug-metabolizing enzymes were studied in dog, monkey, and human small intestines, and in the human adenocarcinoma cell line Caco-2, a commonly used *in vitro* absorption model. Overall, the results demonstrated that both the preparations of small intestines and Caco-2 cells exhibited significant drug-metabolizing enzyme activities, although several differences were noted between the intestinal enzymes in the animals or in the Caco-2 cells and those found in humans.[286]

A recent example of why metabolism is so important is the Roche calcium channel blocker Posicor (mibefradil). Designed to lower high blood pressure and control angina, Posicor was prescribed for millions of people. It was found, however, to inhibit the metabolism of other drugs that many people suffering from hypertension and angina were taking, e.g., cholesterol-lowering drugs, thus leading to dangerously high blood levels of these drugs. Posicor was taken off the market one year after it was released.

One adverse side effect that derails many drugs and causes relabeling and withdrawal is hepatotoxicity (liver toxicity). According to the FDA, drug-induced liver toxicity is the leading cause of liver failure in the US, the most common cause of withdrawing a drug from the market, and more than 75% idiosyncratic drugs reactions result in liver transplant or death.[287] (An idiosyncratic drug reaction is one that is peculiar to an individual, one that occurs very rarely.) One reason this occurs is animal testing. We mentioned Mark Levin Ph.D. and CEO of Millennium Pharmaceuticals and his rat studies in Chapter One but the example is so pertinent we want to bring it to mind again. Levin presented data at the Drug Discovery Technology Conference in Boston, Massachusetts August 2001. In a study conducted at his company, twenty-eight potential drugs were tested in rats. Eleven showed liver toxicity in the rats, while seventeen did not. Normally all eleven would have been tossed aside because it would have been assumed that they would do the same in humans. But because this belief has been shown to be unfounded, all the chemicals went on to be tested in humans. Of the eleven that were thought to be hepatotoxic, two were shown to toxic in humans also, but six were shown to be safe for humans. Of the seventeen that tested safe in the rats, eight were also safe in humans but six went on to be toxic to the liver. Levin concluded that this means the rat data were basically as accurate as "a coin toss." This is why many New Chemical Entities (NCEs) fail in humans and why new predictive methods for testing are needed. Clearly, the animal model aspect of the ADMET testing process is inadequate.

Another reason liver toxicity is a problem is the fact that most Phase III clinical trials involve only about 3,000 patients. In order to detect drugs that may cause liver toxicity, about 30,000 patients should be studied. Since companies rely on the animal tests, they can rationalize not conducting the larger and more expensive clinical trials. The FDA should require the larger clinical trials but because of lobbying efforts by BigPharma, will not.

Nevertheless, procedures that became established after the thalidomide disaster, whereby large numbers of animals are fed large amounts of a drug for a long time, have become ritual; "routine tests of limited value and governed by regulations rather than by rational thought." Reports on the results are submitted to regulatory bodies in conference and are seldom published. Independent scientists rarely repeat the experiments; nobody is motivated to find the very considerable resources needed to do so.[288] While human epidemiological data and chemical structure analysis are utilized in ADMET assessments, ADMET studies continue to be performed on animals and animal-derived tissue, despite frequent admissions by researchers that animal-based ADMET studies often fail to be predictive. It is this failure of the animal-model paradigm that contributes to the following grim statistics.

The number of Britons dying in-hospital from medication errors and adverse effects of medicines shot up from 200 in 1990 to 1100 in 2000, according to a new report.[289] The Audit Commission said this is costing the National Health Service £500 million each year in longer stays in hospitals, "to say nothing of the human cost to patients." According to the report, complications arising from drugs are the most common cause of adverse events in hospital patients and generate adverse publicity for the NHS.

Dr. Karen E. Lasser of Cambridge Hospital and Harvard Medical School and her colleagues studied all new drugs released between 1975 and 1999 and found a total of 56 drugs approved that subsequently acquired a black box warning or were removed from the market. (A black box warning means the drug is dangerous and should be prescribed with caution. The name comes from the fact that in the Physicians Desk reference (PDR) and on drug information sheets, there is a little black box below the drug's name containing the warning.) That represents 10 percent of the 548 new drugs approved during that period. The study suggests a 20 percent ultimate risk of withdrawal or black box warning; one out of five new drugs.[290] The safety of new agents cannot be known with certainty until a drug has been on the market for many years. Lasser has also pointed out that patients in typically-sized clinical trials are not representative of the population that may ultimately take the new drug, such as elderly individuals, children and those with concomitant illnesses.

Elan Corp., the Irish drug firm developing an Alzheimer's drug called AN-1792, was forced to suspend trials after several patients became ill with inflammation in the central nervous system. The drug was studied in mice where it cleared amyloid plaques and in other animals including monkeys where it was shown to be safe.[291] [292] The vaccine appeared to work by interfering with the build-up of amyloid plaque in the brain. Studies of AN-1792 in rodents showed very promising results. The vaccine halted, and in some cases reversed the disease in mice.

According to *The Scientist*, "When Elan researchers vaccinated transgenic mice that had developed AD-like pathology, plaques melted away. Two-and-a-half years of animal experiments yielded further encouraging results. The vaccine prevented and possibly reversed cognitive defects."[293] The drug was tested in nonhuman primates and other animals and deemed safe for humans. Fifteen people, out of 375 in Phase II clinical trials (75 controls while 300 received the vaccine) developed central nervous system inflammation and two suffered strokes. The 15 also showed symptoms of worsening AD. Human data predicted this as the vaccine triggered a peptide normally found in the brain. Many scientists said the vaccine would not work because it would set off a general immune response in the brain.[294] No such symptoms had been seen in the earlier animal studies. "We never saw a hint of this," Dr. Ivan Lieberburg, Elan's chief scientific and medical officer said. "It came as a total shock to Elan."[295]

And there are countless other examples. To cite just a few:

- In 1993, half of the people participating in a 10-person trial of the anti-hepatitis drug fialuridine (FIAU) died and 2 others became severely ill.[296]
- In 2002, a painkiller called Bextra (valdecoxib) caused at least 20 skin rashes that are linked to some rare and life-threatening skin diseases, including

Stevens-Johnson syndrome, toxic epidermal necrolysis, and exfoliative dermatitis, as well as allergic reactions.[297]

- In 2002, Millennium Pharmaceuticals Inc. reported that it would end development of an investigational oral asthma treatment, a 5-lipoxygenase inhibitor called MLN977 or LDP977, when three participants in the 193-patient trial developed elevated levels of liver enzymes that were likely drug related and were similar to those seen with previously developed 5-lipoxygenase inhibitors.[298]

- Between 1976 and 1985, 102 of the 198 new medications, or 52 percent, were either withdrawn or relabeled by the FDA secondary to severe unpredicted side effects.[299]

Given the fact that testing drugs on animals has such a history of failures, it is clear that the process of testing new drugs needs to be vastly improved. *The Scientist* published an article heralding transgenic mice as one solution. Ironically it closed with this: "'There isn't a single genetically manipulated mouse that has been used yet to produce a drug that cures a disease,' says [Kathleen] Murray of Charles River Laboratories."[300]

Fortunately, there is a better way. As Christopher Portier, director of the Environmental Toxicology Program at the U.S. National Institute of Environmental Health Sciences and one of the foremost environmental toxicologists in the U.S., remarked in *BioMedNet News* on the problem of too many toxicologists relying on a stale paradigm to evaluate carcinogens:

> Modern 'biologically-based' concepts are not only more accurate, they also offer faster and less expensive screening. If we're honest with ourselves as scientists, we're looking at more complicated data structures than we've ever looked at before. Toxicology has changed [and] we have to do a better job.[301]

The Better Path: Replacing the Failed Animal Model Paradigm

Graham Lappin, the Head of Research and Development at Xceleron Ltd, York Biocentre, and R. Colin Garner, the Chief Executive Officer at Xceleron Ltd. stated in *Nature Reviews Drug Discovery*:

> The process of early clinical drug development has changed little over the past 20 years despite an up to 40% failure rate associated with inappropriate drug metabolism and pharmacokinetics of candidate molecules. A new method of obtaining human metabolism data known as microdosing has been developed which will permit smarter candidate selection by taking investigational drugs into humans earlier. Microdosing depends on the availability of two ultrasensitive 'big-physics' techniques: positron emission tomography (PET) can provide pharmacodynamic [what

the drug does to the body] information, whereas accelerator mass spectrometry (AMS) provides pharmacokinetic information. Microdosing allows safer human studies as well as reducing the use of animals in preclinical toxicology.

Developing new drugs is becoming an ever more complex and expensive process. Estimates suggest that it takes, on average, 10–12 years to take a molecule from discovery through to regulatory approval; this time period has changed very little over the past 20 years. The costs of drug development are also escalating to in excess of US $800 million per registered drug. Much of this cost is actually associated with those drugs that do not make it to market; therefore the higher the attrition rate, the higher the cost of those drugs that eventually do make it. Unless these costs can be substantially reduced, there will be very few new drugs receiving regulatory approval.

At present, there is an inverse relationship between research and development expenditure by the pharmaceutical industry and the number of drugs receiving regulatory approval. In 2001, only 24 new molecular entities (NMEs) were registered by the US FDA. In 2002, matters were even worse and only 17 NMEs were registered by the US FDA. This is bad for patients who are looking for new treatments for life-threatening diseases such as cancer, and bad for the pharmaceutical industry, who will generate insufficient profits to develop the drugs of tomorrow....

There are many factors that lead to a successful drug, but of particular importance is the way in which the human body absorbs and metabolizes the drug. This area of drug development —known as pharmacokinetics (PK) and pharmacodynamics (PD)—defines the drug's absorption, distribution, metabolism and excretion (ADME) characteristics. Inappropriate ADME parameters can lead to up to 40% of drug candidates failing to make it past the first human studies (Phase I).

At present, methods to define the ADME characteristics of a molecule include *in silico* modelling, x-ray crystallography studies of recombinant cytochrome P-450's (one of the body's key enzyme systems in metabolizing drugs and foreign compounds), *in vitro* metabolism studies including the use of animals and human liver microsomes, hepatocytes or recombinant enzymes, and *in vivo* studies using a range of experimental animal models. The information from these studies is then fed into the candidate-selection process in the hope that the models will have predicted how humans metabolize the drug. The move from animal data to humans is done using a mathematical modelling process known as allometric scaling. Allometric scaling can be very misleading, as it is only about 60% predictive. Allometric scaling models are further complicated because substantial differences in clearance rates are found between animal species, a fact that calls into question which model is predictive of humans. Alternatively, a number of lead candidates might come out of a drug screening programme with similar pharmacological activities and identical animal ADME parameters. Which of these leads would make the best drug?

They then go on to describe human microdosing with accelerator mass spectrometry (AMS) and positron emission tomography (PET) technology and then continue:

The use of the ultrasensitivity of AMS and PET permits new approaches to obtaining crucial ADME data for selecting drug candidates. Microdosing studies are dependent on these ultrasensitive analytical techniques because only they have the necessary sensitivity to follow the fate of a trace drug dose in the human body. PET provides real-time data on drug disposition, whereas AMS is used to analyse drug and metabolite concentrations in body fluids withdrawn at time intervals after dosing. Both AMS and PET require isotopically labelled candidate drugs, in contrast to liquid chromatography/mass spectrometry (LC/MS). However, the latter method does not currently have the necessary sensitivity to measure drug concentrations at microdoses....

The proposals of the EMEA [European Agency for the Evaluation of Medicinal Products] are to be welcomed, as they move the focus of early drug development away from laboratory animals to conducting safe and ethical studies in humans. The move to reduce animal usage... permits some of the resources previously spent on animal studies to be spent on human investigations.[302]

Data from *in vitro* studies, computers, epidemiology, and analysis of the **chemical structure and chemical properties** of the candidate drug have provided useful data about how the drug will perform in humans. But no matter how effective a drug appears in an animal model, *in vitro,* or in a computer model, if it cannot penetrate the body's tissues, move to the target, bind to the target, and exit the body without causing undue harm, it is useless. Hence, the final authority for a whether a drug is useful has always been human studies.

As Jurgen Drews, former president of Global Research at Hoffman La Roche, has said:

For a long time it was considered necessary to carry out ADME studies on rats and dogs, or even on small primates such as marmosets. Yet these experiments were often disappointing in view of their lack of carryover to human beings. Only in recent years have models been developed from comparative analysis of a variety of animal species that allows more precise prediction about effects in man. *Despite any existing uncertainties, ADME studies on human subjects remains the basis for establishing correct dosages for patients and for the development of appropriate dosage schemes.*[303] [Emphasis added.]

Dr M. G. Palfreyman, Dr V. Charles and J. Blander stated:

Mice and humans have more than 95% of their genes in common, yet mice are not men, or women.... Although cell-based and animal models of disease have been the cornerstone of drug discovery, it is increasingly apparent that they are of limited predictive value for complex disorders...One of the major challenges facing the drug discovery community is the limitation and poor predictability of animal-based strategies. Over the last decade, drug discovery has largely been based on finding targets in animal models and then identifying the human homologue...many drugs have failed in later stages of development because the animal data were poor predictors of efficacy in the human subject... One of the overriding interests of the pharmaceutical and biotechnologies industry is to...create alternative development strategies that are less reliant on poor animal predictor models of human disease...Although the species [chimpanzees] share more than 98.9% gene identity [with humans], the expression of genes in the brain was more than five-fold greater in humans than in the chimpanzees....Differences from mice were even greater. These differences reinforce the importance of using human disease models in drug discovery as a real predictor of human efficacy... Discovery of drugs that act on the human central nervous system, are best studied in human-cell based systems.[304]

Referring to the use of human cells, the scientists state: "They are clearly superior to those obtained from animals."[305]

Advances in ADMET technologies—improved *in vitro,* molecular, and cellular assays as well as DNA microarrays, to name a few—are beginning to reshape the drug development process by enabling researchers to predict a lead compound's ADMET characteristics during the discovery phase, well before the preclinical phase.

For example, mutagenicity is studied in bacteria (*Salmonella/*Ames, *E. coli*). The Ames assay is well known, and now the Ames II is available through Xenometrix. There are many *in vitro* means to detect DNA damage that do not involve live animals.[32] The AMES test and its various derivatives is probably the most well known test for gene mutations, but even these are not accurate one hundred percent of the time. AMES uses the bacteria, *Salmonella*, to look for DNA mutations. This method works fairly well; for example, analysis of human cells and *Salmonella* revealed that sunlight caused mutations in the gene *p53*, which led to skin cancer, cigarette smoke likewise damaged *p53* and led to lung cancer, AFB exposure also damaged *p53* and led to cancer of the liver. The bacteria *E.coli* is also used in some AMES tests. Chromosomal mutations can also be looked for in human cells *in vitro*. Another test using bacteria is VITOTOX by Labsystems. It is able to measure both genotoxicity (damage to DNA) and cytotoxicity (damage to cells).

Drugs are metabolized in essentially two ways, called Phase I and Phase II reactions. Phase I includes the chemical reactions known as *oxidation*, *reduction*, and *hydrolysis* and Phase II includes *conjugation* reactions. Enzymes catalyze these reactions. Enzymes are protein molecules that function as catalysts for biochemical reactions. The enzyme cytochrome P450 (CYP) is involved in the metabolism of most drugs. Two CYP isoenzymes, CYP3A4 and CYP2D6 are responsible for metabolizing about 80% of all drugs currently on the market. CYP2C9 and CYP2A1 account for another 15%.[306] Drugs can now be tested *in vitro* with these enzymes.

Many companies are focusing on human-based ADMET tests. Camitro of Menlo Park, California is developing computer models and simulation of drug metabolism. LION Bioscience of Dan Diego and Heidelberg, is developing computer models from *in vitro* data. Genmatics of San Francisco is developing *in silico* modeling. Amedis of the UK is developing software for ADMET studies. D-Pharm/Pharma Logic of Israel is developing computer models. Cyprotex of the UK is developing high-throughput ADMET testing facilities and methods. Pharmagene of the UK, Cell Technologies of Houston and Gene Trace Systems of Alameda, California, are using human tissue for ADMET studies. Amphioxus Quintiles of Durham, North Carolina, MDS Pharma Services of Canada, Quest Diagnostics Clinical Trials of New Jersey and many more are also involved in developing and marketing human-based ADMET tests. The Discovery and Development Services segment of Charles Rivers Laboratories—ironically, the largest purveyor of laboratory animals in the world—has launched an automated *in vitro* ADMET assay service to support drug discovery programs.

Even the massive animal provider is getting into the act:

Jim Foster, the founder's son and CEO, is trying to turn Charles River into more than an animal company. "Our needs move in tandem with the industry," said Jim Foster, the company's chief executive. "Companies need to get drugs to market faster. To do that, they need more nonanimal testing technologies. I don't want to sit here and say, `Hey, there goes our animal business." In the past five years, the lab animal portion of Charles River's business has gone from 80 percent to 40 percent. Earlier this month, the firm bought a lab test, called DakDak, that allows researchers to measure how effectively sunscreens prevent skin damage. The test does in days what would take months in animal studies.... Studying them all in animals is simply an economic impossibility. Animal tests can take months, even years, and quickly run into the hundreds of thousands of dollars. Charles River estimates that DakDak can test five or six products for less than half what it would cost to study one product in animals.... "It is driven by pure necessity and economics," said Melvin Balk, a veterinarian by training and president of the nonprofit foundation associated with Charles River Laboratories.'[307]

The company pION provides technology for predicting solubility, dissolution, permeability and human absorption of chemicals such as PSR4p, which is an *in vitro* tool for measuring drug *permeability* using artificial membranes and PSR4s, which is an *in vitro* tool for measuring drug *solubility*. They also have technology for determining intrinsic solubility and solubility pH-profiles, pKa and logP determination.

LION bioscience has the Absorption Module for the iDEA™ (*In vitro* Determination for the Estimation of ADME) Simulation System. iDEA™ is a computational model developed to predict human oral drug absorption from a compound's solubility and permeability. The iDEA™ Predictive ADME Simulation System is a modular approach to predicting the ADME characteristics of a compound. Each module is designed to model a specific ADME process. The modules interface to each other to form a comprehensive and integrated predictive ADME simulation system.

According to Laura Robinson of LION bioscience, Inc. San Diego:[308]

Historically, out of 250 compounds entering preclinical development, only five are tested in the clinic and one is ultimately approved by the U.S. Food and Drug Administration for use in humans. The role of ADME in 70% of these failures (i.e., for poor pharmacokinetics properties and toxicity) is probably significant....The goal of therapeutics is to achieve a desired beneficial effect with minimal adverse effects. It is now widely recognized that a rational approach towards developing an effective drug is to combine the principles of drug design with pharmacokinetics. The relationship between dose and the therapeutic effect is complex. Not only the potency and pharmacological property of the drug are important but also various other factors govern the ultimate therapeutic efficacy. These factors are based on the physicochemical properties of the drug... substance/formulation and the biological response of the body to these substances. Increased throughput remains the current demand. *In vitro* and *in silico* methods will be used in conjugation with each other to predict aspects of ADME that are usually performed *in vitro* or *in vivo*. These tools may also be used in a high throughput manner as a preliminary screening approach in pharmaceutical development...

The iDEA Absorption Module predicts a compound's absorption characteristic from its chemical structure or chemical structure and *in vitro* data. Each model is thoroughly validated using internal and external data sets to demonstrate its predictive capability. The system is easy to use and has an integrated drawing applet to facilitate inputting chemical structures.

The IDEA Absorption Module consists of the following models:
- Statistical model to predict a compounds Caco-2 permeability from its chemical structure.
- Statistical model to predict a compounds absorption class (e.g., low, medium and high) from chemical structure.
- Physiological model of oral drug absorption.

The physiological module is built upon a proprietary database of 66 clinically tested compounds. This model correlates *in vitro* measurements of permeability, solubility, and human clinical data to predict the oral absorption of drugs in humans. The physiological model predicts the intestinal drug concentration, soluble mass, insoluble mass, mass absorbed, FDp (fractional dose absorbed to the portal vein) and absorption rate from a compound's solubility, measured Caco-2 permeability or predicted Caco-2 permeability and dose. The physiological absorption model accurately predicts human absorption in the different regions of the intestine.

The iDEA Metabolism Module predicts the extent of first pass metabolism for a compound and is built upon a proprietary database of 64 clinically tested compounds. The model correlates a compound's predicted absorption from the Absorption Module, protein binding, and metabolic turnover measured in hepatocytes and human clinical data to predict the bioavailability of drugs in humans. The Metabolism Module accurately predicts a compounds first pass effect in humans.

Tripos' VolSurf calculates ADME properties and creates predictive ADME models. VolSurf predicts a variety of ADME properties using pre-calculated models, computes unique ADME-relevant descriptors, and performs statistical analyses to generate predictive models of bioactivity or property. VolSurf reads or computes 3D molecular interaction fields and uses image-processing methods to convert them into simple molecular descriptors that are easy to understand and interpret. These descriptors quantitatively characterize size, shape, polarity, and hydrophobicity of molecules, and the balance between them. VolSurf's descriptors have a clear chemical meaning, are not sensitive to alignment rules, and have proven to be useful in generating predictive ADME models. Descriptors can be calculated for small, medium, and large molecules, including DNA fragments, peptides, and proteins. Multivariate statistical methods within VolSurf enable the creation of models that relate its descriptors to biological properties. The ADME models included in VolSurf predict drug solubility, Caco-2 cell absorption, blood-brain barrier permeation, and drug distribution. These models have been developed from published experimental data collected from *in vitro* assays that emulate *in vivo* behavior of drugs.[309]

In addition, highly automated cell-based assays can provide a realistic sense of how a chemical can perform in a cellular system. These systems enable scientists to culture living cells very closely related to the cell types found in specific organisms. For example, scientists have discovered that Caco-2 cells, which come from a human colonic carcinoma, have many of the same cellular properties as those in the small intestine. As a result, these cells provide an appropriate *in vitro* assay for the absorption and secretion of drugs.[310] Caco-2 cells have become the standard for predicting drug absorption. A human liver cell line, ACTIVTOX has been used to predict toxicity and metabolism of drugs that were approved based on animals studies, terfenadine (Seldane) and astemizole Hismanal), that went on to harm humans.[311] MDCK, a kidney cell line used to mimic the blood-brain barrier, is also used to predict absorption in cell-based assays.

Scientists have found that a single family of enzymes, known as CYP, is responsible for metabolizing, or breaking down in the body, about 95 percent of all current drugs. Using this information, they can use CYP enzymes in cell-based assays to test lead compounds for metabolic vulnerability. Liver cells from dogs or rats, or immortalized human liver cell lines, such as HepG2, are currently being used. Robert Coleman, chief scientific officer of Pharmagene, a company that uses human tissues to find new drugs insists that data from the primary human cells is more informative than that provided by dog or rat livers, explaining that: "There are significant differences in the way that dog or rat livers metabolize compounds and differences in hepatotoxicity [liver toxicity] too."[312] Pharmagene also uses human tissues for drug toxicology screening, drug-drug interactions, and absorption in the gut.

Now scientists are combining the power of combinatorial chemistry and computational methods to take ADMET prediction a step beyond even *in vitro* to *in silico*. A structure-activity relationship (SAR) is a computer-based technique that allows chemical testing based solely on a chemical's molecular structure. It is one component of the more comprehensive Quantitative Structure Activity Relationship (QSAR), which is capable of quantifying the type of relationship identified. (QSAR dates back to the 1800s when scientists correlated alcohol toxicity with hydrophobicity.)[313] ADMET *in silico* means that scientists can now look at computer models of a chemical's structure and its molecular characteristics and predict some ADMET properties as accurately or even more accurately than *in vitro* assays. Screening *in silico* is taking the place of many animal tests. ComGenex of South San Francisco and Hungary is developing computer technology based on *in vitro* tests using human tissue to predict important metabolic properties of new chemicals, such as pKa, log P and log D. Ferenc Darvas, ComGenex president and chairman said in *Nature Biotechnology,* that "the most promising use of data is to 'calculate structure-activity relationships, convert those into rules, and then reintroduce those rules in a rule-based system for the design and selection of compounds or libraries.'"[314] Along the same lines, Amedis of the UK has developed a structure-activity-based predictive test for carcinogenesis. Chief Science Officer William Bains states, "The prototype software can predict carcinogenicity far more accurately then the Ames test can do."[315]

The idea behind ADMET *in silico* is to develop predictive computer systems that can calculate structure-activity relationships in chemical compounds and convert those relationships into a set of rules that ultimately become part of a rules-based system for designing and selecting drugs. Such predictive systems can dramatically speed up the screening process. Screening that has taken weeks using cell-based assays can be accomplished in a computer model in less than a minute. Today, a wide range of predictive software is available, from GastroPlus, a simulation that looks at the absorption of a drug in the human GI tract by Simulations Plus (Lancaster, CA) to ComGenex's Pallas suite for predictions of pKa, logP, logD, metabolism and toxicity and Pharsight's (Mountain View, CA) clinical trial simulations.

In silico, or computer, models have been made possible by the extraordinary wealth of data generated by high-throughput screening. Technology has created a flood of data for new drug development, and high throughput methods have given rise to more data than a drug company can easily assimilate. The need to organize this avalanche of biological information has sparked the emergence of a field known as bioinformatics. Bioinformatics is the science that uses advanced computing techniques for the management and analysis of biological data. These data, which come from a variety of sources, are placed in huge databases, and scientists can "mine" the data for the information they're seeking.

Toxicogenomics, (the study of the functions of all the genes and how they interact as related to toxicology) is the best way to evaluate medication-caused mutagenesis because it analyzes gene expression patterns and protein expression patterns. DNA microarrays allow an intersection of computers and biology. Thousands of genes interact in order to create proteins and indeed life as we experience it. They do not act alone but in combination with each other. DNA microarrays allow scientists to monitor the entire genome, or at least a very large percentage of it on a single chip. Thus scientists are able to look at how a chemical will influence genes, the proteins they make, and how the gene-gene interactions are effected. Numerous DNA chips are available: Biochip, DNA chip, DNA microarray, GeneChip, and gene array.

Bioinformatics is particularly important as an adjunct to genomic research, which generates a large amount of complex data, involving billions of individual DNA building blocks, and tens of thousands of genes. ComGenex now markets a number of large databases of characterized compounds, including a collection of toxicological data from *in vitro* tests on human fibroblasts of 50,000 compounds. Clearly there is so much good human-based data that relying on animal-based data is a waste of precious time.

Scientists are also using technology to overcome the problem of delivering a medication to the target, and *only* to the target. Drugs cause side effects in part because the drug goes to the whole body, and not just the area where it is needed. Research scientist Tony McHale at the University of Ulster (Coleraine, Ireland) has developed a new technique that may solve this problem through an innovative use of ultrasound technology. Scientists have long been able to place drugs in red blood cells, but the problem has always been to get the red blood cells to release the drug. McHale discovered that by inserting a drug into a patient's red blood cells after they have been exposed to a pulsed electrical field and then applying ultrasound over the target area, the red blood cells burst and release the drug. The technique involves withdrawing 20cc of the patient's own blood, exposing it to an electrical field and loading it with the drug, and then injecting it back into the patient and applying ultrasound to the area of interest, such as a breast tumor.[316]

Many drugs' potencies and therapeutic effects are limited or otherwise reduced because of the partial degradation that occurs before they reach a desired target in the body. Once ingested, time-release medications deliver treatment continuously, rather than providing relief of symptoms and protection from adverse events solely when necessary. Further, injectable medications could be made less expensively and administered more easily if they could simply be dosed orally.

However, this improvement cannot happen until methods are developed to safely shepherd drugs through specific areas of the body, such as the stomach, where low pH (an acidic environment) can destroy a medication, or through an area where healthy bone and tissue might be adversely affected. One way scientists are learning more about the details of how extended-release pills break down and release medicine in the stomach is through the "virtual stomach." Developed by mechanical engineers at Pennsylvania State University working with medical and pharmaceutical researchers, the virtual stomach is a computer-generated program that creates color-coded simulations of the human stomach showing pressures, the motion of gastric fluid, and the path and breakdown of tablets. These simulations enable researchers to analyze the specific processes that lead to release and mixing of medicines from pills in the stomach.[317]

The goal of all sophisticated drug delivery systems, therefore, is to deploy medications intact to specifically targeted parts of the body through a medium that can control the therapy's administration by means of either a physiological or chemical trigger. To achieve this goal, researchers are turning to advances in the worlds of micro- and nanotechnology. During the past decade, polymeric microspheres, polymer micelles, and hydrogel-type materials have all been shown to be effective in enhancing drug targeting specificity, lowering systemic drug toxicity, improving treatment absorption rates, and providing protection for pharmaceuticals against biochemical degradation.

In addition, several other experimental drug delivery systems show exciting signs of promise, including those composed of biodegradable polymers, dendrimers (so-called star polymers), electroactive polymers, and modified C-60 fullerenes (also known as "buckyballs").

GENTEST is a company founded in 1983 that used human cells in genotoxicity assays. In 1985, they began studying xenobiotic metabolism and developed cDNA-expressed human cytochrome P450 enzymes. GENTEST also offers pharmacology and toxicology testing services using *in vitro* products and systems. GENTEST Corporation was acquired by Becton, Dickinson and Company and continues to provide cytochrome P450 screening and toxicology research.

In Chapter 3, we described Pharmagene and how the company is involved in drug development. According to their web site:

Pharmagene believes that it is a matter of logic that the most relevant biological systems in which to test new medicines to treat human diseases are human, thus Pharmagene only works on human tissues, and does no work on animals what-so-ever.

Using human tissue early in the discovery and development process can help improve the success rate of developing new medicines. Information and data predicting potential human side effects, toxicities or likely lack of efficacy due to the absence of key receptors or other target molecules can be generated. This will help cut the overall cost and time of development and crucially, reduce the attrition rate of new candidate medicines as they move from development into lengthy and expensive clinical trials.

Pharmagene's Phase ZERO™ service is a custom-designed pre-clinical research service focused on target identification and validation, and on testing the viability of drug leads and candidates in human tissue...

The bioavailability and biotransformation of drugs can markedly affect their therapeutic activity. The Drug Development Group at Pharmagene has developed a number of human tissue-based assays. Some of these assess drug absorption and metabolism, while others act as predictors of drug-drug interactions and toxicity. Specific assay capabilities include:

Drug Absorption
Drug Metabolism
Cytochrome P450 (CYP450) Induction in human hepatocytes
Drug Safety
Function in human isolated tissue
Gene regulation in human isolated tissues and primary cells
Drug Toxicity in human isolated primary cells...

Phase I and II metabolism of a compound by the liver are key determinants of its pharmacokinetic profile and its suitability as a drug. Evaluation of drug metabolism in freshly isolated human hepatocytes provides essential information for the selection of appropriate drug candidates for use in humans. This is regarded as the industry gold standard assessment prior to clinical testing in healthy human volunteers. Utilization of freshly isolated hepatocytes avoids many of the problems associated with alternatives such as cryopreserved hepatocytes, microsomes, recombinant cytochrome P450 enzymes and S9 fractions.

C2-ADME provides computational ADME/Tox prediction tools[318] and Quantitative Structure Activity Relationship (QSAR) technology.[319]

And there are other companies using other methods: The Microtox® Chronic Toxicity Testing System uses luminescent bacteria that have all metabolic pathways needed for normal metabolism, growth, and cell division to measure the toxic effects of new drugs. MULTICASE Inc. (formerly BIOSOFT Inc.) is a software company that develops programs for use by chemical and pharmaceutical companies to design new useful molecules and to evaluate their toxicity and impact on the environment. Current programs include: CASE (Computer Automated Structure Evaluation), MultiCASE (M-CASE), META, CASETOX and ToxAlert. Areas of current expertise include: carcinogenicity, mutation, teratogenicity, allergic dermatitis and eye irritation, among many others. ToxAlert is based on algorithms derived from powerful artificial intelligence programs. Known as CASE and MULTICASE, these programs (1) analyze the compounds in a "training" database into their structural fragments, (2) identify the biophores, i.e., those fragments responsible for the toxicological endpoint (e.g., carcinogenicity, mutagenicity, rate of biodegradation) for which data are given in the database and (3) compile a dictionary containing the contribution of each biophore to the particular toxicological endpoint. The bioactivity of any compound not in the training database is predicted from the sum of the contributions of the biophores, which it contains.

CompuDrug was established in 1983 on the belief that computational approaches can contribute significantly to life science research. Based upon artificial intelligence and chemistry expertise they have developed a range of interlinked expert systems and knowledge bases useful to pharmaceutical, biotechnology and regulatory research.

CompuDrug software is actively used in these research areas:

• Combinatorial chemistry and rational drug design and disposition
• Virtual structure handling and high throughput prediction experimentation
• Understanding protein structure-function relationships
• Predicting physico-chemical properties

- Predicting metabolism pathways in humans and animals, plants as well in the presence of light.
- Estimating toxic symptoms of organic compounds in human and animals
- Method development and optimization for HPLC techniques

HazardExpert is another toxicity prediction system based on the structure of compounds. HazardExpert predicts different toxicity effects of compounds like carcinogenic, mutagenic, teratogenic, membrane irritation, neurotoxic and other effects. Used together with MetabolExpert, it can predict the toxicity of both the parent compound and its metabolites.

Professor Claude Reiss of Proanima outlines the best way to test a potential new drug:

First assessment level: the molecular responses of the cell to a xenobiotic [drug], on (a) established cell lines, then (b) on primary cultures of human cells of the a priori most exposed organs (liver, kidney, skin, CNS, ...). The responses will be studied at the level of global genetic expression (by means of biochips, proteomics etc.), and at the level of individual genes selected for their specific response ('reporter' genes responding specifically to stresses, to damage of cellular components (DNA repair, chaperones...), involved in metabolic pathways or metabolite transport, etc....Furthermore, the responses of cellular organelles (mitochondria, Golgi...) will be probed, as well as the response of the cellular status (effects on the cellular clock, on the control checkpoints of the cell cycle, induction of apoptosis, ...). The cellular assessment must be completed for cells derived from human sub-populations sharing major polymorphic traits, etc... The thorough evaluation of the molecular and cellular impacts of the xenobiotic allows its activity mechanism to be understood and to predict with high confidence its cellular activity in the long term.

Following the molecular and cellular toxicology study, the assessment will next be extended to perfused tissues and organs, especially those at risk according to the cellular studies.

The results from these studies already allow a meaningful assessment of health risks of the xenobiotic for man, allowing to weigh up whether it is reasonable to take the xenobiotic to clinical trials. The results of laboratory analysis, of imaging techniques and other non invasive examinations, targeted in particular at the most exposed organs (identified during the cellular and organ studies), would then allow the clinical study to be conducted under optimal safety conditions and with a security margin satisfying legal requirements.

Rapid evolution in science, especially biology, has already led to reliable ways and means to investigate human biology and health issues. New concepts appear, new complementary methods are developed, high in performance and precision. Every day, scientific journals bring a wealth of results describing in detail, at the cellular and molecular level, detailed structures of biological agents, their biochemical reactions, the mechanisms of their interactions and their role in the life of the cell, the tissue, and the organ.

The assessment method, building up from molecules and cells to the individual via tissues and organs, is in strong contrast to the top-down approach of the animal model, which faces at the outset the full complexity of the animal. Given the actual state of our knowledge, this complexity is as formidable in mice as it is in primates. Wouldn't it be more logical to go from the simpler to the more complex, from molecules to the cell, then the tissue, the organ, and finally to the whole system, while recognizing that the cell is not simply the sum of its molecules, the tissue or the organ is not simply the sum of the cells, and the individual is not simply the sum of his tissues and organs?[320]

The Power of One: Pharmacogenomics and Personalized Medicine

While advancements made in cell-based assays, computer modeling, as well as the innovative use of technology, are improving the ability of scientists to predict a drug's ADMET characteristics, the ultimate solution for the "ADMET problem" will come in the form of *pharmacogenomics*, a burgeoning field that is enabling scientists to classify patient populations according to their own individual response to a drug.

Pharmacogenomics identifies complex patterns of gene variation in larger populations and attempts to correlate these patterns to different drug response types.[321] Richard Weinshilboum, M.D. writing in *The New England Journal of Medicine* stated:

The concept of pharmacogenetics originated from the clinical observation that there were patients with very high or very low plasma or urinary drug concentrations, followed by the realization that the biochemical traits leading to this variation were inherited. Only later were the drug-metabolizing enzymes identified, and this discovery was followed by the identification of the genes that encoded the proteins and the DNA-sequence variation within the genes that was associated with the inherited trait. Most of the pharmacogenetic traits that were first identified were monogenic — that is, they involved only a single gene — and most were due to genetic polymorphisms; in other words, the allele or alleles responsible for the variation were relatively common. Although drug effect is a complex phenotype that depends on many factors, early and often dramatic examples involving succinylcholine and isoniazid facilitated acceptance of the fact that inheritance can have an important influence on the effect of a drug.

Today there is a systematic search to identify functionally significant variations in DNA sequences in genes that influence the effects of various drugs....

The finding, approximately 40 years ago, that an impairment in a phase I reaction — hydrolysis of the muscle relaxant succinylcholine by butyrylcholinesterase (pseudocholinesterase) — was inherited served as an early stimulus for the development of pharmacogenetics. Approximately 1 in 3500 White subjects is homozygous for a gene encoding an atypical form of butyrylcholinesterase and is relatively unable to hydrolyze succinylcholine, thus prolonging the drug-induced muscle paralysis and consequent apnea. At almost the same time, it was observed that a common genetic variation in a phase II pathway of drug metabolism —N-acetylation — could result in striking differences in the half-life and plasma concentrations of drugs metabolized by N-acetyltransferase. Such drugs included the anti-tuberculosis agent isoniazid, the antihypertensive agent hydralazine, and the antiarrhythmic drug procainamide, and this variation had clinical consequences in all cases. The bimodal distribution of plasma isoniazid concentrations in subjects with genetically determined fast or slow rates of acetylation in one of those early studies strikingly illustrates the consequences of inherited variations in this pathway for drug metabolism. These early examples of the potential influence of inheritance on the effect of a drug set the stage for subsequent studies of genetic variation in other pathways of drug biotransformation.[322]

To fully appreciate the promise of pharmacogenomics, consider again the story of Jeff Smith, the young executive who died from rhabdomyolysis as a result of taking the cholesterol-lowering drug Baycol. The withdrawal of Baycol from the market illustrates one of the most confounding aspects of drug discovery and testing, and that is the knowledge that as little as a third of patients derive the intended therapeutic benefit of a drug, either because most patients will suffer such severe side effects from the drug such that they will be unable to continue taking it, or the medication will be simply ineffective. This fact seriously complicates both the science and the business of pharmaceuticals. Many people took drugs like Baycol and Rezulin and were helped by them, but others died.

The complexities of identifying a drug's pharmacological, pharmacokinetic, and toxicological properties—and eliminating any deficiencies that cause harm—brings a host of scientific challenges to finding safe, effective medicines for the general public. From a business standpoint, investing hundreds of millions of dollars in the development of a drug, only to have to withdraw it from the market due to ADMET complications, has enormous impact on a pharmaceutical company's profitability. (This must be weighed however against the current judicial system that recognizes the animal model as valid. It must also be weighed against the fact that even though some drugs are recalled they may still make the company billions of dollars.)

The list of drugs whose ADMET deficiencies failed to come to light in preclinical (animal) and clinical (human) studies, and which subsequently caused harm, and even death, once introduced into the market, is a long one. It is also a costly one, both in terms of human life and health as well as the financial health of some of the nation's (and the world's) largest companies. Refinements and improvements in ADMET technologies that are eliminating reliance on the expensive, time-consuming, and highly flawed animal model, can go a long way in addressing some of these issues.

Still, we are left with the fact that some drugs are very effective and safe in certain individuals but kill or seriously harm others. These deficiencies will certainly not come to light in animal tests due to their lack of predictive value, and we have seen that they are often not revealed in clinical trials. Is there any way around this dilemma? The answer is yes. And it is light years away from dosing an animal with a chemical and hoping for the best, and then dosing a human based on what is perceived to be favorable animal data. Drug discovery used to go from animal models and animal testing to humans. Today we have the capacity to test human tissues, find gene signatures, use high throughput screening for efficacy and toxicity and then test humans with the appropriate genotype.

The mapping of the human genome offers new challenges and opportunities for the pharmaceutical industry, which currently takes little account of genetic differences and their role in drug response. However, change is in the air. In the future, pharmaceutical companies will need to determine the function of all the genes, correlate genes with disease, find which genes can best be targeted with drugs, and then develop new medications based on this knowledge. We know that people metabolize drugs differently—and thus have different pharmacological and toxicological responses to drugs—because of variations in their genes. As Guenther Heinrich, Ph.D., founder of Epidauros Biotechnologies AG, a company that applies the principles of pharmacogenomics to the drug development process, has concluded based on the analysis of human genes, "It was quite clear to me why drugs don't always work: It's because two unrelated people differ in some three million letters of the biochemical alphabet of the DNA."[323]

Were it not for the Human Genome Project, which unraveled the genetic code, thereby giving scientists the complete chemical instructions that control heredity in human beings, the promise of pharmacogenomics could never be fulfilled. Now that scientists have successfully completed the process of mapping and sequencing the human genome, they can proceed with identifying the genetic differences that determine how individuals metabolize drugs.

Although the genomes of individual human beings are 99.9 percent identical, the small 0.1 percent difference accounts for as many as three million *polymorphisms*. A polymorphism is a variation in the genetic sequence. The most common of these variations is the single nucleotide polymorphism or SNP (see Chapter 3). Many of these SNPs affect protein expression and function, which in turn affects disease inheritance and manifestation in an individual, as well as that individual's ability to metabolize drugs. SNPs are responsible for many diseases, including some forms of Type 2 diabetes.[324] Since 1999, scientists have identified over 1.42 million SNPs that are distributed throughout the human genome—a feat made possible by remarkable advances in mass spectrometry and high-throughput DNA microarray technologies. Scientists have discovered that polymorphisms in known disease pathways can predict a specific drug's efficacy. For example, the presence of a polymorphism in the cholesteryl ester transfer protein (*CETP*) has been found to determine the efficacy of pravastatin in patients diagnosed with coronary atherosclerosis, while the absence of the polymorphism was associated with diminished efficacy of the drug.[325] Polymorphisms in the serotonin neurotransmitter receptor (*5HT2A*) have been associated with the effectiveness of the anti-psychotic drug clozapine.[326]

Genetic polymorphisms in receptors and transporters can also trigger variations in drug response. For example, fluvoxamine, a selective serotonin-reuptake inhibitor, is commonly prescribed for depression. The receptor targeted by fluvoxamine is the serotonin transporter *5-HTT*. Patients with a genetic variation in the *5-HTT*-promoter region respond better to fluvoxamine treatment. Researchers are also exploring the role the receptor *5-HTT* may have in the development of migraine headaches, opening the door to the possibility that pharmacogenomics may be applied to improve migraine therapy. A variation in the expression of the *HER2* receptor gene determines whether or not a metastatic breast cancer patient will respond to trastuzumab (Herceptin). Trastuzumab is an antibody that blocks *HER2*, a receptor for hormones that stimulates tumor growth. The drug has been found to have significant benefit when used in addition to conventional chemotherapy. Overexpression of the *HER2/neu* oncogene, which is seen in about 25 percent of breast cancer patients, is associated with poor prognosis, increased tumor formation and metastasis, and resistance to chemotherapeutic agents. HER2 testing predetermines patients who overexpress *HER2* and who will respond to trastuzumab.[327]

At the present time, the genetic variations related to enzymes involved in drug metabolism represent the greatest opportunities for pharmacogenomics. All drugs on the market today, except for those treating infections, affect less than 500 different targets in the body. Of these 500 targets, more than 200 are enzymes; enzyme disruption has been one of the most successful ways of developing new drugs. A relatively small number of drug-metabolizing enzymes (DMEs) are responsible for metabolizing most drugs, and there are relatively few relevant polymorphisms within these enzymes. As a result of genetic polymorphisms in DMEs, a person may be an efficient metabolizer (EM), a poor metabolizer (PM), or an ultra-rapid metabolizer (UM). EMs are capable of efficient drug metabolism; that is, they are able to maintain plasma concentrations of the drug within the therapeutic range, and thus enjoy the full benefit of the therapy. PMs have metabolic deficiencies, which means that their DMEs allow the plasma concentration of the drug to exceed the therapeutic threshold, thus causing adverse reactions, toxicity, or decreased efficacy. UMs metabolize a drug so quickly that it cannot reach a high enough therapeutic level in the blood, making it ineffective in that individual. By knowing in advance which of the above you are, for the medication being prescribed, your physician can alter the dose and timing of the medication so it works best for you.

The drug 6-mercaptopurine (6MP) has saved thousands of lives but unfortunately cannot be used in everyone, as it is extremely toxic in patients who suffer from an inherited metabolic flaw. The enzyme thiopurine methyltransferase (TPMT), and the polymorphisms that affect the cytochrome P450 enzyme family, CYP2D6, affect a significant percentage of the population. As a result, they have great potential to influence the therapeutic outcomes of drugs commonly used to treat cardiovascular disease, cancer, central nervous system disorders, and pain. A test developed at St. Jude Children's Research Hospital is making it possible for doctors to test patients suffering from acute lymphoblastic leukemia for TPMT activity in order to optimize their therapy and manage their disease more effectively.[328] TPMT is essential for the normal metabolism of thiopurine medications, which include the antileukemics 6-mercaptopurine and 6-thioguanine, as well as the immune suppressant azathioprine. Patients who have inherited the relatively rare TPMT deficiency suffer severe, exaggerated, potentially fatal toxic responses when given standard doses of thiopurine and azathioprine drugs.[329] In these patients 6MP can accumulate rapidly, wiping out essential bone marrow and leading to infections. In 1995, scientists discovered the genetic flaw in an enzyme-producing gene *TPMT* on chromosome 6. A DNA test is now available that tells patients if they are at increased risk for the bone marrow dysfunction.[330]

In a study designed to compare enzyme activity across species, P450 isozymes were used as probes to study *in vitro* metabolism in horse, dog, cat, and human liver microsomes. The researchers found that there were "large interspecies differences in the way the selective P450 inhibitors affect the *in vitro* metabolism of the various substrates in horse, dog, and cat liver microsomes.... Overall, no one species behaved exactly like humans regarding the efficiency of the various inhibitors."[331]

The DNA-based TPMT diagnostic enables doctors to predetermine their patients' TPMT activity levels based on whether or not they have inherited the genes associated with TPMT deficiency. It classifies patients according to normal, intermediate, and deficient levels of TPMT activity. Those patients who have normal TPMT levels are given conventional doses of the drug. Those who have deficient and intermediate levels—about 1 in 300 Whites and Blacks—are given a lower dose. Doctors at St. Jude have found that by decreasing the dose of 6-mercaptopurine by 10- to 15-fold of the conventional dose, the thiopurine is as tolerable and effective in TPMT-deficient patients as it is in patients with normal activity levels. Today, all patients at St. Jude are routinely tested for TPMT activity. The TPMT diagnostic is also being evaluated as a tool to optimize therapy for patients who are taking azathioprine for Crohn's disease and rheumatoid arthritis, and in association with kidney transplantation.

Scientists are equally enthusiastic about the opportunities presented by DMEs in the CYP gene family for developing clinically valuable genomic tests. These include polymorphisms of CYP2C19. Mutations in this gene, which affect almost 25 percent of Asians and up to 5 percent of Whites, result in compromised metabolism of such commonly prescribed medications as citalopram, clomipramine, diazepam, propranolol, omeprazole, and the tricyclic antidepressants. For example, an individual with 2C19 polymorphisms resulting in inactive enzymes show higher levels of the antiulcer drug omeprazole and increased drug response, as measured by the surrogate marketer plasma gastrin.[332] Dempsey and colleagues found that CYP2A6 plays a role in nicotine metabolism, leading to subsequent studies that suggest a genetic factor in nicotine addition and increased risk for lung cancer. CYP2D6, or 2D6 for short, is a DME in the CYP gene family that promises even more opportunities for pharmacogenomics to improve patient therapy. 2D6 is responsible for the metabolism of almost 25 percent of all drugs. More than 20 drugs are known to be 2D6 substrates, ranging from cardiovascular agents to antidepressants, antipsychotics, and morphine derivatives (see Table 7.2).

The 2D6 enzyme is another example of how variations in gene expression or function can have profound effects on the efficacy and toxicity of 2D6 substrates. Between 7 and 10 percent of Whites and 1 and 2 percent of Asians have a genetic mutation that leads to 2D6 deficiency, which can result in either overdose or the inability to maintain therapeutic efficacy with conventional doses of 2D6 substrate drugs. Because many psychotropic drugs have a narrow therapeutic profile and adverse effects are quite common, a test that could measure 2D6 activity levels for patients treated with these agents would contribute enormously to improved clinical management of patients suffering from mental disorders. For example, the conventional dose for the antidepressant nortriptyline is in the 75-150 mg range. However, for PMs (poor metabolizers), the effective tolerable dose is much less—10-20 mg. On the other hand, patients with a genetic variation that results in the inheritance of as many as 13 copies of the gene metabolize the drug so quickly that they need a dosage increase to more than 500 mg to achieve the therapeutic benefit of nortriptyline.[333]

Table 7.2 Medicines affected by the 2D6 gene.

Cardiovascular Agents		
Antiarrhythmics	**Beta-blockers**	**Antihypertensives**
Propafenone	Timolol	Indoramin
Encainide	Metoprolol	Debrisoquine
Flecainide	Propranolol	Guanoxan
Sparteine		
N-propylamaline		
Mexiletine		
Psychoactive Agents		
Neuroleptics	**Tricyclic antidepressants**	**MAOIs****
Perphenazine	Nortriptyline	Amiflamine
Trifluperidol	Amitriptyline	Methoxyphenamine
Fluphenazine	Clomipramine	**SSRIs****
Thioridazine	Desipramine	Fluoxetine
Clozapine	Imipramine	Paroxetine
	Tomoxetine	Sertraline
Morphine Derivatives		
Analgesics	**Antitussives**	
Codeine	Dextromethorphan	
Miscellaneous		
Phenformin	Methoxyamphetamine	Perhexiline

**MAOIs = monoamine oxidase inhibitors; SSRIs = selective serotonin reuptake inhibitors

The 2D6 enzyme also influences the efficacy of prodrugs (compounds that, on administration, must undergo chemical conversion by metabolic processes before becoming the pharmacologically active drug for which it is a prodrug). Ingleman-Sunderberg and colleagues, in discussing the opportunities for individualized drug treatment, note that high doses of the prodrug codeine in UMs (ultra-rapid metabolizers) can trigger adverse effects by generating extensive formation of morphine, while the lack of 2D6 in PMs can reduce efficacy of prodrugs requiring 2D6 activation, such as the analgesic tramadol.[334] A 2D6 diagnostic test kit has been developed in collaboration between pharmaceutical giant Hoffman-La Roche and the genomics company Affymetrix, which, following FDA approval, will soon bring the benefits of testing for 2D6 activity levels to a much wider population.

As a direct application of the knowledge gained from the Human Genome Project, pharmacogenomics involves examining the genetic basis for individual variations in drug response. By identifying the particular gene involved in metabolizing a particular drug, scientists can predict an individual patient's ability to metabolize that drug based on his genetic profile, which is created from a DNA test. As Joanne M. Meyer and Geoffrey S. Ginsburg of Millenium Pharmaceuticals, Inc., wrote *in Current Opinion in Chemical Biology*:

> While the existence of individual differences in disease predisposition, progression, and response to therapeutics is far from a novel concept, our ability to comprehensively measure the molecular markers that track these processes, and draw proper inferences from large amounts of molecular data, is novel. Over the past decade, significant advancements have been made in technologies to discover variation at the mRNA, DNA and protein levels. Indeed, with the advent of glass and nylon microarray technologies for gene-expression studies, it is quite feasible to characterize the expression levels of 30,000 genes in tissue samples from dozens, if not hundreds of individuals.[335]

Pharmacogenomics will allow scientists to isolate the gene involved in a particular side effect, such as rhabdomyolysis in the case of Baycol, and test a patient for this gene before administering the drug to him. This is far superior to testing drugs on a different species (e.g., rats, mice, monkeys, or dogs) from the one intended to take the drug (humans). Meyer and Ginsburg continue:

> Coupled with the advent of these technologies have been extensive efforts to collect appropriate tissues and fluids for mRNA, DNA and protein analysis. These collections have been part of pharmaceutical clinical trials, as well as clinical studies established for the purpose of characterizing biomarkers. The latter studies may involve small numbers of patient samples for initial biomarker discovery efforts, as well as large-scale, disease registry initiatives designed to evaluate and, in some cases, prospectively validate, biomarkers in the relevant patient populations.[336]

With scientists now discovering more each day about the genetic variations between individuals within the same species—humans—and how that influences drug response, what does that say for conducting preclinical testing of drugs on one species and expecting the results to extrapolate to another? Clearly, not much. It should be no wonder, then, that 90 percent of drug candidates that succeed in preclinical studies wind up failing in clinical trials.[337] By addressing the issues of *human* genetic variations, the potential for pharmacogenomics to revolutionize drug discovery, development, testing, approval, marketing, and usage is truly awesome.

The emerging discipline of pharmacogenomics holds the promise of reducing the incidence of adverse reactions, while optimizing dosing regimens. Armed with precise data based on an individual's genetic profile, doctors will be able to administer the exact dosage a patient needs to gain maximum therapeutic effect. This will cut down on hospitalizations, as well as the number of visits to physicians' offices. And most importantly, pharmacogenomics will provide more successful outcomes, thus eliminating the wasted effort and disappointing results caused by ineffective therapy.

Pharmacogenomics will also increase the number of therapeutic drugs available to consumers, as well as the speed with which they are brought to market, by enabling researchers to conduct smaller, more effective, and more cost-efficient clinical trials. Given the fact that the clinical trial phase of drug development is the longest and costliest part of the process, the savings in time and money by compressing the clinical trial phase would mean that new drugs would reach patients sooner at lower costs. Experts believe that pharmacogenomics will change the way clinical trials are conducted, and that by 2007, fifty percent of all clinical trials will involve genotyping. Drugs will need to be tested only on individuals who have the appropriate genetic profile.

Most intriguing of all is the possibility of bringing back drugs that were recalled due to severe adverse effects in some patients. For example, a drug that was recalled because it causes kidney failure in 30 percent of people could now be given safely and effectively to the remaining 70 percent of people identified by their genetic makeup not to be at risk for kidney failure.

Very soon, pharmacogenomics will make today's one-size-fits-all approach to drug selection and dosing as outmoded as an 18th century apothecary's cabinet, delivering a host of social and economic benefits as described by Alan Roses, head of genetics research at GlaxoSmithKline:

> Selection of predicted responders offers a more efficient and economic solution to a growing problem that is leading governments and healthcare providers to deny effective medicines to the few because a proportion of patients do not respond to treatment. The economy of predictable efficacy, limited adverse events, lower complications owing to targeted delivery and increased cost-effectiveness of medicines will improve healthcare delivery and eliminate the need for rationing.[338]

Today, pharmacogeneticists are making dramatic progress in developing tests that will predict which patients are likely to benefit from a medicine, and which patients are likely to suffer an adverse effect. More and more of these tests are becoming available, and they're beginning to make their way from a small number of academic centers and teaching hospitals where they were first developed to physicians' offices across the country. This will create new opportunities—and challenges—for clinicians. Clearly, there is the chance to dramatically improve healthcare delivery. At the same time, clinicians will need to know whether response to a particular drug is genetically based, and then how to use that information to determine an appropriate dosage—or whether to prescribe the drug at all.

Pharmaceutical companies are now developing pharmacogenomic tests designed specifically for use in combination with new drug introductions, paving the way for individually tailored drug therapy, also known as personalized medicine. By 2005, experts contend, gene testing before prescriptions are written will be a routine procedure. And in the not-so-distant future, some say, it will be considered unethical to expose patients to the risks of adverse events without first performing DNA tests.[339]

Clearly, pharmacogenomics is the most ethical way to develop new drugs. At this time, with the cost of a sequencing a genome at $1.5 million, it remains prohibitively expensive. But as the technology continues to evolve, that will change. Already a new approach using a series of methods to sequence single DNA molecules, allows sequences to be read with unprecedented speed. In a special report in *New Scientist*, Eugene Chan, chief executive of US Genomics, says that the company has developed a machine that scans a single DNA molecule 200,000 bases long in milliseconds. He insists that the company expects to be able to read entire sequences one base at a time within half an hour in three or four years. [340] Epigenomics, a company that focuses on the process of methylation (a modification of one of DNA's four bases, cytosine, that normally occurs either with or without a methyl group attached), has developed technology that makes it possible to analyze DNA-methylation at thousands of sites in the genome in one single experiment. According to their web site:

> The sheer amount of data that are generated by the screening of the genome of hundreds of samples per day requires advanced data analysis techniques. At Epigenomics we use machine learning and data mining techniques to extract valuable information from the data and to identify the relevant components of methylation patterns. As a result, it has become possible to classify different types of tissues purely based on methylation fingerprints, which has important applications in tumor diagnosis as well as potentially in most complex genetic diseases.

Right now, there is also another obstacle, and it has to do not with the *science* of pharmacogenomics, but rather the *business* of pharmacogenomics. Some of the knowledge and technology needed to thus classify patients has been available for over two decades. Physicochemical measurements such as ionizability (*pKa*) and lipophilicity (*log P* or *log D*) can be used to predict how the drug will be absorbed from the gut and *in vitro* test utilizing Caco-2 cells from human colon carcinoma cells, can be used to predict absorption and secretion of drugs in the small intestine. But because the drug companies all want to sell a drug to millions and millions of people, they are hard pressed to test their product so as to *decrease* the number of people to whom they can sell it. Under the current business model, Big Pharma wants, and needs, the blockbuster drug to support their massive research and marketing operations. In an article by Susan Warner in *The Scientist*, Robert Toth, senior portfolio manager of the medical technology fund at EGM Capital, a San Francisco hedge fund, was quoted as saying, "In fact there has been some negative lobbying taking place behind the scenes of the pharmaceutical companies that would slow down the adoption of this technology."[341]

Another downside is the FDA. Regardless of scientists' and physicians' publicly expressed doubts about the value of animal studies to predict the pharmacological and toxicological properties of a drug, government regulations in the United States and elsewhere require them to conduct animal studies during the preclinical development phase, particularly when determining toxicity. The FDA has developed these regulations, and data from animal tests are considered a critical element in putting a drug on track for FDA approval. As we have explained elsewhere, Big Pharma likes animal testing for the liability protection it offers, not because it makes drugs safer for humans. Moreover, a report issued by *Obstetrics & Gynecology* indicated that more than 90 percent of drugs approved since 1980 have not been properly tested to rule out possible teratogenic effects. The report found that for the vast majority of new drugs, follow-up studies, also known as post-market surveillance studies, have not been performed. As a result, the report concluded, more than 90 percent of new drugs are still considered to have an "undetermined" risk of producing birth defects. However, because there are usually no regulatory requirements that the companies perform follow-up studies on birth defects once the FDA approves the drug, these studies are generally not done. Because of the revolving door between the FDA and Big Pharma, none of this is likely to change anytime soon without significant efforts from patient advocacy groups and consumer unions.

Using animals to test new drugs is a failed paradigm and should be—and, in many cases is being--replaced by pharmacogenomics, *in vitro* and *in silico* analysis, and other emerging ADMET research methods. If these methods are advanced, the future looks promising.

If you and your sister are diagnosed with the same type of breast cancer on the same day, because of your unique genetic profile, you may receive a very different chemotherapy regime from her. Even though you and your sister have far more genes in common than you and a genetically modified mouse or even a chimpanzee, she may have a gene that would cause a severe adverse reaction to one of the medications you will receive, hence another will be substituted. Or, you may receive a larger and more frequent dose of the same medication as she receives, because you are a rapid metabolizer of that drug. Or, you may both receive very different treatment regimes because, even though the cancer is of the same type, you have genes that will allow it to progress more rapidly than your sister's and hence you need more aggressive therapy. This is not science fiction; these advances are taking place even as you read this, and many are already in clinical use. If we are to expand what is currently being done, more human-based research must be done rather than research with entirely different species. If all these modern-day drug-testing techniques had been in place for the Jeff Smiths of the world, they would still be alive today.

Chapter **8**

How Technology is Replacing Animals in Biomedical Research and the Practice of Medicine

> "Nothing tends so much to the advancement of
> knowledge as the application of a new instrument."
> Sir Humphrey Davy 1778-1827

Bob Sinclair was a happy man, especially for someone in his late 60s who'd suffered not one but two heart attacks in the past five years. Many years ago, Bob would in all likelihood have died after his first heart attack, but advances in technology and clinical research had made it possible not only for Bob to survive, but to enjoy a reasonably active life.

Bob was just returning home from one of his favorite activities—a round of golf with three of his best buddies—when he felt a very slight "hum" in his chest. He strolled into his study, sat down at his desk, pulled out a device about the size of a digital camera and waved it back and forth across his chest. Then he plugged the wand into his telephone line and wired a report to his cardiologist, Dr. Ahmad. The moment the line was free, Dr. Ahmad called him back to reassure him that his automatic internal defibrillator was working just fine—and that he should go out and enjoy the rest of his day.

Automatic internal defibrillators—AIDs—were first implanted in humans in 1980. An AID is a mechanical device that monitors the body's heartbeats. It is powered by a lithium battery and makes a record of the time it shocks the patient, so cardiologists can monitor their patient's condition. By 2001, about 80,000 had been implanted. Bob's AID is different, though. It is a "wand-compatible" device that enables patients to use the telephone—or even the Internet—to report on their condition, rather than having to schedule appointments for frequent check-ups. It can be particularly important for debrillator patients who may get a sudden shock that could be either lifesaving or a sign of malfunction in the device.

This latest generation of defibrillators is just one example of how technology continues to change the face of patient care. In fact, access to technology is the one thing that most separates physicians today from those of 100 years ago and one of the most critical components—perhaps *the* most critical component—in the practice of medicine today. Granted, today's physicians have much more knowledge than those of yesteryear, but all that knowledge comes to no avail if one does not have the means to pinpoint a diagnosis and develop an effective treatment regimen. Many times we have seen a cardiologist listen to a patient's heart and proclaim the presence of a certain kind of murmur, only to have the diagnosis changed after an ultrasound is performed. Today, an anesthesiologist can use end-tidal CO_2 technology to make certain the endotracheal tube is in the correct place and pulse oximetry to monitor a patient's blood oxygen level on a second-by-second basis. These three developments alone resulted in a dramatic drop in negative outcomes.

Like most busy career women, 48-year-old Lekeisha Michaels had become accustomed to the daily stresses of her management position at a financial brokerage firm. So when she became increasingly plagued by vomiting episodes, severe headaches, and vision problems, she went to her internist. Nothing could have prepared her for the frightening diagnosis: meningioma, a tumor that arises in the membranes that cover the surface of the brain and spinal cord.

Lekeisha was not alone. Each year, 100,000 Americans are diagnosed with a brain tumor and face the frightening prospect of brain surgery as the only option. Brain tumors hold a special challenge for neurosurgeons: take out the tumor but don't take out anything else. If Lekeisha had bowel cancer and the surgeon took out a foot of bowel on each side of the cancer, she would probably have a better outcome than if he didn't. But if a neurosurgeon takes out an extra ounce of tissue surrounding Lekeisha's brain tumor, she may survive the operation—but wake up unable to recognize her husband and children. Another challenge with brain tumors is that some are inaccessible via conventional surgical approaches. A new advance in technology has helped neurosurgeons overcome these challenges. Lekeisha was about to go under the knife—but there would be no need for a scalpel.

That's because Lekeisha underwent radiosurgery, in which the surgeon used a Gamma Knife, a tool that bombards the brain tumor and only the brain tumor with radiation, allowing access to otherwise inaccessible tumors without an incision. Brain tumors like Lekeisha's meningioma, as well as acoustic neuromas, pituitary adenomas, and arteriovenous malformations (AVMs) are treated with the Gamma Knife. The computer that operates the Gamma Knife analyzes two-dimensional brain images and directs the radiation accordingly.

The Gamma Knife uses 201 radiation sources that combine simultaneously to create a "spherical ball" of treatment. The shots of radiation act like a scalpel that burns out the tumor. By allowing the computer to operate the knife, it does not matter how many—or how few—times the neurosurgeons has used the device. The Gamma Knife is so precise that it damages and destroys the unhealthy tissue while sparing adjacent normal, healthy tissue. Gamma Knife radiosurgery is also extremely effective against tumors called metastatic tumors, which spread to the brain from cancer in other parts of the body.

Were it not for mathematical modeling, advances in computer technology, oncology, physics, and materials engineering, the Gamma Knife could never have been invented. This brainchild of Swedish professors Lars Leksell and Borge Larsson has come into its own only recently as a brain surgery tool, partly as a result of huge advances in imaging such as magnetic resonance imaging (MRI) and positron emission tomography (PET).

Another innovation in brain surgery can be used in the operating room before, during, and after surgery, giving surgeons an accurate view of a tumor's position at all times. Conventional MRI and CT scanners allowed neurosurgeons to visualize the tumor as never before, but still they could not see everything they needed to. Traditional MRIs, while invaluable in helping doctors diagnose a brain tumor and visualize it, cannot be used in the operating room because strong magnetic forces would suck in the surgical instruments. Now, intraoperative MRI, Polestar N-10, manufactured by Odin Medical Technologies, is allowing neurosurgeons to ascertain precisely where a brain tumor begins and ends. It can pinpoint the exact location and size of a tumor, helping doctors to avoid removing too little tumor or taking out too much tissue, including healthy brain. That information is crucial because during surgery, the brain can shift, making it difficult for doctors to match old MRI films to what they are seeing with the naked eye. This new MRI virtually eliminates the guesswork.

These remarkable tools of technology are but two examples of how computer algorithms and mathematical programming are taking disease treatment to new levels—and even changing the face of the operating theater. Some others we describe below are equally remarkable, clearly demonstrating the power of technology in making surgery safer and more effective, and even revolutionizing how we define surgery. It is largely technology that has advanced medicine to the level it is today, and it is technology that will lead us into the future.

How Technology Has Contributed To Medical Advancement.

Technology has been the foundation of virtually every revolutionary medical advance—and not just since the 20th century. About 1590, the Dutch spectacle-maker Zacharias Janssen discovered the principle of the compound microscope; even today, the microscope remains one of the most important tools in science, and a new robotic microscope is even being used to track changes in cells over time as genes are expressed and the resulting proteins go into action.[342]

In 1851, the invention of the ophthalmoscope enabled physicians to see inside the eye for the first time. In 1854, the development of the laryngoscope allowed better visualization of the larynx. The otoscope, which amplifies examination inside the ear, was designed in 1860.

In the 1900s, technology continued to take the practice of medicine to a new level with such remarkable developments as:

- Nuclear medicine, which is now routinely used for evaluating cancers and hormonal levels of the lungs, endocrine organs and kidneys prior to and after surgery. Nuclear therapy is employed to treat hyperthyroidism and other diseases.

- The tonometer, the device that is puffs air against your eye to measure intraocular pressure, allows early diagnosis of glaucoma.

- Microscopic surgeries, which allow surgeons to reattach severed digits and limbs and save many people from lifestyle-changing injuries. The microscope is also used for the common procedure of placing tubes in a child's ears in order to decrease ear infections and hearing loss. Microscopic discectomy, the removal of a herniated disc in the back, is accomplished with the microscope. The microscope is also used in neurosurgery to allow removal of tumors without damaging delicate nerves. Microvascular surgery allows surgeons to work in very small areas, with minimal destruction of viable tissue. It is invaluable in some cancer surgeries allowing patients with advanced head and neck cancer to use some part of their larynx saving their ability to speak.[343,344,345,346]

- The endoscope allows many procedures that would have required major surgery to be performed non-surgically. This instrument is commonly used to scrutinize the upper GI tract for ulcers or cancer and the colon for early cancers. A laser can be placed on the end of the endoscope and passed into the GI tract via the mouth or rectum. Cancer cells are thus identified because they reflect the laser light differently than normal cells. [347]

- The laparoscope, like the endoscope, allows surgical procedures to be performed less invasively. Appendectomy, cholecystectomy, hysterectomy, hernia repair, kidney removal, and other surgeries were once only possible with a large incision and a prolonged recovery. Laparoscopes allow surgeons to make several very small incisions and insert instruments through them, thus decreasing the wound size, the likelihood of infection, and other complications as well as decreasing recovery time.

- Tissue implants, including artificial eyes, heart valves, penile prosthesis, skin expanders used in order to harvest more skin for skin grafts, artificial blood vessels, pacemakers, and other advances.

- Acoustic microscopy, an extension of ultrasound, demonstrates internal conditions using sound waves without requiring dyes.

- Vacuum-assisted closure devices are used to prevent skin necrosis from snakebite.[348]

- Electronic hearing implants stimulate the auditory nerve, which sends hearing impulses to the brain.

- Computerized canes operate in conjunction with sonar to help the blind avoid obstacles and walk without being guided.[349]

- Impervious wound-edge protectors safeguard against postoperative wound infection.[350]

- Virtual reality flexible sigmoidoscopes help medical residents and other physicians train for live patient examinations.[351]
- Cryoablation uses extreme cold, is used to kill pain-causing nerves and to kill cancerous tissue.
- Time-reversed acoustics employs a reversal of sound waves to destroy gall bladder and kidney stones.[352]

Technology has revolutionized one of the most commonly performed general surgical procedures – the repair of inguinal hernias. Today, prosthetic materials are used in the repair of these hernias. Previously, the hernia was simply sewn back together. The improvement was frequently only temporary and the hernia often recurred. Polypropylene mesh, polyester mesh, expanded polytetrafluoroethylene mesh, and polyester and absorbable hydrophilic collagen film are used today, providing better results than traditional repairs and decreasing the rate of recurrence. Mesh repairs also result in less disability and a quicker return to normal activity due to less tension on the muscles.

Technology has overcome a major drawback of biopsy methods for detecting cancer of the uterus. A simple ultrasound scan can now detect uterine cancers with 96 percent accuracy,[353] whereas traditional biopsy methods sometimes miss the cancer because it samples only one area.

The study of the human brain and diseases of the brain is also being improved dramatically through technology. The combination of magneto-encephalography with MRI, and functional magnetic resonance imaging (fMRI) will enable researchers to learn more about schizophrenia, epilepsy, stroke, autism, and brain damage from chemotherapy in children, through brain mapping. Magnetoencephalography provides millisecond time resolution and identifies the source of neural activity, while fMRI provides high resolution of functional areas of the brain.

A study in which physicians were given a list of 30 medical advances and asked to rank them in order of importance underscores the power of technology in improving patient care. Of the nine examples of technological innovations listed among the 30 medical advances, the physicians ranked eight of them in the top 15, and three of them in the top five (see Table 8.1). Although arguably technology played a role in each of these advances, pure technology received a lion's share of accolades.

The author of the study, Victor R. Fuchs, PhD, Professor Emeritus, Stanford University, noted that the study results might have far-reaching implications for expanding the criteria for quality assessment and shifting the allocation of research and development funds. He said the most surprising finding was "the extent to which the leading innovations were an outgrowth of the physical sciences (physics, engineering, and computer science) rather than disciplines traditionally associated with the biomedical sciences."[354]

Table 8.1

Ranking of medical advances by physicians. Advances made possible mainly due to advances in technology in the area of physical as opposed to life sciences are noted with an asterisk.

1. MRI and CT scanners*
2. ACE inhibitors
3. Balloon angioplasty*
4. Statins
5. Mammography*
6. Coronary artery bypass graft*
7. Proton pump inhibitors and H2 blockers
8. Selective serotonin reuptake inhibitors (SSRIs) and new non-SSRI antidepressants
9. Cataract extraction and lens implant*
10. Hip and knee replacement*
11. Ultrasonography and echocardiography*
12. Gastrointestinal endoscopy*
13. Inhaled steroids for asthma
14. Laparoscopic surgery*
15. Nonsteroidal anti-inflammatory drugs and COX-2 inhibitors
16. Cardiac enzymes
17. Fluoroquinolones
18. New hypoglycemic agents
19. HIV testing and treatment
20. Tamoxifen
21. Prostate-specific antigen testing
22. Long-acting and local opioid anesthetics
23. *Helicobacter pylori* testing and treatment
24. Bone densitometry*
25. **Third-generation cephalosporins**
26. **Calcium channel blockers**
27. Intravenous conscious sedation
28. Sildenafil (Viagra)
29. Nonsedating antihistamines
30. Bone marrow transplant

As Aaron Fenster of the Robarts Research Institute, wrote in *Trends in Biotechnology*:

In the past decade, we have witnessed unprecedented advances in fields such as molecular biology, medical imaging, computer technology and computational techniques. Although advances in each field have provided exciting new insights and capabilities, it is at the interface between these fields that revolutionary advances are being made. In particular, the post-genomic era is providing opportunities for the convergence of these fields, enabling novel imaging technologies and techniques to play a significant role in drug discovery, functional genomics and measurement of pharmacokinetics and dynamics in target tissues.[355]

Nobel Prizes

Considering that medicine is essentially applied chemistry, and is based on the laws of physics, it is not surprising that many of the technological advances are the result of basic science research in chemistry and physics. Many Nobel Prizes awarded for Chemistry, and many that were awarded for Physics, have made contributions to the study of medicine as well. Although an exhaustive review of the Nobel laureates in Chemistry and Physics is beyond the scope of this book, it is worth mentioning briefly the chemists and physicists whose contributions have had monumental implications for the practice of medicine. Even the brief overview of Nobel Prize laureates below demonstrates the critical importance of the basic sciences in medical discovery and treatment.

Physics

1901 W. C. Röntgen
On November 8, 1895, Röntgen proved the existence of x-rays. He never divulged exactly how he did the experiment, but did admit that it was a serendipitous rather than intentional discovery. X-rays had probably been seen by a number of physicists prior to Röntgen; however, he was the first to provide explanation. The medical implications of his explanation – diagnostics x-rays, therapeutic radiation, CAT scanners, etc. – are well known. Less well known is the fact that his discovery also led to the discovery of the electron and the developmental model of the atom. The discovery of x-rays revolutionized the world.[356]

1903 Marie Curie, Pierre Curie and Antoine Becquerel
These three won the prize for their discovery of the elements polonium and radium, and Marie Curie's postulation that the nucleus was the source of the radiation. Like the discovery of x-rays, the discovery of radiation was serendipitous. Becquerel placed some photographic plates in a drawer with what turned out to be a radiation source. When he returned to the drawer several days later, he noticed that the plates had changed. Within three weeks of his discovery he had proven that uranium emitted radiation. He also contributed a detailed experiment, on himself, of the effects of radiation on the skin. The fact that radiation could change the skin was well known but had not been documented in detail. Becquerel placed a small amount of radioactive

material in his waistcoat pocket. He documented the skin changes and continued his experiment on seeds.[357]

The importance of the discovery of radium cannot be overstated because it laid the foundation for the development of diagnostic and therapeutic x-rays, which were later to be used in medicine.[358] This Prize also illustrates another principle we have mentioned before. There are times when animals, humans, or tissue obtained from either will give accurate results. Marie Curie died from leukemia secondary to radiation exposure. Radiation was not thought to be a hazard until women working in a watch factory contracted leukemia at rates far higher than the general population. The women painted radium onto the dials of the watches and in order to maintain a fine point on the brush, they touched the brush to their tongue. Consequently, they developed cancer of the tongue, mouth and jaw. This linked radiation to cancer. It is unfortunate society had to learn of radiation's dangers in this fashion. Exposing tissue to radiation would have revealed its harmful affects. Many cite this as an example of when mice, dogs, cats and other animals would have given the same results as humans. And they are right. But around the same time, animals were also being exposed to asbestos—a very dangerous substance to humans—and "proving" it safe for humans.

1905 P. E. A. von Lenard
Lenard discovered and developed the cathode ray, which has been extensively used in physiology experiments.[359]

1909 Marchese G. Marconi and Karl Braun
Marconi developed technology concerning the thermionic valve, which aided in the performance of physiology experiments.[360]

1915 William Henry Bragg and William L. Bragg
The Braggs introduced x-ray crystallography, which was later used by Watson, Crick, Franklin, and Wilkins to unravel the DNA double helix.[361]

1952 Edward M. Purcell and Felix Bloch
These scientists' research on nuclear magnetic resonance led to the development of the MRI scanner. They discovered the physical phenomenon that "certain atomic nuclei that have been knocked out of alignment in a strong magnetic field by a burst of radiation will realign and emit characteristic resonance frequency signals that provide a kind of chemical signature." This is central to MRI operation.[362] All molecules in your body contain hydrogen. When one enters an MRI machine, all the hydrogen ions point in random directions. The magnet in the machine makes them all align in the same direction. Radio waves are then sent through the body, which results in some of the hydrogen ions spinning. When the radio waves are turned off, the ions take their aligned

position again. The computer measures how long this takes, as every tissue has a different rate for realigning. Then the picture is generated.

A nice example of how physics is tied to medicine is the fact that in 2003, American Paul C. Lauterbur of the University of Illinois and Briton Sir Peter Mansfield won the 2003 Nobel Prize for Medicine for discoveries also related to magnetic resonance imaging. Lauterbur, discovered the possibility of creating a two-dimensional picture by producing variations in a magnetic field, the key to the MRI technique while Mansfield showed how the signals the body emits in response to the magnetic field could be mathematically analyzed, which made it possible to develop a useful imaging technique. Mansfield also showed how extremely fast imaging could be achievable. This became technically possible within medicine a decade later.

As an illustration of what is wrong with the traditional system and mindset of biomedical research, Lauterbur attempted to publish his seminal paper about the MRI scanner in the prestigious journal *Nature* in 1973, but was denied. After being awarded the Prize, he stated: "You could write the history of science in the last 50 years in terms of papers rejected by *Science* or *Nature*."[363] (Lauterbur's article was eventually published in *Nature* only after he had appealed against the rejection. *Nature* also rejected: Krebs paper announcing the Krebs cycle in 1937; Cerenkov's paper on radiation; Hideki Yukawa's paper on the meson; work on photosynthesis by Johann Deisenhofer, Robert Huber and Hartmut Michel; and initially rejected (but eventual accepted) Stephen Hawking's black-hole radiation paper. For more see http://www2.uah.es/jmc.)

Chemistry

1911 Marie Curie
Marie Curie won a second Nobel for her work with radiation in medicine. She and her daughter Irene toured the country teaching physicians how to use the first x-ray machines. Today cancers of the breast, uterus, cervix, mouth, and others are treated with radiation and radiation implants.[364]

1926 Theodor Svedberg
Svedberg won the Prize for developing the ultracentrifuge, which separated particles hitherto inseparable and which is still in use today. That he was honored in the same year he published his article was very unusual and denoted the significance of the discovery.[365]

1929 Hans von Euler-Chelpin and Sir Arthur Harden
These scientists won the prize for contributions to our knowledge of enzymes and nucleic acids. Their research was essential for the development of modern medicine.[366]

1935 Irène Curie and Fédérick Joliot

The husband-wife team won for their discovery that bombarding non-radioactive elements with nuclear particles induced radiation.

1937 Walter Haworth

Haworth won the prize for his research involving vitamins and carbohydrates.[367]

1938 Richard Kuhn and Paul Karrer

These scientists were honored for advancing the knowledge of vitamins and carotenoids.[368]

1939 Adolf Butenandt and Leopold Ruzicka

Butenandt and Ruzicka did extensive research on sex hormones that led to cortisone and birth control pill production. [369]

1946 William Stanley and James Northrop

These two Americans won half of the Prize for new methods of preparing pure viruses and enzymes. The knowledge this revealed about viruses and enzymes created a revolution in medicine and substantiated the field of virology.[370]

1947 Sir Robert Robinson

Robinson conducted research on chemicals such as atropine, quinine, cocaine and morphine in addition to monumental work on steroids.[371]

1948 Arne Tiselius

Tiselius was responsible for the *in vitro* technique known as protein electrophoresis. This, in addition to Svedberg's development of the ultracentrifuge, a project on which Tiselius was an assistant, revolutionized chemistry and medicine. Today, electrophoresis is used in every biochemical, molecular biology and clinical laboratory in the world; it is performed hundreds of thousands of times per day on patients, and nearly everyone has had this process done on their blood at some time in their lives. The Mayo Clinic did approximately 50,000 electrophoresis procedures in 1993.[372]

1952 A. J. P. Martin and R. L. M. Synge

These two Englishmen invented the chemical process of partition chromatography, which was also used by Watson and Crick when elucidating the structure of DNA.[373]

1954 Linus Pauling

Pauling, of vitamin C fame, won the prize for discoveries concerning the nature of the human hemoglobin molecule. (Hemoglobin is the molecule in the red blood cell that transports oxygen). He examined the differences between hemoglobin molecules in patients with sickle cell anemia and patients without the disease. His discoveries in human cells allowed future scientists to elucidate the mechanism of sickle cell anemia. This was indeed a landmark discovery. Pauling's contributions to science and medicine are legendary.[374]

1957 Alexander Todd
Todd's research on cell components revealed new facts concerning nucleotides and nucleotide co-enzymes. This work was very important for a greater working knowledge of the nucleus of the cell and hence important for genetics and molecular biology. It helped explain how DNA could influence genetics.[375]

1958 and 1980 Frederick Sanger
Sanger's studies of lysine metabolism led to award-winning revelations regarding insulin in 1958. His work showed that small differences in the insulin molecule between species accounted for the adverse reactions some diabetic patients had to non-human insulin. Once again, it is the small differences that are so important when using animal data to treat humans. He also contributed to knowledge of nucleic acids, for which he won the 1980 prize. His research was instrumental in allowing the synthesis of human insulin.[376]

1962 Max Perutz and John Kendrew
The Nobel Foundation honored Perutz and Kendrew's lifelong work elucidating the structure and nature of the hemoglobin and myoglobin molecules. The scientists used and perfected x-ray diffraction—a technique that has become a mainstay of such research.[377]

1964 Dorothy Mary Crowfoot-Hodgkin
Crowfoot-Hodgkin used x-ray crystalline methods to determine the structure of vitamin B_{12}.[378]

1976 William N. Lipscomb Jr.
Lipscomb received the prize for contributions to the field of radiation oncology. His work with boron has been used to treat certain types of cancer via radiation.[379]

1982 Aaron Klug
Klug developed crystallographic electron microscopy. He used the technique to study nucleic acid-protein complexes, chromatin, histones, and DNA.

1991 Richard R. Ernst
Ernst earned recognition for his work on nuclear magnetic resonance, the groundwork for the MRI scanner. Ernst expanded on the work of Purcell and Bloch, perfecting the technology to the point that it could be used daily by scientists and physicians. He worked on the "pulse-Fourier transform MR signal detection techniques...added dimensionality to the NMR

spectroscopy...improved the efficiency and accuracy of the acquisition of the MRI data needed to reconstruct the second dimension."[380] We owe the MRI scanner to his contribution.

2002 John B. Fenn, Koichi Tanaka, and Kurt Wüthrich
These three scientists won the Nobel Prize in chemistry for developing methods of identifying and analyzing large biological molecules, such as proteins. Fenn and Tanaka were honored for finding two ways to extend the technique of mass spectrometry so that researchers could identify and analyze large molecules by separating and spreading them out as a cloud in a gas without losing their original structure. Wuethrich was honored for improving nuclear magnetic resonance, so that scientists could develop three-dimensional images of molecules in a solution.

2003 Peter Agre and Rod MacKinnon
Human beings consist of about 70% salt water so it was fitting that the 2003 Nobel Prize in Chemistry was awarded to two scientists, Peter Agre, of Johns Hopkins University Medical School in Baltimore, and Rod MacKinnon, of The Rockefeller University in New York, whose discoveries clarified how salts (ions) and water are transported out of and into the cells of the body. The discoveries have afforded us a fundamental molecular understanding of how, for example, the kidneys recover water from primary urine and how the electrical signals in our nerve cells are generated and propagated. This is of great importance for our understanding of many diseases of e.g. the kidneys, heart, muscles and nervous system.

Defects in the genes encoding aquaporin-family proteins are now recognized to be the basis of number of human diseases. For example, mutations in the water channel of the human eye are associated with congenital cataract formation. MacKinnon was awarded the Prize for his structural and mechanistic studies of ion channels. Inherited and acquired mutations in ion channels are associated with many human diseases, including cystic fibrosis and heart arrhythmias.

The 2003 Prize illustrated how contemporary biochemistry reaches down to the atomic level in its quest to understand the fundamental processes of life.

Computers

Advances in technology are dependent upon advances in physics and engineering, but computer science and chemistry also have an integral role. In fact, the new field of bioinformatics represents a truly multi-disciplinary approach to scientific research, since it combines computer science, physics, math, engineering, and the life sciences. Marvin Cassman, the director of the National Institute of General Medical Sciences (NIGMS) stated, "The future of the biological sciences will be driven by advances in bioinformatics and computational biology." [381]

Today, computer hardware and software giants like IBM, Sun Microsystems, Hewlett-Packard/Compaq, and Silicon Graphics are helping scientists meet the challenges of processing, managing, and manipulating the huge amount of biological data with supercomputers that can hold a terabyte or more of information. (A terabyte is equal to 1,000 gigabytes.) For example, the genomics firm Celera has 110 terabytes of storage in its computer farm, which is about 11 times the amount of information contained in the print version of the U.S. Library of Congress.[382]

To encourage the use of mathematical tools and approaches to study biology, the NIH has added a new center called the Center for Bioinformatics and Computational Biology (CBCB). The CBCB is not the first NIH center of the future. The National Institute of Biomedical Imaging and Bioengineering (NIBIB) was announced in 2000 and is dedicated to advances in medical technologies. NIBIB will coordinate fundamental research e.g., math, physics, and engineering, as it pertains to the imaging of disorders, diseases, and life processes of the body. Ruth Kirschstein, then acting NIH director, stated, "While dedicating an institute to medical technologies...may seem novel for the NIH, it is truly a reflection of what science is today – and where science will be taking us tomorrow."[383]

The pioneering work of scientists involved in the development of artificial neural networks (ANNs) is one of the most stunning examples of the integration of multiple disciplines in the advancement of medicine. ANNs, which grew out of an interest in learning and recognition, and involve scientists from the fields of biology, cognition, physics, computer science, statistics, and probability theory, are becoming an invaluable aid for researchers in analyzing and modeling complex data. They are, in essence, highly sophisticated statistical programs based on pattern recognition. The uses of ANNs are evident in virtually every medical specialty, from anesthesiology to neurology, radiology, laboratory medicine, and cardiology. In cancer management, ANNs are utilized to predict the course of cancer on an individual basis, thus enabling clinicians to customize a treatment protocol based on those predictions.

ANNs are also being used to improve cancer diagnosis. Mammograms have been criticized for being very difficult to interpret; a study in the September 18, 2002 issue of the *Journal of the National Cancer Institute* demonstrated that the interpretation of mammograms varies widely among radiologist practicing in a community setting, with younger, more recently trained radiologists having two to four times more false-positive interpretations than older radiologists. When used in conjunction with a radiologist's interpretation of a mammogram, for example, ANNs allow for more accurate diagnosis of breast lesions.

ANNs are also speeding up the process of determining the type of bacteria that is causing infection in a patient, so that the patient can begin the proper antibiotic treatment as quickly as possible. While the use of cultures currently provides accurate diagnosis, the process can take days—even weeks, during which the patient may be using the wrong antibiotic, the technique using ANNs takes only minutes.

By combining an electronic stethoscope with an ANN, scientists can distinguish harmless heart murmurs in children from those that represent serious cardiac pathology. [384] Scientists hope that in the future ANNs can even be used in "reverse genomics"—that is, quantifying the combined role of genes and the environment in disease incidence. In combination with epidemiology, ANNs can lead researchers to a greater understanding of how to avoid disease.[385]

Nanotechnology

The emerging field of nanoscience and nanotechnology, which builds upon knowledge from the fields of molecular biology, chemistry, physics, engineering, computer science, and electronics, is another example of the further integration of multiple disciplines for the advancement of medicine. Nanotechnology can be described as the science of assembling materials one atom at a time. Such inventions as the scanning tunneling microscope, when combined with the atomic force microscope, enable nanoengineers to see the atoms they are working with and piece them together in different ways.

Once considered the domain of science fiction writers, nanotechnology got its jump start when a third form of pure carbon was discovered in 1991. Previously, carbon was thought to exist in only two pure forms—diamonds and graphite. Now, nanoengineers are manipulating these carbon molecules, known as buckminsterfullerenes (and commonly referred to as "bucky balls" because their spherical structure containing 60 carbon atoms are arranged like the hexagonal pattern on a soccer ball) to act as atomic soldiers in the war on disease.

Although some applications are decades away, scientists believe that it is only a matter of time before they will be able to use the principles of nanotechnology to build machines to fit inside cells and repair DNA or other cellular structures. Already, researchers are inserting drug-coated fullerenes inside the HIV virus to prevent it from replicating.[386] Biomedical scientist Shuming Nie, who holds a joint appointment at the Georgia Institute of Technology and Emory University, is testing the use of nanoparticles to dramatically improve clinical diagnostic tests for the early detection of cancer. The nanoparticles, called quantum dots, glow and act as markers on cells and genes, which enables scientists to rapidly analyze biopsy tissue.[387] Scientists are also exploring the possibility of using nanorobots to kill bacteria mechanically by chopping them up, which could eliminate the problem of bacteria mutating and becoming resistant to antibiotics. In addition, scientists are working on loading fullerenes with drugs or radioactive atoms and then aiming them—like smart bombs—at cancer cells.

Scientists have used nanotechnology to make cancer-destroying nuclear molecules; monoclonal antibodies conjugated to alpha particle-emitting actinium-225. The molecules explode inside cancer cells and destroy them with blasts of radiation. Dr. David Scheinberg, from the Memorial Sloan-Kettering Cancer Center in New York said: "We have found an effective way of containing and then delivering this highly potent element directly into cancer cells." The technology was tested on human cancers *in vitro* as well as on mice. The mouse studies merely duplicated the *in vitro* work.[388]

Technology—like artificial neural networks and nanoscience—continues to be the driving force behind the most remarkable and worthwhile advancements in biomedical research today. And while it is true that animal models have been used to test whether x-rays and MRI scanners can visualize tissues, in most cases this was done after the devices were tested on humans. In many cases, such as with artificial mitral valves, animal models derailed the technology. As you will see, it is technological innovation combined with human-based research that is making a difference in patient care.

How Technology is Enhancing Medical Knowledge, Diagnoses, and Treatments

Although he has no name yet, he will be like every other human being. His eyes will open and close. Blood will course through his body. His sunburn will cause blisters. His cells will replicate and die. But there will be one crucial difference between him and any other person on earth. He will live only inside a computer.

At the Oak Ridge National Laboratory in Tennessee, computational engineers are busy creating this Virtual Human Being, which will be the most complex computer model ever attempted. Virtual reality "total immersion" software currently being developed, will enable scientists to observe, through the Virtual Human Being, the inner workings of the human body as never before. They will be able to see the interconnections between different organs, the human body's reaction to different chemicals, and even the way disease affects different organs. The Virtual Human Being will provide invaluable medical information to researchers. It will be a whole new way of viewing the human body and how it operates, and a crowning achievement in the field of mathematical modeling, in which computers simulate parts of the human body as mathematical equations. And while the Virtual Human Being will likely be years in the making, scientists have already created a host of computer simulations that are providing new insights into the way the human body works.

For example, Denis Noble at the University of Oxford has created a virtual heart that not only beats on the computer screen, but also can develop diseases, which Noble can treat with virtual drugs. Already, pharmaceutical companies have used this heart to test for adverse reactions.[389] At the University of California, Davis, researchers have developed a computer simulation that shows how branches and bends in blood vessels disturb smooth-flowing blood and contribute to heart disease. They hope to use this simulation to predict the risk of some types of heart disease by imaging a patient's aorta by CT (computed tomography) scan, then putting that image into a computer model and seeing how it performs under different conditions.[390] John Tyson of Virginia Tech and Bela Novak of the Budapest University of Technology and Economics are developing mathematical models of the molecular mechanisms that control the way yeast cells grow and assume various shapes. By studying how cells grow and divide under normal circumstances, we can better understand how the process goes awry in cancer.[391]

By studying the brains of 56 people, scientists determined that MRI can be used to measure hippocampal volume and thus distinguish individuals with stage I or II Alzheimer's disease. These findings may help to identify individuals who will develop Alzheimer's disease decades in the future.[392] By studying the MRI scans of 89 patients who were diagnosed with symptomatic lacunar infarcts or were neurologically normal and free from stroke but reported headache or dizziness, scientists discovered that severe white matter high intensity lesions were independent predictors of stroke from arteriolosclerosis. This means that if people have white matter lesions, they should undergo MRI exams frequently to see if they are at risk of stroke.[393] It will also give these patients an opportunity to make the lifestyles changes that may help counteract these risk factors.

Predicting the course of multiple sclerosis is very challenging if not, currently, impossible. MS patients suffer not only from the physical disability but also from the mental torture of not knowing when their condition will worsen. Scientists have found that an MRI brain scan might predict which people with potential MS symptoms probably have the disease and which ones will develop significant disability as time progresses.[394] The studies revealed that if the patient had more than 10 abnormal markings on the MRI, the patient was more likely to have considerable disability in the future. It also showed that patients, who developed more MRI abnormalities during the first 5 years after diagnosis, were also more likely to progress to severe disability. Hopefully, this will allow more accurate targeting of patients needing aggressive intervention.

Functional MRI (fMRI) has revolutionized the way research on the brain is carried out. Based on traditional MRI, fMRI allows scientists and physicians to see which areas of the brain are active. It works by measuring levels of oxygen throughout the brain. The more input a neuron is receiving, the more oxygen it uses. Increased blood flow means more oxygen is needed and the very subtle magnetic difference between oxygenated and deoxygenated hemoglobin produces the signal, which is read by the MRI. By using fMRI, scientists have been able to determine that children process words differently than adults. Lead investigator Bradley L. Schlaggar, M.D., Ph.D., instructor of neurology and pediatrics stated, "A fundamental objective of neuroscience research is to understand how the human brain develops. We need such knowledge to understand how normal brains develop and to learn what goes wrong in pediatric neurology-related disorders. Only then can we develop clinical interventions to treat these children."[395]

Dean Shibata of the University of Washington administered intermittent vibrations on the hands and used fMRI to scan the brains of 10 deaf students in order to learn how deaf people sense vibrations. The fMRI revealed activity in the region of the brain that processes vibrations but also in the auditory cortex, the brain area used in hearing. This study demonstrates brain reorganization or "plasticity." When an area of the brain is not being used for what it is normally used for, it can be used for other things.[396] In a similar study, Laura Ann Petitto and Robert Zatorre of McGill University and their colleagues used PET scanners to study deaf people. People who are deaf used the left hemispheres of their brains to process sign language, just as hearing people do with spoken language. This study isolated which part of the left hemisphere is used, the left inferior frontal cortex and the planum temporale, and found it was identical in both groups. The finding that the planum temporale was involved in deaf people was surprising; as most scientists believed that this area, which has input from the ears, would be used exclusively for processing spoken language.

Synthetic Aperture Magnetometry (SAM) maps areas of the brain and nervous system that are activated by pain. The technology is helping scientists understand the causes of pain and develop ways of treating it. Previously much of this type of research was conducted by administering powerful electric shocks to animals, including cats, monkeys, possums and rats or by ligating nerves. By using SAM, scientists were able to actually evaluate pain in humans. They placed the head of a patient suffering pain inside a hood containing electrodes which emitted electromagnetic signals that were picked up by the brain and projected as colored areas on a screen, thus enabling experts to identify the brain region involved in the pain experience. Dr. Qasim Aziz, who conducted the research at Hope Hospital, Salford, said: "This is a very important scientific breakthrough in the assessment of human gut complaints like abdominal pain in Irritable Bowel Syndrome. The work will encourage research groups to replace their current animal testing with suitable and more appropriate human studies."[397]

CT angiography or xenon-enhanced CT cerebral blood flow measurements in conjunction with standard CT may be used to determine treatment for patients who present in the ER with stroke. Dr. Howard Yonas and associates studied 51 patients who presented within 24 hours of stroke symptom onset. They found that, "Patients with reversible cerebral blood flow and no initial infarction are theoretically most likely to benefit from the effects of successful thrombolytic therapy," while patients with normal blood flow are unlikely to benefit, and may in fact, if such therapy was instituted, actually increase their risk of bleeding complications and hemorrhage. Dr. Yonas told Reuters Health, "I can't imagine any reason to not recommend doing all three tests when patients present...Our challenge is to extend the window for treatment beyond three hours, and to make the therapy more effective even before three hours."[398]

PET scans measure brain activity by revealing the amount of glucose metabolized in each region of the brain. This is useful in studying Alzheimer's disease (AD) as drops in glucose activity in particular areas of the brain are characteristic of AD. In a 16-year study, 284 patients in the United States and Europe were evaluated—the largest PET scan study of Alzheimer's diagnosis to date—to determine if positron emission tomography (PET) scanning of the brain can predict, with a high degree of accuracy, whether someone will develop Alzheimer's long before major symptoms begin to appear. The scientists concluded that PET accurately predicted whether patients would or would not develop Alzheimer's disease in nearly 90 percent of all cases. Dan Silverman, MD, PhD, an assistant professor in the Department of Molecular and Medical Pharmacology at the University of California-Los Angeles and the lead researcher on the study stated, "We wanted to test the sensitivity of PET in evaluating the brain for the presence of Alzheimer's disease and other dementias...PET appears to be particularly valuable in the early stages of Alzheimer's, which is when clinical diagnosis has been most challenging and least accurate."[399]

By monitoring PET scans of healthy humans, as 13 men and seven women volunteered to undergo 20 minutes of constant pain caused by an injection of highly-concentrated salt water into their jaw muscles, scientists at the University of Michigan were able to study how the brain's painkiller system works. They determined that not all brains handle pain the same way. Researchers recorded the level of pain the volunteers felt every 15 seconds during the injections and completed a pain questionnaire about their experience at the end of the experiment. The scientists found that individuals showed different patterns of mu-opioid activity (the brain's mu-opioid system controls chemicals called endogenous opioids, which bind to receptors and hinder the spread of pain messages in the brain). There were differences in both the amount of chemicals released and the timing of the release. The volunteers who experienced the largest change in the mu-opioid system between the placebo injection and the painful one tended to report the least pain. The scientists stated that, "This may help explain why some people are more sensitive, or less sensitive, than others when it comes to painful sensations. We show that people vary both in the number of receptors that they have for these anti-pain brain chemicals, and in their ability to release the anti-pain chemicals themselves."[400]

PET delivers real time data that can be used to quantify drug distribution and kinetics and probable mode of action on other body functions like blood flow and metabolism. It allows non-invasive evaluation of a drug's interactions in the body, including where the drug goes in the body and what it does when it gets there. Perhaps most interesting is the ability of PET scanners to measure drug effects in the brain. PET can access the capacity and occupancy of brain receptors and transporter molecules. PET can also allow scientists to evaluate what the body does to the drug (pharmacokinetics). PET is made possible because of chemistry's and physic's ability to label a drug or molecule that serves as marker for function with a radioactive isotope that emits positrons such as ^{11}C, ^{13}N, ^{15}O and ^{18}F. PET is noninvasive and safe.

By using PET scans, scientists were able to clarify the mechanism of migraines. Dr. Michael A. Moskowitz examined migraine sufferers who experienced auras prior to the onset of their severe head pain. He found that the auras were linked to changes in the brain called cortical spreading depression. This phenomenon is associated with massive release of chemicals that cause inflammation and increased blood flow to one side of the brain's outer membrane. This in turn makes the blood vessels feeding the membrane dilate thus irritating the nerves.[401]

By combining PET with a hydrophobic radiofluorinated molecular imaging probe dubbed called FDDNP, (a chemical marker) scientists were able to identify amyloid plaques and tangles (the brain lesions associated with Alzheimer's disease) in living patients. The plaques and tangles are believed to cause Alzheimer's by disrupting cell function and killing brain cells. But until now they could only be identified at autopsy.[402] The scientists studied nine living patients and examined the brain of one after death. The PET scan detected high concentrations of FDDNP in the memory centers of all nine Alzheimer's patients who had been injected with the chemical marker. If this marker proves accurate, it could help scientists develop treatments and preventive measures for Alzheimer's.

Clinically, it has been established that major depression and obsessive-compulsive disorder (OCD) are two very different psychiatric illnesses, yet both respond to treatment with selective serotonin re-uptake inhibitors. To find out why this is the case, scientists performed PET and MRI scans of patients with either major depression or OCD, and then again after several weeks of treatment with a serotonin reuptake inhibitor. The scans revealed that even though the treatment was the same, certain regions of the brain were involved in OCD while different regions were involved in patients with depression.

Given Imaging has developed a wireless endoscopic camera, which can be used to detect cancer and polyps and can help determine the causes of bleeding and anemia. The "pill" is a swallowable capsule that contains a tiny camera that takes 2 pictures per second as it travels through the intestine. The "camera pill" may make endoscopy obsolete as it can take pictures of the area of the small bowel that can be reached by endoscopy as well as areas that cannot. The wireless camera was developed using light-emitting technologies, image sensors and application-specific circuits. The capsule transmits the images to a data recorder worn around the patient's waist.[403]

Electron Beam Tomography (EBT) scanners are being used to screen for CAD (Coronary Artery Disease) and other causes of premature death. An EBT scan creates precision three-dimensional, digitally enhanced images of a patient's heart, lungs, colon, and other vital organs, as well as cardiac arteries, and can uncover asymptomatic disease not recognized by standard screening tests. EBT technology is most valuable for measuring the calcium build up in the main arteries of the heart, which is a leading cause of coronary artery disease. Another advanced imaging technique known as multislice spiral computed tomography (MSCT) has been shown to be a reliable way to detect blockages in the coronary arteries, providing an accurate, noninvasive alternative to conventional angiography, which is performed by threading a catheter near the heart and injecting a dye into the arteries around the heart.[404]

In addition to improving diagnostics, technology is helping scientists predict disease progression and outcome with greater accuracy—and profoundly affect a patient's quality of life. For example, PET scans are helping physicians predict whether preoperative chemotherapy will be successful in patients with gastric cancer.[405] FDG (18-fluorodeoxyglucose) PET has been shown to be a powerful prognostic tool in predicting outcomes for patients with osteosarcoma, a form of bone cancer.[406] The higher the initial FDG uptake in a tumor, the poorer the prognosis. This finding could change the course of therapy offered and may improve chances of survival among children with the disease. This study indicates FDG PET can be used to identify patients at first diagnosis of the disease who may have a poor prognosis with the therapy usually prescribed. These patients can then be treated more aggressively.

In addition to improving diagnostics, technology is changing how clinicians treat patients, and these breakthroughs are resulting in improved outcomes and quality of life not only for people who are suffering acute and chronic disease, but also for those who are physically challenged as a result of disease, injury, or birth defect.

Direct infusion of radioactive microspheres (yttrium-90 insoluble glass microspheres from TheraSphere, MDS Nordion, Ottawa) into the hepatic artery is proving effective for patients suffering from metastatic or primary liver cancer. Apparently it does so without damaging the liver. An interventional radiologist performs the procedure. She places the catheter in the liver then infuses the TheraSpheres into the hepatic artery and the beads stick next to the tumors. The beads then release their radiation over the course of about a week, producing a highly localized effect, killing the tumor but sparing normal tissue. This technique is being used in patients who failed first and second-line chemotherapy. The procedure is performed on an outpatient basis, thus allowing patients a better quality of life than staying in a hospital.

Radiofrequency ablation of liver tumors, such as hepatocellular cancer or metastatic colon cancer or other cancers that have metastasized to the liver, has obviated the need for surgery in some patients. A needle probe is inserted into the tumor and an alternating current is applied through the needle. The current oscillates in the radio frequency spectrum. This causes heating of the surrounding tissue thus killing it. The tumor can usually be seen via ultrasound, MRI or CT scan thus the needle can be placed with precision. If the tumor is large or located in a place that is not easily accessible then the procedure will be performed in the operating room. Access to the tumor can be gained by using a laparoscopic technique, but even if an open technique is needed the morbidity is still much less than conventional surgical removal. Sometimes a pump filled with anticancer chemotherapy is also placed, allowing the medication to infuse directly into the liver.

Technology is also improving the quality of life for people where tragedy has already struck. For example, a virtual reality system is significantly improving hand impairment in stroke patients. In the new system, for which a patent application is pending, the patient dons two gloves, equipped with sensors that are linked to virtual hands on a computer monitor. By moving the gloves, the patient tries to do things with the virtual hands such as play a piano keyboard, grab a butterfly, or shake hands. In a study involving four patients who had experienced a stroke one to four years previously, all of them showed improvement on measures such as finger speed and finger strength after just three weeks of therapy. The scientists documented up to 140 percent improvement in range of motion of the thumb and up to 118 percent improvement in the ability to move a single finger.[407]

Scientists at Johns Hopkins, Harvard, and MIT are working on artificial vision research that aims to replace the seeing apparatus of the eye, or at least some of it, with computer chip-driven microelectrodes. A pair of glasses fits on the patient's face. A digital camera is located on or in the glasses. The camera communicates via radio waves to a chip with approximately 100 platinum electrodes, each the size of an eyelash, implanted on the back wall of the patient's eye. The signal processor and microelectrodes stimulate neurons in the retina in a pattern picked out by the camera. This technique will not help people born blind, or those with a damaged optic nerve; they would need chips placed in the visual center of their brain. But to those who can be helped by this research, it will seem like a miracle.

Light enters the eye through the lens and cornea. It then strikes the retina, where over 150 million photoreceptors (rods and cones) and one million neural cells are located. The light stimulates the rods and cones to send electrochemical signals via the optic nerve to the visual cortex of the brain. In another project designed to restore vision to the blind, surgeons have implanted silicon chips into the eyes of three blind men in an experiment to help them see again. Each chip is the size of a pinhead and contains 3,500 solar cells that act like the eye's natural photoreceptors. At this writing, the patients have shown no signs of rejecting the implants. In an earlier experiment, three other patients received the implants after they lost their vision through retinitis pigmentosa, a condition that causes degeneration of the retina. The recipients should get enough vision to recognize faces or see objects in a room.

Technology in the form of the cochlear implant has helped more than 25,000 deaf people to hear. In a person with normal hearing, sound waves enter the ear through the external auditory canal then flow through the middle ear until they reach the hair cells of the organ of Corti on the basilar membrane.

The hairs bend and so create impulses in the cochlear nerve fibers attached to the hairs. The cochlear nerve transmits the impulses to the temporal lobe, the hearing center of the brain. The brain interprets the signals as sounds. In deaf individuals, the cochlear implant receives sound through a tiny microphone and sound processor and transmits it to an electrode in the cochlea, which in turn stimulates the auditory nerve.

Cochlear implants have been shown to benefit children who are profoundly deaf because of mutations in the gene encoding connexin 26 (GJB2).[408] GJB2 mutations cause half of the cases of severe to profound deafness observed in Caucasian families. Cochlear implants can be safely placed in deaf children younger than 2 years of age, with outcomes comparable to those seen in older children.[409]

A prosthetic device may make speaking easier for many amyotrophic lateral sclerosis (ALS) sufferers. Patients with ALS know what they want to say and how to form the words, but their muscles do not conform to their wishes. A dental device called a palatal lift that works by lifting the soft palate up to properly route air through the mouth may give ALS patients hope for improved clear speech and reduced nasality. These devices may lessen or eliminate nasality in other speech disorders as well.[410]

For scientists using bionic technologies to restore at least some degree of any lost function to persons with missing or nonfunctional limbs, the Six Million Dollar Man of television fame is no longer fiction. A device called Bion is a single-channel stimulator about the size of a long grain of rice that is controlled by an external-radio frequency. When injected into muscles involved in coordinated movements, Bions can control these muscles, given the appropriate motor commands.[411]

Continuing medical science's long tradition of self-experimentation, Oxford University Professor Kevin Warwick has had surgeons fit him with cyborg technology by implanting a silicon square with 100 electrodes into an incision in his wrist. The wires are linked to a transmitter/receiver device to relay nerve messages to a computer by radio signal. Professor Warwick hopes that the procedure could lead to a medical breakthrough for people paralyzed by spinal cord damage.

Whether in the operating room, the clinician's office, or the research laboratory, these and other extraordinary achievements illustrate how far we have come, and how far we can go, by focusing resources on the development of technology. The examples cited in this chapter represent merely a fraction of all that technology has brought us in terms of improved patient care. On the other hand, animal-modeled research has contributed little if anything to the cures and treatments we are seeking, which makes the abandonment of this outdated paradigm all the more urgent. (For more examples of how technology is changing the way medicine is practiced see www.curedisease.com.)

Technology and Alternatives to Using Animals as a Heuristic; Knowledge for the Sake of Knowledge as an End in Itself; and for Spare Parts

Studying animals in order to advance knowledge is, to the first approximation something one cannot argue with, as clearly knowledge of some sort will be gained from animal experiments. The question we, and we think society, is asking is: "Is this knowledge worth having?" Indeed we would suggest that there is a difference between knowledge and information and that animal experiments generate information or data but precious little knowledge. Knowledge implies information worth having. What benefit is it to society for a researcher to learn yet another piece of minutia about the mouse liver, kidney or lung? Considering there can never be enough money to fund every research project, like those mentioned in this book, we cannot justify spending the money to experiment on animals just to increase the amount of data in the universe.

Using animal models to generate ideas, or as a heuristic, is equally dubious. Certainly one can perform hundreds of experiments on animals in hopes of getting an idea about what kind of study to perform on humans in order to learn more about human disease. But is this the best way to generate such ideas? It seems human studies involving technologically sophisticated devices like fMRI and PET scanners would be more effective and of course less likely to lead one down the wrong path. No research project is without risk. The data gained can be used appropriately or inappropriately. As long as researchers believe rats and humans are essentially the same animal, just dressed up differently, there will be a strong temptation to extrapolate data. Further, in our experience, most good, new ideas come about as a result of hard work, careful study and occasional serendipity. Many ideas have been thought of, then tried on animals with disastrous results, but fortunately were pursued anyway to the eventual benefit of humankind. Using animals to generate ideas is a crutch with a broken leg of its own. Science has yet to explore even a small percentage of what current technology has to offer and new technologies are appearing on a regular basis. If a scientist is looking for new ideas, we suggest he look there.

An investigation into the value of so-called *basic science* research resulted in an article that was summarized in the *Times Higher Education Supplement:*

> Key evidence that has helped persuade policy-makers to fund basic biomedical research the world over cannot be relied on, a new study has found. Analysis of work by US researchers Julius Comroe and Robert Dripps, which is often cited by funders, has shown their methodology to be ambiguous. The original 1970s study purported to demonstrate that 62 per cent of key research articles that were judged to be essential for later clinical advances were the result of basic, as opposed to applied, research. This was widely interpreted as justification for funding laboratory-bench projects, since many would lead to benefits at the hospital bedside. But work by Jonathan Grant, associate programme director at Rand Europe, and

colleagues at Rand and Brunel University's health economics research group has shown fatal ambiguities in the study. Among the problems was a lack of clarity over whose opinions had been surveyed, how clinical advances were assessed and how a "key article" was defined. "It is an insufficient evidence base for increased expenditure on basic biomedical research," Dr Grant said. The Comroe and Dripps study was published in the journal Science in 1978, but it has become influential among research policy-makers in recent years.

The proportion of UK research-council spending on basic research has increased over the past decade, from 42 per cent of civilian research-and-development spending in 1991-92 to 61 per cent in 1998-99. Similar patterns are found in the US and other G7 nations.[412]

Basic science research is usually a euphemism for the animal model. Much of the funding for the animal model has been justified based on the Comroe Dripps report but this is not the first time it has been pointed out that the report was self-serving. In the final analysis the animal model as a heuristic is just not that useful especially when one considers the harm factor—harm to humans—associated with its application.

Now, just a brief word about using animals as spare parts or as incubators as we already covered this in some detail in previous chapters and in our first book *Sacred Cows and Golden Geese*. Animals are frequently used as living incubators for producing chemicals, such as insulin and monoclonal antibodies. They are also used as tissue donors for human use, such as pig valves in aortic valve replacement. There are risks involved in using animals as living incubators and tissue donors, including the risk of allergic reactions, as well as transmitting pathogens that could cause serious illness to humans. Fortunately technology has provided us with better and safer products. Human insulin is far superior to the insulin from pigs and cows for diabetics and is now produced from bacteria. Mechanical aortic valves function longer and more reliably than valves from pigs. Monoclonal antibodies, as we have mentioned earlier were essentially useless when scientists were producing them from animals but since scientists have been producing them as pure human monoclonals, they are invaluable.

The same is true of using animal cells as a growth medium. According to the Associated Press a medical ethics committee said it would be unethical and risky to treat people with the ES cells approved by President Bush for federally funded research. The approved cell lines, created for possible future disease treatments, were initially grown on mouse cells. That could expose humans to an animal virus their immune systems couldn't fight, the panel said. The experts said that safer stem cell lines now exist, but those would not be eligible for federal funding.[413]

Technology and Animals in Education

Medical student and aspiring surgeon Dan Pauly is a typical young man of his generation. A computer is as natural a tool for him to use as a typewriter was to his parents and grandparents. He grew up with the Internet, cell phones, personal digital assistants (PDAs), and other sophisticated electronic tools. So when Dan takes his seat in front of the console, puts on his 3D glasses, and grabs his joystick, one might think that he's taking a break from his studies with a round or two of *Laura Croft Tomb Raider.*

But Dan is not playing a game. Far from it. He is actually taking part in a virtual reality session that is part of his medical training, and he is working with a computer model of an inner ear and other complex anatomical structures developed by a team of physicians, engineers, and educators at the University of Illinois.[414] The model uses computer renderings of these structures that, when coupled with the 3D glasses, allow Dan and his fellow students to observe and manipulate images that appear to rise off the screen in three dimensions. The virtual reality images are a vast improvement over the two-dimensional drawings and photographs that appear in medical textbooks, providing students an opportunity to get a much better feel for the complex anatomy of the human body.

The University of Illinois virtual reality medicine lab is one way that technology, just as it is revolutionizing biomedical research and the practice of medicine, is also changing the way physicians of the future are being trained. In the process, what is being left behind is the archaic tradition of the "dog lab" where an animal, usually a dog, was used as a four-legged learning tool. Today, fewer and fewer students are participating in these procedures, in which a dog is anesthetized and the students place catheters in the veins, arteries, and heart to measure pressures and volumes and administer drugs to observe the effects.

The vast majority of animals used in the life sciences—and they number in the tens of millions on an annual basis—involve drug testing and modeling human disease. However, animals are also used in other scientific endeavors, such as subjects of dissection exercises in education.

Since 19th century British zoologist Thomas Henry Huxley decided that dissecting animals was the best way to teach the biological concept that form follows function, dissection has been part of the educational curriculum. In the days of Huxley, animal dissection may have been valuable, since back then we were just learning about the gross anatomy of organisms. Today, however, as we have seen in earlier chapters, biology is focusing on the cellular level—a level not seen in dissection. It is more about receptors and G-proteins than discovering what the pancreas looks like and where it is located. But even if dissection is used for identifying gross structures, it is not the preferred way. There is now a plethora of educational materials, such as CD-ROMs and DVDs, highly realistic, three-dimensional models and computer simulations that offer a virtual reality experience, and CT and MRI scans of human anatomy—all of which provide far better visualization. Learning anatomy on worms, starfish, and frogs just isn't all that helpful. When we were in school the standing joke was "What would the teacher think that brown piece of tissue was?" because no one, not even the teacher, thought it was the same thing twice.

In addition to its limitations in only showing gross anatomical structures, there are other problems with the "frog lab," which, despite the large number of high-quality alternatives available, remains a fixture in the education curriculum. Biology classes focus on *human* biology, and there are vast differences between frogs and humans. Frogs have a three-chambered heart, while humans have a four-chambered heart. If their optic nerves are cut, frogs will be able to see again within weeks. Performing the same procedure on a human will result in permanent blindness. Some frog species change in color in response to changes in the surrounding temperature, light, and humidity. Frogs breathe through their skin as well as their lungs. Their bulging eyes allow them to see in all directions, and some species can leap up to 20 times their body length.

Frogs represent about half the animals used in dissection, and the use of frogs in such high numbers is harmful to the environment. Because attempts to breed frogs in captivity have proven unsuccessful, frogs used for dissection must be captured in the wild, which upsets the balance of nature and causes many different problems for humans. As part of a complex ecological cycle, frogs are both predator and prey. Frogs eat mosquitoes and other insects, and in turn, frogs are an important food source for bats, snakes, turtles, fish, and herons. When the frog population declines, mosquitoes and other insects—which carry disease and destroy food crops—become too numerous. Meanwhile, the animals that prey on frogs decline in number because they do not have enough food to eat, which affects the animals that prey on them, and so on throughout the ecosystem. The worldwide population of frogs is in serious decline. Several years ago, the collection of huge numbers of frogs in Bangladesh caused insect overpopulation, resulting in serious crop damage and the spread of disease. In the United States and Mexico, the collection of the American bullfrog and the leopard frog (the ones most commonly used in dissection) is threatening the future of these species while upsetting the balance of nature in wetland areas.

Animal dissection may also cause other kinds of human health problems. Animals used in dissection are often embalmed with formaldehyde, a chemical preservative linked to cancer of the throat, lungs, and nasal passages. Formaldehyde can also cause eye damage and trigger asthma attacks and bronchitis, and it has been linked to human cancer, birth defects, and reproductive problems.

Investing in non-animal alternatives, which can be used repeatedly, is a much better use of school (and taxpayer) funds. The alternatives are available to students, teachers, and school districts on a free-loan basis through the National Anti-Vivisection Society's Dissection Alternatives Loan Program. Those that require the use of a computer offer an additional advantage, providing students not only an opportunity to learn about biological processes, but also to hone their computer skills as well. (See NAVS website (www.navs.org) and *The Use of Animals in Higher Education: Problems, Alternatives, & Recommendations* by Jonathan Balcombe, for a partial list of what is available.)

Today, not a single one of the top ten medical colleges in the United States, including Harvard, Stanford, Yale, Duke, and Columbia universities, use the traditional dog lab to train doctors. As of this writing, 91 of the country's 126 medical schools now have entirely non-animal curricula. Medical students and physicians have been surveyed and asked if they think learning techniques, procedures, and basic physiology is best obtained from animals or humans. Not surprisingly, the overwhelming response has been that human observation is the best teacher.

Surgeons learn how to be surgeons by watching other surgeons perform procedures on humans. Medical students, like surgery residents, observe numerous procedures, such as chest tube insertions, before ever doing one. When the time comes, they will not be alone, but will probably have two or three physicians watching them to ensure that they are performing the technique properly. Only after multiple insertions, under direct supervision, will the by-then resident be allowed to do one alone. There is no need to use animals to teach basic medical techniques and principles, and indeed there can be harm. For example, there are many differences between inserting a chest tube on an anesthetized dog and into a human, who has a different anatomy than a dog. If a physician treated the human the way a dog would be treated, there would be serious complications.

Physicians who receive advanced training in emergency patient care through Advanced Trauma Life Support (ATLS) courses frequently use animals. Now there is a trend toward eliminating the use of animals in ATLS courses. A growing number of medical centers are using non-animal methods exclusively for ATLS training. These centers are pioneering the use of human cadavers to teach such techniques as inserting airway and chest tubes, tapping fluid from the chest, and other procedures. The American College of Surgeons has endorsed the use of cadavers for ATLS courses.

Realistic simulators are replacing animals in teaching lifesaving procedures. SIMULAB, for example, has introduced SIMULAB® TRAUMA MAN ™ Surgical Trainer. TRAUMA MAN is an anatomically correct human mannequin made from an elastomeric composition and is designed specifically for surgical training. Physicians can use TRAUMA MAN to practice peritoneal lavage, chest tube insertion and pericardiocentesis, and cricothyroidotomy. Medical simulators, like flight simulators, place trainees in a virtual environment that mimics the look and feel of performing an actual medical procedure. SIMULAB offers SIMUVIEW Suture Trainer, a two-dimensional laparoscopic simulator that allows surgeons to perform laparoscopic training without setting up traditional videoendoscopic camera equipment. It can be used to practice laparoscopic cholecystectomy and laparoscopic Nissen fundoplication. The Simulab Breast Probe model simulates the breast and axilla for probe equipment demonstration.

Immersion Medical's CathSim® has six learning modules that provide a complete visual, tactile, and auditory learning experience. These simulators also provide a thorough evaluation following each trial run, saving information in a database and allowing individual users to track their progress. Immersion Medical has also developed simulators for endoscopy and endovascular procedures, such as placement of electrical pacemaker leads in the heart. By using these simulators, a doctor-in-training can practice these very tricky procedures repeatedly without risk to patients.

A number of studies have documented the significant improvement in trainee skill resulting from use of the simulators. One study, for example, found that novice bronchoscopists performed more thorough exams on a mannequin following training with Immersion Medical's simulator than did skilled physicians with two years of training without a simulator.[415]

There are many benefits to using non-animal technologies to train tomorrow's physicians and surgeons. First, they provide a superior learning experience that ultimately results in better patient care; they can be less costly than using live animals; they don't pose a potential human health threat, nor do they pose a threat to the environment. And there may be a less quantifiable benefit as well. Many students oppose animal dissection on ethical grounds, but they believe that they have no choice if they want to earn a degree in the life sciences. To avoid the issue, they may be more likely to choose an alternate career. How many outstanding young scientists are we losing as a result? We don't really know. But in a field such as health care, where one is deeply involved in caring for people—often at incredibly stressful and critical times in their lives—a strong sense of compassion, combined with a skilled hand, is a welcome trait indeed.

Animal Experiments Benefit Animals? By Dr. Jean Greek

As a veterinarian who is opposed to animal experimentation, I am frequently told that animals benefit from experiments done on animals. Even if this were so, I fail to see how tormenting a "lab" dog for the benefit of my "companion" dog would be appropriate. Putting more value on certain animal lives is no different than the grievous ethical lapse that resulted in such blights on medical history such as occurred with the Tuskegee study. In the 1950's in rural Alabama, a group of doctors decided that "mankind" would be best served by allowing a group of poor, African-American men to go untreated for syphilis. They felt justified that the good that they were doing outweighed the harm they caused. Besides, the men who died from this hideous disease were not ones that society deemed very important. Surely, no one would question the immorality of using these men as uninformed test subjects for the rest of us.

Why should my beloved pet cat be allowed to enroll her less fortunate cousins in a feline variation of the Tuskegee experiment, even if she might benefit?

Furthermore, the argument that animals benefit from laboratory experiments on other animals is a distractor. The National Institutes for Health is not doling out its billions for Fluffy's benefit. The monies spent on research that is intended to benefit animals is miniscule when compared to the monies poured into research for that is intended to serve mankind's interest. Particularly when one removes the research dollars that "help" animals grow more rapidly into chicken sandwiches or pork chops, very little effort and very few dollars go into medical research to help animals.

Because there is a legal mandate that all new human drugs be tested in animals, it is not surprising that many people have the mistaken idea that veterinarians use this data and apply the information to their animal patients. There are a number of reasons that this does not occur. The test species is often not one that is seen commonly in clinical practice. These days the test species may very well be an animal such as a genetically modified mouse that does not even exist in nature. Animals used to screen for toxic reactions are given artificially high doses over very short time periods. Data gleaned from such studies is rarely published in veterinary journals and even if it was would not help much in a clinical setting where I am giving a lower therapeutic dose over a much longer time period. The animals used in such studies never have a natural version of the disease being treated. Therefore it is not apparent if animals would even benefit from the drug being studied. Finally, much of the animal experimentation is proprietary. That is, even if I thought the information might be beneficial to my animal patients, I may not be able to access it.

In the real world of veterinary medicine, the opposite is more typical. I hear of a drug that has been used in the human variant of the disease that I am treating and then try it in my patients. Sometimes it works, sometimes it does not. Sometimes my patients require much higher doses, such as occurs with antihistamines. Sometimes they don't tolerate the medication even at very low doses, such as with acetaminophen. Accutane can be very toxic to human livers. Dog livers love it, but you have to monitor for toxic effects to the eyes. This does not occur in man.

The converse is also true. Dr. Steven A. Goldman of the Weill Medical College of Cornell University in New York said in Science News, "even where things work wonderfully in animal models, it's not uncommon to fail in human trials."

An example of how research to benefit animals should be conducted comes from Purdue University. Obsessive-compulsive disorder (OCD) was highlighted in the movie *As Good As It Gets* starring Jack Nicholson. People suffering from OCD demonstrate repetitive behavior such as locking their door seven times before they go to bed, always sitting in the same place in a restaurant, and so forth. Dogs also seem to suffer from something similar in that some may chase their tails or demonstrate some other repetitive behavior.

According to *New Scientist*, "Andrew Luescher of Purdue University in West Lafayette in Indiana is recruiting affected dogs to test whether drugs used to treat humans with OCD will work on them. He also plans to use brain imaging techniques to diagnose the condition." By studying these dogs, with the consent of their humans, we will be able to learn more about the disease and test, under very controlled conditions, if a specific drug helps.

This is typical. It does not require that animals be specifically bred with a disorder nor does it require that the animals be housed in confining cages, on cement all day, without love and affection. Just as in human research, animals can be studied as they present to the vet with a disorder. This is how most human research is conducted. We do not need to create babies with heart disease; we study those unfortunate enough to have been born that way in hopes of learning something that will help them and others that come after them. The same can be, and is done in vet medicine. This is true for operations, for drugs, and other therapies.

Another fallacy purported by the vested interest groups to defend animal models is refuted by the fact that a drug that works well in humans and becomes profitable to the company will then become available and cheaper for veterinary community to prescribe. For most human drugs, the veterinary market is the tiniest economic blip. Prices are set in response to the human demand. If there is a veterinary demand, monies earned from that are merely icing on the cake.

Animals and humans do have things in common; hearts, brains, lungs, bones and so forth. It should not come as a surprise that these organs get sick nor that some animals can take the same drugs as humans. The reason animal testing does not work is not that animals and humans are totally different. However, species will vary in their responses to drugs and disease. You cannot know if an animal responds like a human until a drug has been used in both that species and in man. In one case a drug may kill humans and dogs but cure rats, cats and monkeys while in another situation a drug may cure the human but kill the monkey, rats and dog and a third drug may affect the species even differently from the first two.

Neither do animals need to be killed in order for vet students to learn to practice medicine. Physicians don't kill humans to learn operations or anatomy. Neither do students at the Western School of Veterinary Medicine. Animals that have died of natural causes are donated for the students to learn on, as has long been the case at medical schools. Students are taught surgery by performing necessary surgeries on actual patients under the watchful eyes of their teachers. This is exactly what is done in medical schools.

The next time a supporter of animal experimentation assures you that animals benefit from animal experiments, tell him not to do the animals any more favors.

Chapter **9**

The Urgent Need to Focus Resources on Non-Animal Modalities

> The spectacles we wear behind the eyes are
> our greatest barrier to understanding.

Steve Samuels was diagnosed with pancreas cancer on his fiftieth birthday. He had lost 30 pounds from his normally fit 210 pounds on his large former football-player frame. After seeing his internist, Steve consulted three cancer specialists in the large metropolitan city where he lived in an attempt to find out all he could about the disease and his options. All three said his life expectancy was less than one year. He searched the Internet and found many miracle cures, but none that were supported by reputable medical professionals or institutions. Neither did he find anything promising about treatment options that the three specialists had not already mentioned.

He journeyed to a large tertiary-care center, a university teaching hospital, in another city to see yet a fourth cancer specialist, Dr Ell, that the previous three specialists had said was the foremost expert in the country on pancreatic cancer. Dr Ell looked at the biopsy results, the scans, and all the other information Steve had hand carried on the 1500-mile trip. Yes, there were some ongoing clinical trials with new drugs that had shown promise in animals, and yes, Dr Ell would attempt to enroll Steve in these trials. But Dr Ell cautioned Steve to be realistic. Steve now weighed 166 pounds.

Two days later, Steve underwent his first treatment with a new form of chemotherapy. He was treated with the new drug every third day for a month. He did surprisingly well with the treatments, experiencing a little discomfort after each infusion but all in all, tolerating the treatments well. At the end of the second month he was re-examined by Dr Ell and re-scanned. No improvement. Dr Ell then suggested a second and third experimental drug to be taken concurrently. Steve weighed 138 pounds.

Steve underwent the additional chemotherapy but found it far more difficult than the first. He experienced constant nausea, dry retching and could not eat. The drugs also made all his muscles ache, lowered his red blood cell count, and caused other blood tests to be abnormal, in addition to apparently being the cause of an unrelenting fever. Steve was hospitalized for the remainder of the treatments so he could be given blood, monitored intensively and given nutrition intravenously. When his weight deteriorated to 98 pounds the treatment was canceled. Steve lived only another month and a half. At his funeral, many did not recognize their previously vibrant friend.

In our lifetime we have lost relatives and friends to cancer, heart disease, Parkinson's, Alzheimer's, renal failure, liver failure, depression, multiple sclerosis, AIDS, stroke, and other diseases. The suffering of the sick is not an abstract thing to us. We doubt it is to you either.

In the US in 2001, diseases of the heart killed 699,697 people. Cancer killed over 500,000, cerebrovascular diseases (such as stroke) over 150,000, respiratory diseases 123,974, diabetes mellitus 97,707, Alzheimer's disease 53,679, chronic liver disease and cirrhosis 26,751, essential (primary) hypertension and hypertensive renal disease 19,054, over 25,000 infants died, and the list goes on.[416] Many more suffered as a result of these and other illnesses. It has been estimated that adverse drug reactions are the fourth leading cause of death.

Despite the billions spent on medical research over the past thirty or so years, we have seen very few cures for diseases like multiple sclerosis, epilepsy, diabetes, cancer, heart disease, stroke, AIDS and so forth. It is only prudent to question why this is the case.

The last week of April and first week of May 2003, Sharon Begley of *Newsweek* had two articles published in the *Wall Street Journal*. Both discussed the role of animals in biomedical research. She wrote: "Lab mice, after all, have responded quite well to an experimental Alzheimer's vaccine that blocked the formation of the amyloid plaques believed responsible for the disease. Lab rats with paralyzing spinal-cord injuries have walked again, albeit awkwardly, after treatments. And we've cured cancer in enough rodents to fill several New York City subway systems. For people, however, there is no cure for spinal-cord injury, Alzheimer's, Parkinson's disease, multiple sclerosis, cystic fibrosis, osteoporosis, brain and other cancers ... the list goes on."

Begley suggests that the biomedical research industry has broken its contract with the taxpaying public. That contract being the taxpayers give the researchers billions of dollars to search for cures and treatments to diseases that afflict society and researchers are expected to produce said cures. Begley quotes immunologist Ralph Steinman of Rockefeller University, New York, as saying: "Patients have been too patient with basic research." Most basic research has been conducted on animals. Begley explains that one reason for this lack of translation from basic research to humans is that top science journals prefer to publish the kinds of studies that can be performed on animals as opposed to the kind performed on humans. She quotes Dr Steinman again as saying: "Most of our best people work in lab animals, not people. But this has not resulted in cures or even significantly helped most patients."

Begley then quotes Rockefeller's James Krueger as saying: "Human experiments are much more time-consuming and more difficult than animal studies. There are also funding issues. It's much easier to write a successful grant proposal for animal experiments. Animals are homogeneous, and let you say 'aha!' in a neat, clean experiment."

Begley ends her first article by saying: "From 1998 to this year, the budget of the National Institutes of Health doubled. The 2004 budget request is $27.9 billion. Millions more in private money gushes into biomedical research. Despite those billions, it's the paralyzed rats that walk again. Solutions, anyone?"

In her second article Begley states: "About 30% of NIH's research budget supports clinical research on patients. The rest goes to basic science, from molecules in test tubes to tumors in lab mice." Begley's articles voice the concept we have been expressing for years. What is significant is the fact that the person saying this is a nationally renowned science journalist. We hope the decision-makers in government listen. But we have our doubts.

Neil Munro wrote in the *National Journal*:[417]

> In the six years since 1997, Congress has doubled the National Institutes of Health's medical-science budget, which this year stands at almost $28 billion. Now Congress wants results.

> The money flows to scientists at NIH and also to research centers scattered throughout legislators' districts. The rising tide of funds has helped to boost many local economies, but, so far, the money has produced limited benefits for patients, in part because scientists direct so much of it to their colleagues for basic research. NIH's research promises a big payoff someday, but, given the complexity of human biology, converting hopes into therapies can take 10, 15, or even 20 years.

> In Congress, the debate over the benefits of increased NIH funding is shaped by politicians' ambivalent approach to their oversight of the science sector.... Liberal Democrats are reluctant to regulate scientists, academics, and their allied professionals, partly out of ideological sympathy for intellectual exploration, and partly because those groups help generate many jobs. Free-market Republicans are as loath to regulate job-creating universities as they are to regulate job-creating companies, even when university researchers challenge social conservatives' positions on human experimentation and genetic engineering.... Administration officials and legislators want better management at NIH, but they are reluctant to second-guess scientists' spending policies. They want NIH to develop treatments more quickly but are loath to shift money away from basic science and into near-term therapies. They want more transparency in NIH's activities, but they also want to minimize regulation of science and technology.

> These policy dilemmas were fully visible on Oct. 2 at a joint House-

Senate hearing on a possible reorganization of NIH. Sen. Judd Gregg, R-N.H., chairman of the Senate Health, Education, Labor, and Pensions Committee, lauded the institutes' scientific accomplishments but also questioned funding priorities: "Does [the NIH] peer-review process adequately balance results to the population as a whole, the health care results?" he asked. "Where are we closest to getting something, versus just the academics and the basic science?"

....At the joint hearing, Varmus said the directors of the 27 centers "are under tremendous pressure from their constituencies to try to fund more grants [for them] rather than donate money to a common pool." During his term from 1993 to 2000, he said in a later interview, "we got very little support for trans-NIH activities."

....Each of the 27 NIH centers has its supplicants and lobbyists, all hoping to promote cures for particular diseases—and funds for their own projects. The centers distribute their grants according to the advice of peer-review groups drawn from pools of academic and research-center experts. This gives NIH officials free access to the best scientists' expertise, and has led to medical advances that have extended the lives of millions of Americans. But the advice comes entangled with the peer-review scientists' professional, financial, and personal interests. As a safeguard, NIH officials try to minimize conflicts of interest in the peer groups, and they keep control of funding decisions. But most of the NIH officials making the decisions are also scientists, and they have their own ties to the complex of professional and commercial centers within the scientific community.

....In 1992, at age 24, Will Ambler was paralyzed in a motorcycle accident. Doctors don't have a cure for his spinal cord injury, so he sought help from various scientists. But he found none willing to turn away from the laboratory to test possible treatments on patients, Ambler said from his home in Solvang, Calif. This focus on science rather than therapy, he said, is driven by scientists' preference for professional success, and also by NIH funding policies. NIH "provides funding for scientists if they show scientific progress; they don't have to deliver [therapeutic] results," he said.

....Zerhouni [NIH Director Elias Zerhouni] is also keenly aware of the complaints from Gregg, Ambler, and many others about the slow conversion of science into health care. The answer, he said, "is not so much a question of incentives, [but rather] removing the obstacles." *Still, NIH will remain focused on science, not therapies,* he said. "We're not changing the balance, we're supercharging the NIH." (Emphasis added)

Expanding scientific knowledge is not synonymous with creating new therapies. It is very disappointing to read that the Director of a government institution whose mission is finding treatments and cures would rather fund science research for science's sake than research focused on finding cures.

Any child will tell you his puppy is not exactly like him. A well-educated adult should be able to expand on that childhood observation and explain that because of the process of natural selection in evolution, different species evolved to fill different niches and therefore have different anatomies and physiologies. As scientists, we can explain how regulatory genes and gene expression can take two organisms with 99% of their DNA in common and produce on the one hand a human and on the other a chimpanzee or even a mouse. We can also explain why animals are examples of *complex systems* and therefore why a mouse or chimpanzee cannot be used to model a human suffering from AIDS or cancer. Very small differences between two species will be multiplied exponentially until the two systems are very different in the property being examined, for example drug toxicity. As we have seen, even small differences between humans can lead to disaster when taking drugs.

We live in a very exciting time. Scientific advances are daily taking us places our parents never dreamed we would go. Personalized medicine is a reality and will continue to grow in its application, provided society funds the necessary research. It is possible that someone reading this book will live to see the day when his annual checkup consists of a physician waving a wand over his body and diagnosing all his ills. We can also expect treatments to be noninvasive or minimally invasive with many diseases being prevented at birth or before. This future will not be seen if society continues to waste resources on misleading experiments in animals.

William Russell and Rex Burch, concerned about the use of animals in medical research proposed in their book *Principles of Humane Experimental Technique*, published in 1959, what has come to be known as the *Three Rs*: reduction; refinement; and replacement. Their goal was to: reduce the number of animals used in experiments; refine the experiments so less pain and suffering was involved; and to eventually replace animals in medical research. The Three R's were interesting from an animal welfare perspective, but today have little to offer humanity. The National Anti-Vivisection Society has proposed the Three R's be replaced with the *Three A's*: Accuracy; Accountability; and Advancement. We support this proposal. Society must demand research and tests that are accurate, that predict human response and that are useful for medical research and testing. We must hold accountable those who continue to assure the public that animal models are reliable and needed, because they profit from the paradigm. And finally we need to demand that instead of relying on an outdated, unreliable, and dangerous paradigm, the animal model, scientist use advanced techniques such as we have discussed that will truly lead to tomorrow's cures. Humanity is drowning in a sea of disease. It is time to stop throwing dogs overboard, and instead, start giving patients the life jackets we have described in this book. Human lives depend on it.

Appendix

The following is from the PBS program FRONTLINE. The transcript and video for *Dangerous Prescription* can be found at: http://www.pbs.org/wgbh/pages/frontline/shows/prescription/. We thank FRONTLINE for allowing us to reprint some of the transcript from the program.

"I think Americans need to recognize that every time they put a pill in their mouth -- especially a new pill that they've never taken before -- it's an experiment," says Dr. Raymond Woosley, vice president for Health Sciences at the University of Arizona.

"When a drug goes on the market, only about 3,000 patients have ever been given that drug," says Woosley, who directs a national center that studies drug side effects. "We will never know all the toxicity that can occur, especially the one [patient] in 10,000 or one in 20,000 that could be seriously harmed. Our detection will only happen after the drug is on the market and exposed to a huge number of patients."

"The FDA is wholly dependent on trust -- trusting that the company is providing all the truth, all the time," retired FDA drug reviewer Dr. Leo Lutwak says. "And that the company is not hiding information. And that the company is not covering up information."

When the FDA approved the release of the higher-dosage Baycol -- known as Baycol .8 -- in the summer of 2000, the agency was unaware that Bayer had information suggesting that patients on Baycol had a significantly higher risk of developing rhabdomyolisis than patients on other statin drugs. Bayer declined to be interviewed by FRONTLINE.

FRONTLINE also recounts the biggest safety disaster in the FDA's history: the approval and removal of the diet drugs known as Fen Phen. Fen Phen was a combination of fenfluramine (also sold under the brand name Pondimin) and phentermine. Redux was a slightly modified version of fenfluramine called dexfenfluramine. In "Dangerous Prescription," FRONTLINE speaks with scientists and former FDA officials who say the agency had evidence of the dangers of Redux before the drug was released but chose to approve it anyway.

Dr. Stuart Rich, a cardiologist at the Rush Heart Institute in Chicago, recalls that the FDA's decision over whether to approve Redux for U.S. distribution occurred around the same time that he and his colleagues in France were wrapping up a three-year European study of the drug. The study showed a strong correlation between pulmonary hypertension and diet drugs -- particularly Redux.

"What was particularly shocking to me was that on the heels of reporting that this drug caused a fatal, incurable disease in Europe, that the company was planning to put it on the American marketplace," Rich tells FRONTLINE. "When I had heard this, I'd said, 'Well, you can try, but it's never gonna get in this country. The FDA would never permit a drug that had little benefit [and] terrible risk on the American marketplace.'"

Dr. Lutwak, then still employed at the FDA as a drug reviewer, agreed. "I thought it was an open and shut case," he says. "This was a dangerous group of drugs with very little, if any, benefit."

FRONTLINE recounts the internal review process that led the FDA to approve Redux over the concerns and objections of its own drug reviewers -- a decision that Lutwak says left him "disturbed." Although Lutwak eventually agreed to an approval of Redux with a number of restrictions, he was quite worried.

"I became concerned about the system," he says. "And I was particularly concerned about the potential effect on thousands and millions of people who would be using the drug."

The documentary also examines the impact of the Prescription Drug User Fee Act -- legislation passed by Congress that allows drug companies to pay a fee of more than $500,000 with each drug application so that the FDA can hire more drug reviewers -- thereby speeding up the drug approval process. Critics say the law has pushed the FDA too close to the pharmaceutical companies it is charged with regulating. FRONTLINE speaks with a former FDA safety officer, who recounts being pressured to tone down or alter negative drug reviews in order to speed approval of a new drug. Another tells of suffering agency retribution and retaliation for recommending against a drug's approval.

"This system has created a very unhealthy relationship between the industry and the FDA, where the FDA says, 'We have to be nice to these people because they are paying our bills,'" says Sidney Wolfe of Public Citizen's Health Research Group. "The culture at the FDA has become 'please the industry, avoid conflict, look upon our role as getting as many drugs approved as possible.'"

FRONTLINE: We understand that the Food and Drug Administration only gets about 1 to 10 percent ... of adverse event reports reflecting what actually occurs out there. Isn't that a dangerous situation ... to not really have a good picture of what's occurring?

Steven Galson, MD, Acting director of the FDA's Center for Drug Evaluation and Research: Right. I think that, first of all, the estimates for the proportion of cases that we get is a little bit broader than that. Some people think it's more than 10 percent. But nonetheless, the general point is correct -- that we get a small proportion. We'd like to get more. But the system is imperfect. Without being able to require people to make those reports, if we don't have the authority to do that, it's hard to increase it beyond that. Again, we could do better if we had more case reports. But we're trying to do the best with the system that we have.

FRONTLINE: How well is the safety of the American public assured today by the system we have for approving and monitoring drugs?

Steven Wolfe, MD Director of Public Citizen's Health Research Group since its founding in 1971: In the 31 years that I've been monitoring the Food and Drug Administration, what has gone on in the last five and six years is unprecedented. There have been an unprecedented number and percentage of drugs taken off the market; in many cases, drugs with known problems before they came on the market.

There's an unprecedented turnover of top scientists and physicians at the FDA. We now have three former FDA scientists on our staff. The absence of congressional oversight to sort of hold the FDA accountable has also been devastating. So the outcome of all of this is that we've had more drug safety-related problems in the last four or five years than really almost any comparable period of time.

The sad thing is these were preventable. They could have been avoided. In most, if not all of the cases, there were strong danger signals even before the drug came on the market that there was a problem. In all cases, once they came on the market, there was a very dangerous and reckless slowness to respond to the signals that came after marketing -- signals in the terms of deaths and serious injuries to people who took the drug once it was on the market. So I think the combination of problems in the pre-approval phase, combined with a very defective system for post-market safety surveillance have really been devastating.

At one time, 10 years ago, I would have said -- and did say -- that the FDA was the gold standard, that no country was doing a better job, either in the approval of drugs in the first place, or, secondly, in finding out as quickly as possible once they came on the market. That's no longer the case. Other countries that formerly were looking up to our gold standard are now outperforming us, and protecting people in those countries much more than we are protecting Americans. ...

If the mistakes that the FDA were making were in the area of lifesaving drugs that there wasn't any substitute for, where you would say, "Yes, there's a risk, but you've got a benefit that clearly outweighs it," that would be a whole different thing. It turns out that the FDA's done a very good job with drugs that are truly breakthrough [lifesaving] drugs. They've put them on a faster track, and there really haven't been problems there.

The problems have all been with drugs where we already have 10-20 drugs, painkillers, on the market; where we already have 10 or more drugs, diabetes drugs, on the market. The drug in question, from the start, in many cases, is not really a breakthrough. ...

So the FDA has gotten in trouble and gotten the American public's health in trouble by a series of mistakes involving drugs that we already have many other examples on the market that are just as effective, just as safe or, in fact, as it turns out, safer. ...

So the FDA seems to have made a number of mistakes in the area of drugs that we really didn't need. Twenty years ago, if any of these drugs such as Duract, Posicor, Rezulin, and a number of other of them came on the market or came up for consideration with the kinds of questions they had, the FDA's response would have been, "We're not going to approve this drug. We're going to take a better look at it."...

Twenty years ago, if a question came up about safety, it was much more likely that the FDA would say, "No. Let's wait a minute. Let's get more information." More recently, the scrutiny over drug safety has weakened. In the study that we conducted of FDA physicians, they told us in 1998, compared with several years before, the standards were lower for safety and for effectiveness. In other words, the decision to approve a drug was more lax, more risky in a sense, in the late 1990s than it had been even three or four years before. We focused on those people that had been around long enough to be able to compare what was going on then with what was going on earlier.

So if you relax the standards and don't pay as much attention to early warnings about safety as you should, and if you relax the effectiveness standards and say, "Well, the drug is only this much better. It's statistically significant. Even though it might not be clinically important, we'll still approve it," that's a real relaxing of the effectiveness standards. If you relax both the safety standards and the effectiveness standards, you're looking for trouble. And that's what's happened.

FRONTLINE: I would imagine, as most people do, that if a new drug is coming on the market, it's got to be better and safer than other things that are already there.

Steven Wolfe For close to 30 years, we have supported legislation that would say a new drug cannot be approved unless there's evidence that it's either safer and/or more effective than an existing drug. Such legislation was strongly fought by the industry, and it's never passed. So right now, if you want to bring a new drug to the market, you don't have to even do a study to compare it to the state-of-the-art drug. ...

So although FDA doesn't have the authority to require head-to-head safety and efficacy studies on a drug, if it turns out that there is some evidence, prior to approval, that the drug is more dangerous, they can -- and have in the past -- say no. They just aren't saying no often enough in the present.

FRONTLINE: What don't we know about a drug at the time it's approved?

Paul Seligman, MD, MPH, Director of the Office of Drug Safety in the FDA's Center for Drug Evaluation and Research: There are a lot of things that we don't know about a drug at the time that it's approved. First of all, because of the limited number of people who were studied during the clinical trial phase, rare adverse events are often difficult to pick up during that phase.

For example, for a serious side effect that occurs once in every 10,000 prescriptions, if you have a clinical trial that only studies 350 individuals in three separate arms, it may be very difficult to understand or to pick out that piece of critical information.

Once a drug is marketed and used in tens [of thousands], hundreds of thousands, or even millions of individuals, it's more likely for that rare adverse event to occur.

There are also lots of other things that we don't know at the time a drug is approved. For example, it's hard to fully characterize the entire range of use of a particular medication, once it is on the market.

The general population is a complex one. People have many underlying illnesses. They use many different kinds of drugs. They have many different kinds of diets. They use different kinds of dietary supplements or herbal medicines. All of the potential interactions, underlying illnesses -- co-morbidities, as they are called -- can contribute to the underlying risk profile of the drug, and can result in an unintended or unpredicted adverse event. ...

FRONTLINE: Are Americans as safe and protected as [they should be by our drug safety system]?

Raymond Woosley, MD, Vice President for Health Sciences at the University of Arizona, he was a top candidate to become FDA commissioner in 2002: I think Americans need to recognize that every time they put a pill in their mouth, especially a new pill that they've never taken before, it's an experiment. How big an experiment depends on the pill and how well it's been studied. Unfortunately, many of the pills we take have not been studied adequately. Even the old ones that we think we know a lot about, we're learning every day that we missed something along the way.

At the same time, I have to say we know more about a new medicine today when it goes on the market than we've ever known before. But we've also learned from the science that there's an awful lot out there that we need to learn. We assume that a medicine is going to have the same effect on one person as the next. Now we know, with better data and more time, that there's huge variability between the response of one individual and another. The average medicine only works and has the right effect in only about 60 percent of people. Many people have side effects. We didn't know how many until we started looking carefully, and some of those side effects are deadly.

FRONTLINE: Why don't we know everything we need to know about drugs at the time they come on the market?

Raymond Woosley: We don't know everything we need to know about medications because we've relied upon the market. The market is going to find out what's good about medicines. It's never going to ask all the questions about what could be wrong with it. As long as we mostly depend upon the marketplace to study the medications, we're never going to know all the warts. I mean, why, if I'm a stockholder in a company, I don't want my company looking for bad news. I want them to find the good news and invest in finding that. That's what we have. But when we're dealing with health and we're dealing with medications, we have a responsibility to find out all about these medicines. So it's society's responsibility. It's the National Institutes of Health, it's the FDA, it's the [Department of] Health and Human Services' responsibility to provide that other half that the free market isn't going to provide us, to tell us the downside, because the marketplace will push these and tell us all the great things about them. ...

The toughest part of this is, when do you put a drug on the market? Do you wait until all the answers are in? Well, a lot of people can suffer, waiting for those medications. So that's the hard job that the FDA has to deal with. How much evidence do we need to be fairly certain that there's going to be more benefit than harm? That's the risk-benefit ratio.

When a drug goes on the market, only about 3,000 patients have ever been given that drug. We will never know all the toxicity that can occur, especially the one in 10,000 or the one in 20,000 that can be seriously harmed. Our detection of that will only happen after the drug is on the market and exposed to huge numbers of patients. ...

FRONTLINE: I get the sense that sometimes there's not a great deal of intellectual honesty in this whole industry, including among the regulators. Is this a problem?

Raymond Woosley: It is. It's a serious problem, not having independent thought, even in the regulatory side. We have regulators who recommend a drug go on the market, and then they're the same ones who have to make the decision to take it off. That means they've got to say, "I made a mistake, I let this on the market and there's some problem I missed," and that puts them in a terrible situation. ...

We need for the pharmaceutical industry something analogous to the National Transportation Safety Board, so that when a plane goes down they go in and analyze what happened. They may find that the plane was the problem and the manufacturer, or they may find that the regulations were inadequate. But they're independent. When a drug comes off the market, we have no analysis to say, "Should it have ever gone on the market? Was it a mistake at the agency? Was it a mistake at the industry? Was it something that was totally unpreventable? Did the system work?"

I think it's important for people to know that drugs will always have to be taken off the market. That's not a signal that there's a problem. Medications will never be tested completely in our system, and that's OK. But we have to find the problem and we have to see could we have done it better, could we have done it differently. We don't ask the drug company, "Did you make a mistake in developing this drug?" or the FDA, "Did you make a mistake in approving this drug?" It should be another body to make that determination. So independence is not going to be there; we have to add it. ...

FRONTLINE: Is the balance of the FDA out of whack, in your opinion?

Raymond Woosley: I think the FDA is so grossly underfunded for its mission that it is out of balance because of user fees. User fees enable the agency to hire people to work for the industry. The other budget has been so limited and so cut -- the other budget being that which is there for safety -- the number of people hired at the agency to protect, to analyze data and drug safety, is criminal. The number of people required to study 3,000 drugs that are on the market is far more than the 17 or 20 -- however many they have now. The teams that are needed to do drug safety are infinitely more than what they've got right now.

We don't have a safety system in this country. We've got a good voluntary report system, but it is not a full system. We need other tools, like other countries. In France, a very small country, they've got 30 sites where they've trained people to go and look at the medical records, talk to patients to find out what happens when you take a medication. So if it looks like there's a problem, they can actually pick it up very quickly.

In the United Kingdom, they have a network of general practitioners who report their findings on every new drug they use, so that you can not only pick up signals, but you have an estimate of how large is the signal. You know that 100,000 people took the drug and one or two people were hurt, 10 people, whatever. You have the ability to quantify the problem.

We don't have that. We know that for every adverse event that is reported to the FDA, about 100 never get sent in. We only get 1 percent of serious reports sent in, and many of those are sketchy. That's why it takes a while, too long a while, to detect these problems. ... The system works, it's just too slow. It's too cumbersome. We have to do too much else to verify that a signal is real, because we don't have the other tools. ...

FRONTLINE: What would be an ideal drug safety system?

Raymond Woosley: The ideal drug safety system would be one that had the ability to look at drugs throughout their lifespan, as soon as they go on the market, to have studies designed to look for problems that could not have been detected before marketing. It would involve spontaneous reports for those rare reactions. It would involve a French-type system, where you go in and look at subsets to see what happens.

And then even think long-term toxicities -- I mean, there is a possibility that there are side effects with medicines that will take 10, 20 years. We're now in an era where we're taking drugs for 20, 30 years. We're taking drugs to lower cholesterol. We're starting them in our 20s and 30s. That's never happened before. No one in our society really has taken medications for that long a time before. There's no way we will be able to pick up toxicities unless we have controlled trials where we have groups to compare, and that means we need the ability to do randomized, long-term safety trials. Those are very expensive to do.

We need community-based studies. We need to look in subsets of the population. Those aren't being done now. We don't look at women. ... We need to be doing targeted studies in Hispanics, in Native Americans, because there will be toxicities unique to those populations that will be totally missed if we just look at everybody in the country.

There are many things we need to do. There needs to be a team of people independently funded.

FRONTLINE: By not doing these things, what's the cost?

Raymond Woosley: The cost of not having this kind of a safety system is we take drugs off the market that shouldn't be taken off the market. ... We lose 100,000 lives every year. We lose $137 billion because we don't have an adequate safety system.

FRONTLINE: How is the pharmaceutical industry making its inroads into the FDA? Where is it exerting its influence?

Sidney Wolfe, MD Director of Public Citizen's Health Research Group since its founding in 1971: The pharmaceutical industry's influence gets exerted in a number of ways. One, starting 10 years ago [with the Prescription Drug User Fee Act (PDUFA)], the influence was exerted by their directly funding, paying cash right up front, for FDA review. So in many ways, the FDA started looking upon the industry as their client, instead of the public and the public health, which should be the client.

A second way in which the industry influence occurs is by having leaders in the drug division who are spineless and gutless, and who don't like controversy. I have heard over and over again, directly from these people, "Why can't this be settled on a scientific and medical basis?" They don't like to take on the very awesome forces of the drug industry and a lot of its indentured servants, so to speak, in academic medicine. So the attitude by the leaders there [is], "avoid conflict" -- and avoiding conflict means doing what the industry wants.

A third way in which the industry's influence has been allowed to grow considerably is the absence of congressional oversight. Up until 12 years ago, whenever the FDA would make a mistake -- such as the series of mistakes they've made in the late 1990s -- there would be a congressional hearing. They would have to explain to the legislative branch of the government what went wrong. They would be -- properly, and in the best public health sense -- on the defensive to try and explain what went wrong.

No one is there in the Congress [now]. There have been essentially one or two days of oversight hearings in 12 years, as opposed to maybe the previous 12 years with dozens and dozens of oversights. So they're getting away with no congressional oversight.

Those are some of the reasons. And the culture at the FDA has become, "Please the industry. Avoid conflict. Look upon our role as getting out as many drugs as possible." ...

FRONTLINE: What evidence is there that it's the pharmaceutical industry influence that is changing these attitudes in the upper levels of management at the FDA, that's overruling the scientists, that's putting the business interests first?

Sidney Wolfe: The FDA is an agency of the Public Health Service. Its primary mission is to improve the public health. You have to be very cautious when -- through a combination of being funded directly by the industry, as opposed to through the U.S. Treasury, and congressional influences which are pro-industry as opposed to pro-consumer -- it starts moving in a way that is very favorable to the industry.

The positive opinions of the pharmaceutical industry of the FDA have never been higher than they were at least from 1997 to 2001. The last year, they've been complaining a little, because there's been a smaller number of drugs approved. But one way of gauging how favorable the FDA is acting towards the pharmaceutical industry is just to ask the pharmaceutical industry what they think of the new FDA, the FDA from, let's say, 1995-1996 through 2000-2001. They love it. They gave a former FDA commissioner an award for doing a terrific job. You would not have seen these things 10-15 years ago, when the FDA was in an appropriately vigilant and appropriately adversarial attitude with industry. The FDA, obviously, has to work with the industry, and that's good. But when the FDA starts getting taken over in many ways by the industry, that's not good. In response to the questionnaire that we sent out to the physicians at the FDA, they themselves told us that, many times, they believe that industry influence was operating on the people above them, and getting their bosses to overturn some of the decisions that they had made against approving a drug.

So there are lots of sources of evidence about the fact that the pharmaceutical industry has an almost unprecedented finger or thumb on the FDA in the last few years, compared with any time in the past. ...

FRONTLINE: What's the concept [of user fees]? How does it work?

Sidney Wolfe: For the first 86 years of FDA's existence, from 1906-1992, all of FDA's funding came through the U.S. Treasury. In other words, everyone -- industry, people -- paid their taxes, and FDA got appropriations out of the budget.

Starting in 1992, unfortunately, a law was passed that said for a large proportion of the work done by the FDA on new drug applications, the money's going to come directly, quid pro quo, from the industry. If they want a drug reviewed, they pay directly to the FDA to have the drug reviewed.

This system has created a very unhealthy relationship -- even more unhealthy than it used to be -- between the industry and the FDA, where the FDA says, "We have to be nice to these people, because they are paying our bills." It's developed an unhealthy sort of client relationship between the government and the industry which, I think, has resulted in some drugs getting approved that shouldn't; drugs being put on a faster track than they should have.

I think that, in general, it's been a very bad idea. We strongly favor ending this experiment, which has had, in the 10 years that it's been in existence, some of the worst things happen in terms of drug safety we've ever seen. I think that's not the only explanation. But direct cash funding from the pharmaceutical industry to the FDA turns out to be a very bad idea.

FRONTLINE: You were under consideration to be commissioner of the Food and Drug Administration. You've got pretty strong ideas about making drugs safer and as beneficial as possible. ... How did it go?

Raymond Woosley: I was very proud that I was considered as a candidate for the Food and Drug Administration's commissioner position. ...

Unfortunately, it was a very complicated process. ... As I look back over my interview and the other interviews, it was very clear that people like myself, who care about drug safety, had become too controversial. Just like Senator Kennedy didn't want to take somebody right out of the drug industry, the drug industry didn't want someone like myself, who was going to focus on toxicity and side effects. So it became clear that I wasn't going to be able to meet a broad enough constituency. ...

FRONTLINE: How did Secretary Thompson tell you that you couldn't get this job? What did he say?

Raymond Woosley: Secretary Thompson told me that I was a candidate, that I would be very high on his list, but that it was going to be a long process, that there were other considerations, that I might not be the final candidate, and that it would be a long time before I would know. He didn't say that someone was going to veto me; he did say that I was a candidate that would be acceptable to him, and now he's very proud of that. But he also said that it wasn't just his decision.

FRONTLINE: Did he imply to you that you would not be accepted by some other powerful constituency, that it would be a problem?

Raymond Woosley: ...It became clear that anyone who had focused on drug safety couldn't make it, just like people who had come right out of industry couldn't make it. Too far on the extremes to be acceptable. ...

To me, the greatest sadness is that people who care about drug safety and food safety to the level that they get involved and they try to make a difference can't be acceptable to regulate the agency. I think that's one of the main criteria that should be used. Of course the regulators have to serve, but they also have to regulate and they have to protect. To me, protection is first; serve has to be second. You've got to take risks. You can't just be risk-averse and unwilling, because people need medications and they need access to foods, so it's the ability to balance risk and benefit. To work in drug development and focus on drug safety, you become identified with the risk and not the benefit.

FRONTLINE: Is the balance of the FDA out of whack, in your opinion?

Raymond Woosley: I think the FDA is so grossly underfunded for its mission that it is out of balance because of user fees. User fees enable the agency to hire people to work for the industry. The other budget has been so limited and so cut -- the other budget being that which is there for safety -- the number of people hired at the agency to protect, to analyze data and drug safety, is criminal. The number of people required to study 3,000 drugs that are on the market is far more than the 17 or 20 -- however many they have now. The teams that are needed to do drug safety are infinitely more than what they've got right now. We don't have a safety system in this country.

FRONTLINE: Why is the safety part resisted so adamantly? How do you explain it?

Raymond Woosley: The budgets of the FDA are determined by lobbyists who call for money to be spent in certain ways. The user fee is negotiated to be spent on reviewers. Until recently, none of the money that was sent by the pharmaceutical industry for user fees could be used for drug safety. Now that's changing -- not to the rate I'd like to see it. Some of the money can now be spent for drug safety, but that was impossible until recently. It's only because many of us have screamed that that has to change has it changed. ...

FRONTLINE: What's the lobbying in terms of safety?

Raymond Woosley: Nothing. They're not lobbying for safety. ... The pharmaceutical industry doesn't lobby for safety. They lobby for rapid review, rapid access to the marketplace. They haven't lobbied for drug safety; no one has. There are groups, consumer groups, that have spoken out, but not with a uniform voice. Large constituencies haven't joined together to say, "Stop the harm." When the papers came out from the Institute of Medicine talking about medical errors and medical harm, I thought surely there would be action taken and the agency would be given money to increase its safety net. But it hasn't happened. There's a lot of lobbying for helping the agency serve. ... No lobbying [is] being done to help it get its safety mission accomplished. ...

FRONTLINE: You worked at the FDA for five years. Can you describe the kind of pressure, day-in and day-out, to recommend approval of new drugs that would come your way for evaluation, versus having an objective opinion?

Michael Elashoff , PhD. (A biostatistician, Michael Elashoff was a drug reviewer for the FDA from 1995 to 2000. Elashoff says he found himself marginalized at the FDA after he voiced his concerns about a new flu drug called Relenza. In this interview, Elashoff speaks out about the culture of the FDA's drug approval process and why he felt Relenza should not have been put on the market. This interview was conducted on Feb. 19, 2003.): For the most part, when drug applications came in, there was the presumption that the drug was going to be safe and effective, and was going to be approved. So, when during the course of the review you find something that suggests some problems, typically the other reviewers and the FDA management would not want to really explore those problems, and would kind of view it as a hassle on the way to drug approval. That was a pretty much constant pressure for most reviews. Also, when it would come time to write the official review, there would be times when the management -- it would review my drafts [and] would want to take out various sections where [I] commented on lack of efficacy or safety problems; or [management would] want [me] to tone down the language, so that they could more easily have a written justification for why they're approving the drug.

FRONTLINE: How general or pervasive was this in review?

Michael Elashoff: It was pretty widespread. You know, many drugs really had pretty good safety and efficacy. So of the remainder, the ones where there are potential problems, I'd say in nearly all the cases I was familiar with -- both that I worked on, and other people in my division worked on -- there would be pressure to approve those drugs, or soften the language in the reviews and on the labels, so that they could have a more easy justification for why they're approving it. So I would say it was very common.

FRONTLINE: How subtle or overt was the pressure that was put on you?

Michael Elashoff: I was told very explicitly, "Don't write in your review that you're recommending against approval. Write that the data is unclear, you could go either way." So it was quite explicit. ... It was pretty typical that, at the start of a review, the division director would say, "You know, I don't really see any issues with this drug. Some small things may come up in the course of your reviews. You have to do a careful review, but I don't see any roadblocks on the way to approval." That would set an overall tone for the review, where potential problems were really de-emphasized in the meetings to discuss the data. There was just an overall expectation from the top that it would be approved. You knew that if you found a problem and wanted to pursue it, it would take a lot of extra effort, a lot of extra meetings, a lot of extra justification for why something wouldn't be approved. Whereas, if you felt the drug was safe and effective, very rarely would someone challenge you on that.

FRONTLINE: What was the drug company that made Relenza coming to the FDA for approval for? What it was supposed to be?

Michael Elashoff: Relenza was intended to be a treatment for the flu. Glaxo Wellcome did a large number of studies to demonstrate that it would significantly reduce the course of symptoms once you got the flu -- would get your temperature down and all of the other flu symptoms; would get you up and back to work faster. That was the promise of Relenza.

FRONTLINE: What was your responsibility in reviewing Relenza?

Michael Elashoff: It's actually fairly extensive. My responsibility in the evaluation of Relenza was to look at the clinical trials that Glaxo Wellcome had performed; assess whether they had demonstrated that the drug was safe and effective; try and establish what a reasonable estimate of the treatment effect was, what the risks and benefits were. Basically, [to] review the claims that they're making in their application.

FRONTLINE: What was your complaint with Relenza, in terms of its efficacy and safety?

Michael Elashoff: Simply stated, Relenza just didn't work in the United States' clinical trials, and really didn't even come close to working. You think the flu can be seven to 10 days, and it maybe knocked half a day or less off the duration. Even that wasn't established statistically. So it was pretty much no different from placebo as far as efficacy, and it had some potential safety concerns, especially in people with underlying lung disease. Like any new drug, it had potential risks that weren't even characterized. It wasn't studied in very many patients. For a self-limiting disease, where most of the patients that were studied were reasonably healthy, less than one day of benefit for potential risk doesn't really seem like something anyone would want to take. Glaxo had these expectations for what their drug was going to do in patients who had the flu.

FRONTLINE: How did the drug stack up? In your view, how did it perform in their clinical trials for all of these?

Michael Elashoff: In the largest trial, which was the only one done in the United States, it really had no effect at all on the symptoms of influenza. It had no effect on influenza complications. It had no effect on basically any aspect of the flu, so that you really couldn't distinguish it from placebo in the trial. To me, it was almost a complete wash.

FRONTLINE: In terms of safety, what were the risks that were seen in clinical trials and that you were concerned about, as far as getting into a large population?

Michael Elashoff: One of the concerns during the review was that Relenza had the potential to cause bronchospasm, or constriction of the airway. It was observed in several patients in the clinical trials. That was a concern, since there weren't really very many patients studied. It was a very controlled population under the strict clinical trial monitoring. So the concern was that, once the drug got under less supervision in the larger market, then incidents of those types of problems would be magnified.

FRONTLINE: Why is bronchospasm such a concern?

Michael Elashoff: Bronchospasm is potentially fatal, particularly in patients with asthma or other underlying lung condition. So after the drug was released, there were cases of people with asthma or other lung problems who took Relenza, and subsequently died. ...

FRONTLINE: You weren't too impressed with this drug -- is that fair to say? What was your overall impression?

Michael Elashoff: It was pretty much a placebo that had side effects. I would summarize it that way. ...

FRONTLINE: What did you present to the advisory committee?

Michael Elashoff: I told the advisory committee that, in my view, the drug was not effective, either for the symptoms of the influenza or for the complications due to influenza, [and] that in the high-risk patient population that was studied, it was actually slightly worse than placebo in terms of efficacy. The advisory committee had a fair amount of discussion about Relenza, because it had had a lot of advance hype around it. Ultimately, they decided that it was not worth approving, and voted 13-4 to reject the drug.

FRONTLINE: Were you the only person who spoke at the advisory committee meeting? Were there other people who made presentations for or against?

Michael Elashoff: Well, Glaxo presented, and they were obviously for it. The FDA medical reviewer made a presentation. Her conclusion was it could either be approved or not approved. It was a fairly borderline drug.

FRONTLINE: Were there other parties that weighed in on this at all?

Michael Elashoff: There were influenza experts on the advisory committee, so there was a lot of internal discussion in the committee meeting about why the drug -- which had looked so promising in earlier studies -- wasn't working in the current study. There was a fair amount of discussion about its safety, its efficacy. I think there were a lot of people on the committee who had had a lot of experience, both in clinical trials and in influenza specifically. Ultimately, they just concluded that the drug and the clinical trials hadn't established either safety or efficacy.

FRONTLINE: How much of a deciding factor was your testimony at the advisory committee meeting?

Michael Elashoff: You'd really have to ask the advisory committee members who voted on it. I think my testimony may have been the only one that brought up certain potential problems with the drug. But since they're pretty bright people, I would think that anyone giving [that] presentation -- and I only spoke for about 15, 20 minutes -- would have turned the tide. They had read the results of the clinical trials. So I think even in the absence of any presentations, they would have come to the same conclusion.

FRONTLINE: You referred to the clinical trials conducted in the United States. Were there more promising or more successful clinical trials that had been conducted elsewhere that had better results?

Michael Elashoff: There were two other studies -- one in Europe, one in Australia -- where Relenza showed some efficacy. One of the issues was, why isn't it showing efficacy in the United States? One of the most promising hypotheses was that people who take other symptomatic relief medication -- Tylenol, aspirin, cough syrup -- in the United States basically masked any effect of Relenza. So Relenza had no impact on symptoms over and above those baseline medications that people take when they have the flu. In Europe, in particular, there was a very low rate of people taking those other medications. I guess [there's] just a different cultural environment there. So in the context of not being allowed to take anything to relieve your symptoms, you might notice some effect of Relenza. But in the context of a typical flu, where you have to take other things to manage your symptoms, you wouldn't notice any effect of Relenza over and above those other things.

FRONTLINE: What happened to you after the advisory committee meeting?

Michael Elashoff: The next day after the advisory committee, several people in FDA management told me that they blamed me for the drug getting turned down in the advisory committee; that I wouldn't be allowed to present at the advisory committee meetings in the future for any other drugs. At the time, I was also scheduled to be the reviewer for another flu medication, Tamaflu. That review was taken away from me. I guess they were worried that I might apply the same level of review to that application as I had for Relenza. So they gave it to someone else.

FRONTLINE: Where was that message coming from? Who was behind the message to you?

Michael Elashoff: It was mostly coming from the higher-level FDA management, filtered down through my boss, who agreed with my position, but didn't particularly want to fight it out with all of the other higher-level people. ...

FRONTLINE: When you got that message, what did you think about the place where you were working?

Michael Elashoff: I was really pretty disappointed in the whole place. There had been previous instances where I thought things had got approved where there were really potential problems. But this was, in my mind, pretty much a no-brainer -- where a drug really just had no efficacy at all, had potential safety problems, and where the advisory committee had really voted pretty overwhelmingly against it. You know, I think that was the first time that our own advisory committee had ever voted to reject a drug, but then look like it would be approved. So it was personally very disappointing, but it was also really hard to see any motive behind it. It was really kind of a mystery why people at the FDA would be pushing so hard for a drug that had so little benefit and risks on top of that, especially when it was being targeted at otherwise healthy people. Even under the kind of most favorable view of efficacy, it would knock about one day off the course of a two-week flu. So, in my presentation, I said I thought the drug had pretty much no effect, and the most favorable view of the data suggested maybe one day of effect. That's not really too much of a difference.

FRONTLINE: Why would they want to push so strongly to get that drug approved, even when there had been a public advisory committee where experts had really come to the same conclusion that Relenza had no effect?

Michael Elashoff: It was pretty puzzling.

FRONTLINE: Did you have any explanation for why this happened to you? Did you figure out a way to make sense of it?

Michael Elashoff: I guess the fact that Glaxo is a very large and influential drug company, and that they stood to make a lot of money on this drug. If it looked like it was going to be turned down, then Glaxo would go to the highest levels at FDA and really make a big complaint, and start trying to make life pretty miserable for all the reviewers of Relenza. If that's not why, I'd really like to know why. But I think in the past, when applications from large pharmaceutical companies had seemed problematic, it would be pretty standard for the company to complain to the head of FDA, or the head of the review divisions. Those complaints would make it down to the individual reviewers, basically saying, "Why are you giving this particular drug such a hard time?"

FRONTLINE: Was it dangerous for reviewers, if they cared about the FDA, to oppose a drug -- especially from a big drug company?

Michael Elashoff: I think it was pretty well understood that if you were advocating turning a drug down -- particularly if it was from a large pharmaceutical company -- that that wouldn't be good for your career, as far as promotions. It wouldn't be good for your career, scientifically, as far as being able to review other drugs in the future that had potential problems.

FRONTLINE: Did you feel like you were getting punished for your opinions, for expressing what you felt was the truth about a drug?

Michael Elashoff: Yes, I was punished for my views on the drug, which was, in one sense, rather silly, because it was the drug that didn't have the efficacy. It didn't really have anything to do with me pointing it out that it ultimately got rejected in the advisory committee. But I took it, not so much as punishment, but a strong encouragement to leave the FDA, because in all my performance evaluations and reviews, I still continued to get the highest grades. So it was pretty clear that they weren't going to do or say anything on paper that would indicate they were unhappy with my review. But that they would continue to make my working life more and more difficult -- not doing reviews of controversial drugs, not speaking in front of the advisory committee, having my review subject to extra levels of comment and potentially removing comments from my reviews.

FRONTLINE: What does what happened to you say about the FDA and the culture there, and the interest in honesty and truthfulness and safety?

Michael Elashoff: What happened to me would be pretty alarming to people who use prescription drugs; that they really shouldn't have a lot of faith that drugs that are approved have really been demonstrated to be safe and effective to the standards that -- at least I thought before I went to FDA -- that they were trying to uphold. I'm not sure what someone can do about that. I mean, if you're prescribed something, it's difficult to go back and review the underlying clinical trials and come to some other conclusion. So when you're taking medication, you're pretty much taking it on faith that it's been really thoroughly reviewed, and that all of the safety and efficacy concerns have been really explored, have been documented in the labeling, have been communicated to physicians. In Relenza, when it was ultimately approved, clearly the risks/benefits weren't communicated to people. Relenza was not by any means an isolated incident. I think it was pretty typical for drugs that had problems to get pushed through to approval. As far as the FDA culture, I think people who didn't like that kind of environment ultimately would just leave.

FRONTLINE: How did your fellow scientists at the FDA react after you made your presentation at the advisory committee meeting?

Michael Elashoff: A lot of the other reviewers at FDA thought that they liked the fact that I made a stand on Relenza, but said they wouldn't have done it themselves, and that it wasn't going to be good for my career at FDA in the future. So in one sense, it was gratifying to have people say that they agreed with me and liked what I did. On the other hand, it was fairly disheartening to know that no one else is really going to step up and do the same thing on drugs that they were reviewing that had similar problems. ...

FRONTLINE: So you think, to really do your job, you had to stand up? And to not do that would be shirking responsibility?

Michael Elashoff: Officially, that is the responsibility of every reviewer at the FDA. Your responsibility is to review the scientific data, and come to a conclusion about the safety and efficacy of the drug. Just because the unwritten rule is that things should be fast-track to approval doesn't mean -- ultimately, I just felt a responsibility to do a real review. If I felt the drug was going to be potentially unsafe and offer no benefit, then I wanted people to be aware of that.

FRONTLINE: Was it a moral thing for you? Was it a conscience thing?

Michael Elashoff: I didn't really ever consider not doing it. To me, it's surprising when I heard other reviewers saying they would experience the same types of things and would ultimately back down. To me, I think those are the people who need to explain why they did what they did. Does the FDA have a problem? The FDA has a big problem. It's pervasive. It's throughout the entire FDA review culture. I didn't see it getting any better, which is ultimately why I left. ...

FRONTLINE: Is there room for bad news at the FDA? Or do administrators at the FDA only want to hear good news?

Michael Elashoff: There is no room for bad news, particularly when large pharmaceutical companies are involved. I think with smaller biotech companies, particularly where it's their first drug application, I saw a little more intellectual honesty about the pros and cons of drugs. But for large pharmaceutical companies, it was pretty clear. I mean, it's called the drug approval process. It's not called the drug review process. So that really sets the mindset on what the job is.

FRONTLINE: Do you have any opinion about why the FDA tends to be that way?

Michael Elashoff: Well, in the past, the drug companies weren't paying a sizeable fraction of FDA's budget. So now when drugs come in for review, there's a large user fee attached to that. I suppose FDA management views themselves as increasingly reliant on those user fees, and if they're too tough on large companies, then maybe a large portion of their budget goes away. When I started there in 1995, I didn't perceive the same level of pressure as I did when I left in 2000. So definitely something changed during the five years I was there, and that also coincided with the User Fee Act.

FRONTLINE: Can you prove it, or is it just a sense? Because you say this and then the guy we interviewed this morning says, "No, that's not a problem here at all. We don't care where the money comes from. It's all the same to us."

Michael Elashoff: I think most reviewers at FDA you would talk to or most reviewers who have left FDA that you talk to would find it's pretty well understood that the large pharmaceutical companies kind of have a substantial influence on the review process. I don't think anyone is really surprised about that. Someone who would disagree maybe isn't really involved in reviewing drugs, because I think nearly every application I was involved with or I knew about, where it looked like there were concerns about the drug, it was always understood that there would be high-level complaints from the company to FDA management. Those complaints would come down to the reviewers. There would be both subtle and rather overt pressure to change the reviews, change the recommendations, soften the language. Since it happened numerous times, I think it's pretty clear that they have a large influence. Whether the user fees directly contribute that influence or whether it's indirect through lobbying, I really couldn't say. But it's influence, nonetheless.

FRONTLINE: We've had this study that suggested that morale was not great among some of the people at the FDA, that there certainly were frustrations. A lot of reviewers had expressed about having their opinions rewritten or being asked to soften language. Yet the person we interviewed this morning said, "No morale problem at all here, everybody is happy, just the weird bird here who is not happy--"

Michael Elashoff: Well, the unhappy ones leave, so it's a self-selection process. The people who stay for the long term are those who aren't unduly upset about the fact that drugs are getting approved that shouldn't be, or that reviews are being influenced either by drug companies or FDA management. The whole promotion environment is such that people who raise concerns about drugs don't get promoted. So you have a whole set of people at the top who probably didn't have any morale problems, because they didn't see what they were doing as anything different from what they were supposed to be doing. The ones who had ethical concerns -- there's no reason to stay around in an environment such as that for year after year, when it's really so hard to make a difference. So those people would leave, and the ones who stayed might think this is how the drug approval process is supposed to go. ...

FRONTLINE: The person we interviewed this morning expressed shock that somebody would be treated like you were, and if it's happening, it shouldn't be happening. You know, "This is just a small problem. We should correct it, but it can't be something that happens a lot here." Is that fair?

Michael Elashoff: That's a joke. I mean, it happens all the time. I guess the only reason it doesn't happen as frequently as it might otherwise is people start censoring themselves. They say, "OK, after the first time I noted a problem and it's been glossed over, well, why bother the second time?" So you have this process where people will stop raising the concerns by themselves, based on what happened to themselves previously or what they perceive happening to other people. It only takes a couple people to be made an example of. Other people see pretty clearly the writing on the wall, and won't let that happen to them. You may have 20 reviewers in a particular division, most of them potentially concerned about at least one drug they've reviewed in the past. They see, "OK, someone who makes a stand on something is going to really be forced out." So the next drug that comes along and they see problems, I think many people will be less likely to pursue those problems. Then it does become an isolated incident, when it gets as far as actually trying to get a reviewer to leave FDA based on a review they wrote. I don't think the management has to do that a lot of times before everyone gets the message.

FRONTLINE: Should we, as Americans, be concerned that the FDA is not doing a great job protecting our safety; that safety has been compromised?

Michael Elashoff: Safety has definitely been compromised. Efficacy has been compromised, too. I think the whole drug review process, in a lot of cases, is compromised.

FRONTLINE: Are Americans being exposed to drugs that are not worth it, that are not safe, that are not effective?

Michael Elashoff: Certainly. ... I think proof that people are being exposed to unsafe or ineffective drugs comes when drugs are pulled off the market for problems, where in most cases, warning signs were seen at the earliest stages of the review. It would just take either more people to die after taking medication, or just such a public recognition of the fact that a particular drug just wasn't effective or had many safety problems. When those drugs are pulled off the market, that's only the tip of the iceberg, as far as what other drugs are causing similar problems that there's just not an awareness of yet. ...

FRONTLINE: Are you just a complainer? Are you just one of those guys who is never happy with anything? You're always going to try to dot every "i" and cross every "t" and have total perfection and yell and scream when he doesn't get his way?

Michael Elashoff: That's kind of how an administrator characterized the people who make a stink. Well, I reviewed about 20 drugs when I was at FDA and recommended that three of them not be approved. Ultimately one of those was, in fact, not approved. Two of them were approved and are on the market. So in the other 17 cases, I felt that the drug was safe enough, effective enough to be on the market. I think that would argue against someone who says that anyone who recommends turning a drug down is just making too much of small issues. [According to Steven Galson,] there's not such a crisis in the FDA; they're just little problems. It's like, we could go out and find all the examples of people like you, and it would just not be an accurate picture of what's happening inside the FDA. It would be a distorted picture. But behind each drug that gets approved when it shouldn't, or each drug that is ultimately taken off the market, you have lots of people who experience serious adverse events or died. So even if it were just a handful of cases, that's something pretty alarming, if those drugs are going through. It's really not just a handful of cases. It's a significant number of drugs that are approved when they shouldn't be. And for each drug, you have deaths and other problems that could have been prevented. ...

FRONTLINE: Are people getting hurt as a result of this, as a result of the way the FDA operates?

Michael Elashoff: Certainly. You can point to Relenza, where a year after it was approved, there was new language added to the label, warning of people who had died as a result of bronchospasms after taking Relenza. What do you say to those people when the drug never should have been on the market, and when they weren't actually deriving any benefit from taking it in the first place? That's just one drug, one example, [with] measurable consequences of people dying as a result. Then you multiply that by the number of drugs, the number of reviewers, the number of companies, and it becomes a pretty large problem. ...

FRONTLINE: What's sort of the rule of thumb that you advise people on, if any?

Michael Elashoff: I don't know. If I were asked for advice, it's hard to think of an easy answer. But the message is you'd have to view the drugs that are approved and the claims that are made in the label very skeptically. Don't take them at face value, and really do your own investigation into whether the drug is as safe and effective as it's purported to be. Although as I'm saying that, it's a rather preposterous thing to tell people to do that every time they get a prescription, every time they get a new drug, to go into that level of detail of reviewing the data. The way the review process is supposed to work is that someone at FDA is supposed to have already done that for people, and already come to a real conclusion about whether the drug is safe to be on the market. So if you can't trust in that and people have to be their own FDA reviewers, I don't know. I don't know what I would tell those people.

The producer of FRONTLINE's "Dangerous Prescription" offers two stories, not included in the documentary, about how pharmaceutical companies have been known to handle bad news. **Andrew Liebman** is a Boston-based documentary filmmaker and the founder of Resolute Films. He has been producing programs for FRONTLINE since the early 1980s and also works extensively for DISCOVERY Channel.

Andrew Liebman
...But drug safety isn't just in the hands of the FDA. Americans -- and the Food and Drug Administration itself -- rely on pharmaceutical companies to be honest about what works and what doesn't. The ways in which pharmaceutical companies can "spin" bad news about their products, or influence the distribution of that news, in order to control damage and impede important information from reaching consumers and doctors, are revealed in two cases that didn't make it into the program.

What Bad News?
The first of these stories is about patients getting "less effective drugs" when better choices are available. If your doctor prescribes a less effective drug, you're not being helped as much as you could be helped. And when you think about it, that means you are being harmed.
About 50 million Americans have hypertension (commonly known as high blood pressure) -- and an estimated 30 million need some sort of medical treatment to bring their problem under control. Patients who fail to lower their blood pressure face increased risk of heart attacks, strokes and diabetes -- so the treatment of hypertension has become one of the largest markets for drugs in America and everywhere else in the developed world.
By some estimates, there are as many as 180 different prescription medications used in the United States to treat hypertension. Almost every major drug company has at least one product for lowering blood pressure, and doctors are generally happy to have these choices. But having so many choices does create a problem. Some drugs are bound to be more effective than others -- so doctors urgently want to know what's best.
Unfortunately, pharmaceutical companies rarely conduct clinical trials that fairly and objectively compare other companies' drugs against their own. And the FDA doesn't conduct such trials either, because the agency is not in the business of doing medical research -- only reviewing the results submitted by pharmaceutical companies.

With Americans spending $16 billion a year on blood pressure medicines, and no objective information to show which ones were most effective at reducing the problems caused by high blood pressure, about 10 years ago the National Heart Lung and Blood Institute (a division of the National Institutes of Health) started a long-term clinical trial that would honestly and fairly compare the effectiveness of the leading types of blood pressure medicines. The study, called ALLHAT (short for Anti-Hypertensive and Lipid-Lowering treatment to prevent Heart Attack Trial) enrolled over 42,000 Americans, lasted for some eight years, and cost over $140 million.

It was the kind of study that only a government agency could organize --
comparing four major classes of competing hypertension drugs, each of which
lowers blood pressure in its own unique way. The drugs included: a diuretic (one
of the oldest and cheapest treatments for hypertension, and widely available as
a generic drug); Lisinopril (one of the popular, widely prescribed "ACE inhibitors,"
a class of drugs that includes Capoten, Vasotec Lotensin, Monopril, Univasc,
Aceon, Accupril, Altace, Mavic); Norvasc (a "calcium channel blocker" made by
Pfizer and the country's largest selling treatment for hypertension according to a
Pfizer annual report); and Cardura (an "alpha blocker").

According to ALLHAT's principal investigator, Dr. Curt Furberg, "since the early
1990s, ACE inhibitors and calcium channel blockers had captured maybe a
third or maybe 40 percent of the market" for treating high blood pressure,
cutting into the prescriptions for older drugs that had a long track record of
effectiveness and that were much cheaper. "And there wasn't good evidence
that the newer drugs were better, or even as good," says Furberg, "so this study
was undertaken to help us figure that out."

About six years into the study, its organizers halted treatment with one of the
drugs, Cardura, because an early data analysis showed that patients on Cardura
were 25 percent more likely to develop cardiovascular disease than patients on
diuretics, and twice as likely to develop heart failure. It wasn't that Cardura was
bad, but for most people it was clear that diuretics were significantly better.

The study continued with the three remaining drugs until the summer of 2002,
and then in December of last year the results were announced at a packed
press conference in Washington. The news was dramatic.

While all the drugs helped lower patients' blood pressure to about the same
degree, according to the ALLHAT results patients on Norvasc -- an expensive and
highly-advertised product -- were 38 percent more likely to develop heart failure
than patients on the cheap, tried-and-true diuretics. And patients on Lisinopril
(also more expensive than diuretics, and just coming off patent) were 15
percent more likely to develop strokes, 19 percent more likely to develop heart
failure, and 11 percent more like to have angina than patients on diuretics. So,
as a first-line treatment, the cheapest, oldest and least-promoted drug was
significantly better at preventing the serious problems that can arise from
having high blood pressure.

"ALLHAT demonstrated that, in the past, we didn't spend our drug dollars
wisely," says Furberg. "We put too much money into drugs that are now shown to
be inferior. And we need to learn more from that. And I think it's important for
society to step in and not just leave it to drug companies to promote their
drugs."

In Furberg's opinion, the fact that millions of people took -- and are still taking --
less effective drugs means that tens of thousands of Americans have been
developing health problems that could have been prevented by a more effective
drug.

"If you eliminated all the ACE inhibitors and calcium antagonists [calcium channel blockers] for the first-line treatment of hypertension," says Furberg, and if patients were put on diuretics, "we would avert maybe 60,000 events per year -- 60,000 heart failures or strokes. These are devastating complications. So, if you want to know what has happened over the past five years, we'll you can multiply by five. So we're talking about a large number of people who unnecessarily have suffered these events because we didn't have the knowledge we have today."

Furberg does note that many patients need to combine two or more different drugs to adequately lower their blood pressure -- so there's an important role for less effective drugs. And some patients don't tolerate diuretics so they need other options. But for the vast majority of people who have just been diagnosed with high blood pressure, according to ALLHAT, diuretics were the best as a first-line treatment -- and also the cheapest.

Given the ALLHAT data about calcium channel blockers and ACE inhibitors, the question was, how to get doctors to change their prescribing habits? For that to happen, first they would have to get the news.

But as Furberg soon discovered, the maker of one of the less effective but highly popular hypertension drugs wasn't going to let its market share slip away without a fight.

On the same day that the NIH scientists announced their results to the nation, Pfizer, the manufacturer of Norvasc, started a quiet campaign to counter the study results. First, the company issued a press release highlighting all of the study findings that were positive for Norvasc -- but leaving out the findings that were negative. (The release did mention that patients should first be started on diuretics, but it didn't mention that starting patients on Norvasc would lead to more heart failure.)

Then the company sent to television stations a videotaped interview with Dr. Michael Berelowitz, vice president of Pfizer's Metabolic and Cardiovascular Group, who declared that the ALLHAT study was an affirmation for Norvasc. "This study confirms what I think we have felt all along," Dr. Berelowitz says on the tape. "And that is that Norvasc is a safe, effective, well-tolerated agent for lowering blood pressure. ... Accepting that diuretics are safe and effective and decreased cardiovascular disease, ALLHAT looked to see how the new agents -- calcium channel blockers like Norvasc, and an ACE inhibitor -- compared to the diuretic. And these agents were equally effective."

Compare Dr. Berelowitz's statement in the video to a statement made by the NIH research team that conducted the study. "Each of the newer drugs had significantly higher rates of one or more forms of cardiovascular disease," the ALLHAT team said. They went on: "Because of their superiority in preventing one or more forms of cardiovascular disease and their lower cost ... diuretics should be the drugs of choice for the initial treatment of hypertension in most patients requiring drug therapy."

In the eyes of Curt Furberg, who had spent almost 10 years organizing and supervising the ALLHAT study, Pfizer was not telling the whole story. "I have problems with any drug company pushing an inferior product," says Furberg. "I don't think that's in the best interest of the patients. This is a difficult issue that somehow I have to deal with, society has to deal with: how we handle the situation where we have good knowledge that there is a difference between drugs and whether we should allow both of them to be out there competing, or whether we should put some restriction on the inferior drugs."

It's not hard to imagine why Pfizer might have responded to the ALLHAT study the way it did. Norvasc is a very profitable drug. According to the company's summer 2002 quarterly report, "Sales of Norvasc, the world's largest-selling medicine for hypertension and angina and the fourth-largest selling pharmaceutical of any kind grew 8% ... to $931 million in the first quarter, compared to the same period in 2001."

In light of Pfizer's campaign to put its own positive spin on the ALLHAT study, Furberg decided to hit the road and start a "counter campaign" -- to make sure that doctors and patients got the entire story about ALLHAT. That meant getting himself booked on radio talk shows and traveling to medical conferences to set the record straight on the study.

Unfortunately, Furberg says, he has to play the same public-relations game the pharmaceutical companies play, or his message is going to get lost in the company's PR campaign. He has to go to the media, visit the offices of influential doctors -- and get them to look at the data. "One of our biggest problems, to tell you the truth," he says, "is that diuretics don't have any champions. They're all generic drugs nowadays and drug companies don't make much profit on them. By and large, companies are only going to promote what earns them profits. And sometimes that's not good for your health and safety."

A Doctor Feels the Heat

In our documentary segment about the Fen Phen disaster, we met Dr. Stuart Rich, a respected cardiologist and pulmonologist from the Rush Heart Institute in Chicago. During the mid-1990s, Rich played a central role in conducting the International Primary Pulmonary Hypertension study -- a large study of European men and women who were taking diet drugs, including Pondimin, which was on the market in the United states, and a closely-related "sister drug," Redux, which was not yet on the American market.

One of the main goals of the study was to evaluate the connection between these drugs and pulmonary hypertension, a devastating side effect that reduces the lung's ability to absorb oxygen, leading to constant shortness of breath and ultimately death. While a few cases had been reported around the world, drug manufacturers had long claimed that Pondimin and Redux only rarely caused pulmonary hypertension. Furthermore, they said, the benefit of losing weight was far more significant than the risk of developing the side effect.

In their three-year study, Dr. Rich and his colleagues found that Pondimin and Redux posed a "significant risk of dying from pulmonary hypertension," according to Rich. "And the risk went up the longer you took the drugs." Those results, and the fact that on average most people only lost a small amount of weight when they took these medicines, made Rich an opponent of FDA approval for Redux -- particularly for long-term use.

While Rich was appalled by the drug company's determination to put its drug on the American market, he was even more upset when the FDA acquiesced and approved the drug in the summer of 1996. "My reaction was despair," he told us. "Why despair? My specialty is I treat patients with pulmonary hypertension. These are the sickest cardiovascular patients that exist. They're young people. They're tragic stories. We have some treatments ... but it's a death sentence. And it's a slow death, drowning, months to years."

Rich's only comfort was knowing that the European study would soon be published in *The New England Journal of Medicine* -- one of the most prestigious medical journals in the world. The drug company may have pushed this controversial product onto the market, thought Rich, and the FDA may have gone along with the idea, but doctors would soon read the study's findings about Redux when the *Journal* came out. Then, he hoped, doctors would stop prescribing the drug so often.

But getting out a clear message to consumers and the medical community about the risks posed by these diet drugs proved to be more difficult than Rich imagined.

The day before his article officially came out, Rich got a phone call from a newspaper reporter who had received an advance copy of the *Journal* and wanted Rich's reaction to an accompanying editorial -- which Rich hadn't seen yet. (As was the custom at *The New England Journal of Medicine*, the magazine's editors had invited two prominent scientists to write an editorial about the European study to put it into perspective and help doctors determine whether and when the risk of using the diet drugs would be justified by the benefits.) Much to Dr. Rich's dismay, the editorial claimed that the benefits of using Pondimin and Redux far outweighed any risks and compared the risk of taking the diet drugs to taking penicillin for an infection. In effect, the editorial advised the medical community not to pay too much attention to Rich's study, and not to stop prescribing the drugs.

When Rich heard who the authors of the editorial were -- Dr. JoAnn Manson and Dr. Gerald Faich -- he realized immediately that both had financial ties to the drug companies that were making and/or selling Redux. And both had done work with those companies specifically in connection with Redux. "This was one of the greatest scandals that ever hit *The New England Journal of Medicine*," says Rich.

To guard against such potential conflicts of interest, it had been the *Journal*'s policy to always ask editorial writers whether they had any "ongoing financial associations" with the company producing the product. In this case, the two scientists who authored the diet drug study editorial had told the magazine's editors -- in writing -- that they had "no financial interest or equity in any pharmaceutical company producing anti-obesity agents."

As word of the editorial controversy spread, the *Journal's* editors asked the two scientists to explain their written statement that they didn't have any financial interest in the company. In their defense, both authors downplayed their financial connections to the companies, and pointed out that the *Journal* had defined "ongoing financial associations" as "equity interest, regular consultancies, or major research support" and that their associations were neither "regular" nor "ongoing" but more occasional and not relevant to their editorial.

Despite the authors' explanations, a few weeks after publishing the pulmonary hypertension study the *Journal's* editors, Dr. Marcia Angell and Dr. Jerome Kassirer, ran a new editorial acknowledging that the authors may have misinterpreted the *Journal's* definition of "financial associations," but the editors also cast doubt on the credibility of any editorial written by someone with the kinds of financial ties that the authors had. (You can read the original *Journal* article [free registration required to read the full text] on the study and the accompanying editorial on the *New England Journal's* Web site. And you can also read the editors' follow-up editorial.)

But by that time, the damage may have been done. Thanks to the editorial that had run with the study article, many doctors around the world may well have dismissed the study's results and decided not to worry about prescribing Pondimin and Redux.

The *Journal* affair wasn't the only development that interfered with getting the story out about the European diet drug study, says Rich. The drug manufacturer, he says, tried to stop him from talking to the general public.

The news that popular diet drugs carried significant risks prompted NBC's *Today* show to invite Rich to appear on their morning program to talk about the study. Host Bryant Gumbel asked him to tell the country about the study and put it in perspective. "What I said," Rich recalls, "was nothing that was not mentioned in the paper: that the drug carried a very high risk of developing this fatal disease, that it should not be prescribed lightly."

A couple of hours after the live broadcast, Rich returned to his office where, he says, he received a phone call from a senior executive at Wyeth Pharmaceuticals.

"He told me he saw my interview on the *Today* show and warned me that it was very dangerous for me to talk to the press about that, that if I had any issues regarding their product that I wanted to publish in a scientific journal, so be it. But if I spoke to the media about their drug, bad things would happen. 'Bad things would happen' was the exact phrase he used. ... And I never talked to the press again. Because I didn't know what they had in mind. ... They are a very big, a very powerful company."

Rich has told his story under oath in several legal depositions as part of lawsuits brought by Fen Phen victims against the company.

For his part, the senior Wyeth executive has testified under oath in at least one deposition and denied having ever threatened Rich.

We will never know whose version of the facts is correct -- because none of the parties can prove one way or the other that they are being truthful. One thing is certain, however. Dr. Rich didn't speak to the popular press about Redux and Pondimin for many years after that appearance on the *Today* show -- and until now, he never told anybody in the media the details about that phone call.

References

[1] *Science* vol 278, Nov 7, 1997 p1041

[2] GAO/PEMD-90-15 FDA Drug Review: Postapproval Risks 1976-1985

[3] Lumley and Walker (Eds). *Animal Toxicity Studies: Their Relevance for Man* Quay 1990 p73

[4] *JAMA* 2002;287:2215-2220

[5] *Mutagenesis* 1987;2:73-78

[6] *Fund Appl Toxicolo* 1983;3:63-67

[7] *J Am Parapl Soc* 11;23-25, 1988

[8] *Circulation* 1996 pp2326-2336

[9] *JAMA* 2001;286:2673 and *Nature Medicine* 2002;8:5

[10] New Stroke Drug Fails in Humans December 5, 2001 CHICAGO (AP)

[11] *JAMA* 2002;288: 321-33

[12] http://www.usnews.com/usnews/issue/021118/health/18hrt.htm

[13] JENNIFER COUZIN The Great Estrogen Conundrum. Science 2003;302:1136-8

[14] *Public Affairs Quarterly* 1995;9:27-137

[15] Dogs Key to Understanding Advanced Prostate Cancer June 15, 2002

[16] Re: A rational for animal studies *BMJ* 18 February 2002

[17] From Sally Satel, MD: Medicine's Race Problem published in Policy review and republished in Ridely, Matt (Ed) *The Best American Science Writing 2002*. HarperCollins 2002.

[18] *J Clin Oncol* 2002;20:1439-1441,1491-1498 and Toxicity of 5-FU-based chemotherapy more severe in women than men. 2002-04-04 14:51:51 EST (Reuters Health) By Steven Reinberg

[19] See report at www.gao.gov/new.items/d01286r.pdf

[20] From Groopman, J: The Thirty Year's War published in The New Yorker and republished in Ridely, Matt (Ed) The Best American Science Writing 2002. HarperCollins 2002

[21] http://www.washingtonpost.com/wp-dyn/articles/A37557-2003Jun26.html?nav= hptoc_p   NIH Officials Investigated For Possible Ethics Breach By Rick Weiss Washington Post Friday, June 27, 2003; Page A27

[22] Public Citizen. 23 June 2003. Drug Industry Employs 675 Washington Lobbyists, Many with Revolving-Door Connections, New Report Finds. http://www.citizen.org/hot_issues/issue.cfm?ID=579

[23] New York Times, May 30, 2003 http://www.nytimes.com/2003/05/30/business/30DRUG.html?ex=1055727962&ei= 1&en=efb1bfd6b1b233e6

[24] Bodenheimer, T. N Engl j Med 2000;342:1539-44

[25] Nestle, M. *Food Politics*. Berkeley, CA: Univ. Ca Press; 2002

[26] USA Today September 25, 2000, p1, 6 (For more see *JAMA* 2003;290:113-114)

[27] *N Engl J Med* 2000;342:1516-1518)

[28] see N Engl J Med 2000 vol 346 p 1901-02 and *BMJ* 2002;324:1474

[29] vol 338 p101-106

[30] see Scope and Impact of Financial Conflicts of Interest in Biomedical Research: A Systematic Review by Justin E. Bekelman, AB; Yan Li, MPhil; Cary P. Gross, MD JAMA. 2003;289:454-465
[3131] see Science 1986;231:242-246 and N Engl J Med 1996;334:368-373
[32] Science for Sale? 11-15-02
http://www.pbs.org/now/transcript/transcript_scienceforsale.html
[33] Drug Discovery & Development Nov 2002 p34
[34] JAMA 1989;262:2716-20
[35] JAMA 1990;264:2564-6
[36] NEJM 1991;324:1640-3
[37] JAMA 1998; 179;1200-1205.
[38] New Scientist vol 177 issue 2386 - 15 March 2003, page 44
[39] taken from http://www.talkorigins.org/faqs/modern-synthesis.html 6-23-2003
[40] Science 2001;294:2285
[41] JAMA 2001; 286;2213
[42] JAMA 2001;286;2323
[43] Mark, Jonathan. What it means to be 98% chimpanzee: Apes, People and Their Genes. University of California Press 2002 p27
[44] LaFollette, Hugh and Shanks, Niall. Brute Science: Dilemmas of Animal Experimentation. Routledge: 1996.
[45] LaFollette, Hugh and Shanks, Niall. Brute Science: Dilemmas of Animal Experimentation. Routledge: 1996.
[46] LaFollette, Hugh and Shanks, Niall. Brute Science: Dilemmas of Animal Experimentation. Routledge: 1996.
[47] Weissman, Gerald. The Year of the Genome. Times Books 2002 p30 and references therein.
[48] Science (vol 296, p 1661)
[49] www.newscientist.com/news/nes.jsp?id=ns99992352
[50] http://www.sciencemag.org/feature/plus/sfg/resources/res_epigenetics.shtml
[51] Press Release: "Ras Gene Causes Cancer Via Different Pathways in Humans vs. Mice: Finding May Present a New Target for Anti-Cancer Drugs 8/14/2002
[52] www.ornl.gov/hgmis/
[53] JAMA 2001;286:2290
[54] Public release dated 10-18-2002 "Novel Gene Mutation Causes Huntington's-Lik Systems, Providing Window to How Brain Cells Die" Contact: Trent Stockton tstockt1@jhmi.edu
[55] Public Release dated 8-22-2001 "Mayo Clinic Proceedings feature primers on medical genomics" Contact: John Murphy
[56] "Unraveling the Genome," Newsweek June 24, 2002 pg76
[57] www.xensei.com/users/chi/2001/hpr/hpr_pressrelease.htm
[58] Ham, Becky. "The genome is cracked, now what? Proteomics: the next frontier. Science 2/20/01 www.msnbc.com/news/528872.asp
[59] www/xensei.com/users/chi/2001/hpr/hpr_pressrelease.htm
[60] www.xensei.com/users/chi/2001/hpr/hpr_pressrelease.htm
[61] www.xensei.com/users/chi/2001/hpr/hpr_pressrelease.htm
[62] Ham, Becky. "The genome is cracked, now what? Proteomics: the next frontier. Science 2-20-2001. www.msnbc.com/news/528872.asp
[63] www.xensei.com/users/chi/2001/hpr/hpr_pressrelease.htm

[64] Public release date: 8-6-2002 "Structure of key receptor unlocked; Related proteins will fall like dominoes" Contact: Joanne Dowter Johns Hopkins Medical Institutions
[65] Public release date: 8-7-2002 "Discovery may lead to new HIV drugs, says Jefferson virologist" Contact Steve Benowitz steven.benowitz@mail.tju.edu Thomas Jefferson University
[66] *New Scientist* vol 179 issue 2409 - 23 August 2003, page 36
[67] The cancer revolution in *New Scientist* vol 179 issue 2409 - 23 August 2003, page 36
[68] Press Release Date 9-25-2002 "Study: genome-wide scanning unravels complex birth defect" Johns Hopkins Medical Institutions
[69] Public Release Date 6-19-2002 "Gene expression profiles predict survival of lymphoma patients after chemotherapy" NCI Press Office
[70] *Nature* 2000;403:503-511
[71] *J Natl Cancer Inst* 2001;93:1364-1365,1392-1400
[72] *Proc Natl Acad Sci USA* 2001;98:11462-11467
[73] VARIAGENICS website
[74] GCI website
[75] Ham, Becky. "The genome is cracked, now what? Proteomics: the next frontier. *Science* 2-20-2001. www.msnbc.com/news/528872.asp
[76] Public release date: 7-24-2002 "Breakthrough in profiling yeast genome" Contact: Howard Bussey hbussey@po-box.mcgill.ca
[77] Reuters July 12, 2001. Will Dunham. *Huge Genetic Variation Found in Human Beings*
[78] *Science* July 12, 2001
[79] *JAMA* 2002;287:1662-1670 and Reuters Health 2002-04-02 16:00:57 EST
[80] Charlene Laino MSNBC April 2, 2002
[81] *JAMA* 2002;287:1662-1670 and Reuters Health 2002-04-02 16:00:57 EST
[82] Scientific American.com October 10, 2002
[83] Scientific American.com October 10, 2002
[84] Source: In Brave New Medical World, Gene-Based Medicine Becomes Reality by John Casey, Medical Writer CBSHealthWatch. Copyright: © 2001 Medscape, Inc. Posted On Site: Oct. 2001. Publication Date: Oct. 2001
[85] Source: In Brave New Medical World, Gene-Based Medicine Becomes Reality by John Casey, Medical Writer CBSHealthWatch. Copyright: © 2001 Medscape, Inc. Posted On Site: Oct. 2001. Publication Date: Oct. 2001
[86] *J Natl Cancer Inst* 2002;94:681-690 and Reuters Health 2002-04-30 16:36:11 EDT
[87] Reuters Health 2002-04-30 17:12:54 EDT
[88] Ananova 08:25 Monday 22nd April 2002
[89] Nat Genet 2002;June 17. http://gnetics.nature.com
[90] Reuters Health Jan 30, 2002 and *Nature* 2002;415:484-485, 530-536
[91] Ananova Story filed: 23:54 Sunday 3rd March 2002
[92] Ananova Story filed: 21:01 Thursday 14th February 2002
[93] *Cancer* 2002;94:323-330 and Reuters Health 2002-02-01 13:49:46 EST
[94] Reuters Health Jan 30, 2002 and *Int J Cancer* 2002;97:230-236
[95] Reuters Health Jan 14, 2001 and *Natl Med J India* 2001;14:335-339
[96] *Journal f the National Cancer Institute* 2001;93:1458-64 and 1437-39
[97] *JAIDS* 2001;27:472-481
[98] *J Acquir Immun Defic Synd* 2001;27:472-481
[99] WESTPORT, CT (Reuters Health) Nov 26, 2001 and Circulation 01;104(22):2641 [Abstract]

[100] *N Engl J Med* 2002;347-1135-1142,1196-1199

[101] Public release date 6-26-2002 "New cholesterol disorder discovered—As predicted from gene's role" Contact: Wallace Ravven wravven@pubaff.ucsf.edu University of California—San Francisco

[102] *Pharmacogenetics* 2002;12:627-634

[103] Reuters Health Jan 22, 2002

[104] UCSD News Release 11-11-02 "UCSD Bioengineers develop first computer model that predicts disease variant based on genetic defect" Media contact: Denine Hagen dhagen@ucsd.edu

[105] Gorner, Peter. "Wisconsin clinic to form huge gene bank." *Chicago Tribune* September 20, 2002, Section 1, pg8

[106] Gorner, Peter, "Wisconsin clinic to form huge gene bank." *Chicago Tribune* September 20, 2002, Section 1, pg8

[107] www.genetronics.com/tech_98/gene-therapy/htm

[108] Public release date: 6-27-2002 "New gene therapy protocol: First successful treatment for 'bubbl babies' Contact: Roberta Elliott relliott@hadassah.org Hadassah, the Women's Zionist Organization of America

[109] Public release date: 6-27-2002 "Gene therapy may offer release from sterile isolation for patients lacking immune systems" Contact Lisa Onago lonaga@aaas.org American Association for the Advancement of Science

[110] Leroux, Charles. "Affairs of the heart." *Chicago Tribune,* September 17, 2002.

[111] Public release date: 8-12-2002 "Gene therapy may increase cancer cure rates, medical physicists show" Contact: Ben Stein bstein@aip.org American Institute of Physics

[112] Public release date: 6-10-2002 "Genetic engineering could salvage once-promising anti-cancer agents" Contact: Vince Stricherz vinces@u.washington.edu University of Washington

[113] Public release date: 7-2-2002 "New method of turning off viruses may help control HIV infection, says Jefferson scientist Contact: Steve Benowitz steven.benowitz@mail.tju.edu

[114] Taken from MSNBC website

[115] For more information, go to http://www.nobel.se/medicine/laureates/2001/press.html

[116] *Science* vol. 210 Nov. 7, 1980 p 621-3

[117] **Science vol. 218, Nov. 19, 1982 p765-8**

[118] *Science* vol. 222, Oct 28, 1983

[119] *Science,* vol.231, Jan. 10, 1986 p126-129

[120] *Science,* vol.234, Oct 31, 1986 p5434

[121] *Science,* vol. 238, Oct 23, 1987, p484-5

[122] Holloway, Marguerite The Satisfaction of Delayed Gratification. *Scientific American* Oct 1991

[123] *Science* vol. 242,Oct. 28, 1988

[124] *Science* vol. 246. Oct. 20, 1989 p326-7

[125] *Science,* vol. 254, 1991, p 380

[126] *Science* vol. 258, Oct 23, 1992 p542-3

[127] *Science* vol.262. Oct. 22, 1993 p 506

[128] *Science* vol. 266 Oct. 21, 1994 p 368-9

[129] *Science* vol. 270, Oct 20, 1995. P 380-1

[130] *MJA* vol. 165 2/16 Dec. 1996

[131] *Nature* vol. 383 Oct. 10, 1996

[132] *Science* vol.278, Oct. 10, 1997 p214, 245-51

[133] *ATLA* 2002;30:219-227

[134] www.iivs.org/svclist.html

[135] www.iivs.org/svclist.html

[136] Mandavilli, Appoorva. "Taking tissues out of the trash" BioMedNet News www.news.bmn.com 9-19-2002

[137] Angus, JA. Human Vascular Response in Disease: Pharmacodynamic Analyses in Isolated Tissue in *The Pharmacology of Functional, Biochemical, and Recombinant Receptor Systems*. (Kenakin, Terry and Angus, JA, Eds.) Springer 2000 pp. 15-49

[138] Angus, p. 15

[139] SAN ANTONIO, Texas (Reuters Health) Dec 13, 2001

[140] *New Scientist* May 26, 2001, p17 and *Proc Nat Acad Sci* vol. 98, p 6342

[141] NEW YORK (Reuters Health) Dec 10, 2001 and *Science* 2001;294:2163-2166

[142] *J Infect Dis* 2002;185:1055-1061 Reuters Health 2002-04-19 16:32:56 EDT

[143] *AIDS* 2001;15:2221-2229 and NEW YORK (Reuters Health) Dec 13, 2001

[144] *Nature Medicine* 2001;7:1313-19

[145] *Antimicrob Agents Chemother* 2001;45:2229-2237 and WESTPORT, CT (Reuters Health) Aug 24, 2001

[146] Ibid

[147] The NIDA-funded study, led by Dr. Phillip Peterson, appears in the November 2001 issue of Drug and Alcohol Dependence.

[148] May 28 issue of the Proceedings of the National Academy of Sciences and press release from Johns Hopkins

[149] Independent London Local Newspapers Ltd. www.londonlocals.uk Animal World Section 8-5-02

[150] *JAMA* 2001;286:2212

[151] NEW YORK (MedscapeWire) Nov 21, 2001 and WESTPORT, CT (Reuters Health) Nov, 21, 20001 and *J Natl Cancer Inst* 01;93:1747-1752

[152] Reuters Health Jan 30, 2002 and *N Engl J Med* 2002;346:302-304, 311-320

[153] *The New England Journal of Medicine* 2001;345:9-16,25-31,55-57 and NEW YORK, Jul 05, 2001 (Reuters Health)

[154] Grabley S and Thiericke R. *Drug Discovery from Nature* 2000 Springer-Verlag Berlin Heidelberg, p. 44

[155] Grabley and Thiericke, p. 44

[156] http://dtp.nci.nih.gov/branches/btb/ivclsp.html

[157] Drug Discovery Technology Conference syllabus Boston August 12-17, 2001

[158] Drug Discovery Technology Conference syllabus Boston August 12-17, 2001

[159] Mandavilli, Apoorva. "Taking tissues out of the trash" BioMedNet News www.news.bmn.com 9-19-2002

[160] http://www.pharmagene.com/home.htm

[161] *Science* 2002;295:1637

[162] Khalik, Salma. "Breakthrough by NUS scientists: safe stem cells" The Straits Times Interactive 8-7-2002

[163] Khalik, Salma. "Breakthroughs by NUS scientists: safe stem cells" The Straits Times Interactive 8-7-2002

[164] *Discover* June 2002, p55-59

[165] FLORENCE, Italy (Reuters Health) Nov 02, 2001

[166] *Neurology* 2001;57:62-68 AND WESTPORT, CT (Reuters Health) Jul 17, 2001

[167] Reuters Health 2002-04-16 18:00:29 EDT

[168] 2002-04-17 18:00:38 EDT (Reuters Health)

[169] *JAMA* 2002;287:175

[170] *New Scientist* Feb. 2, 2002 p12

[171] *The Medical Letter* 2001;43:84

[172] *Hematol Oncol* 1997;19:183

[173] *N Engl J Med* 1998;338:1119

[174] http://www.ananova.com/news/story/sm_382867.html

[175] Nat Biotechnol. 2002 Dec;20(12):1261-4. Epub 2002 Nov 11.

[176] Public release date: 9-16-2002 "Rice researchers develop first fully automatic method to track 3-D movement of cancer cells" Contact: Jade Boyd jadeboyd@rice.edu Rice University

[177] Congress's Office of Technological Assessment 1986

[178] Mandaville, Apoorva "Taking tissues out of the trash" BioMedNet News www.newsbmn.com 9-19-2002

[179] *Environ Health Perspec* 2001;109:509-14

[180] *Science* 2001;293:608-9

[181] Altman, Lawrence, MD. *Who Goes First? The Story of Self-Experimentation in Medicine.* University of California Press 1998. p. 9.

[182] Altman, Lawrence, MD. *Who Goes First? The Story of Self-Experimentation in Medicine.* University of California Press 1998. p. 10.

[183] Doctor's Guide. November 2002. Pfizer Medicines Receive FDA Approvals for Pediatric Use.

[184] Reuters Health 2002-10-15. "Low plasma folate increases risk of early spontaneous abortion."

[185] Sonali Paul Reuters MELBOURNE May 23, 2002

[186] Reuters Health 2002-04-22 9:31:06 EDT

[187] Reuters Health 2002-11-27 14:00:59-0400. "Single nucelotide polymorphism predisposes to type 2 diabetes."

[188] Arch Otolaryngol Head Neck Surg 2002;128:655-659.

[189] EPA: Toxic Chemicals Raise Cancer Risk, By H. JOSEF HEBERT. The Associated Press. June 1,2002

[190] Reuters Health 2002-09-10. "Long-duration, high-intensity smoking is associated with breast cancer risk.

[191] M S Wolff *Envir Health Perspect* 1997;105, suppl 4:891-96; *BMJ* 2000;321:1403-4.

[192] Release date June 24, 2002 "Importance of Early Environmental Exposure Pinpointed in Study of Breast Cancer Development." Contact Lois Baker, ljbaker@buffalo.edu.

[193] Public release date 29-Aug-2002. "New UNC study suggests multivitamin use during pregnancy cuts childhood tumor risk." Contact: David Willamson 919-962-8596 University of North Carolina at Chapel Hill.

[194] *Pediatrics* 2002;109:904-908 and 2002-05-17 13:07:51 -0400 (Reuters Health)

[195] Am J Epidemiol 2002;155:1023-1032.

[196] [196] *Pediatric Hematology and Oncology* 2002;19:197- 203 and Reuters Health 2002-04-22 16:29:09 EDT

[197] 2002-05-27 5:00:08 -0400 (Reuters Health) and *J Infect Dis* 2002;185:1244-1250.

[198] Genetic mutation linked to high bone density 2002-05-15 17:14:14 -0400 (Reuters Health) and *N Engl J Med* 2002;346:1513-1521,1572-1573

[199] Reuters Health 2002-08-28 14:00:16-0400 "APOE epsilon4 allele linked to cognitive change in old age."

[200] Altman, Lawrence K., Who Goes First? The Story of Self-Experimentation in Medicine, University of California Press, 1998, p. xi.

[201] Altman, Lawrence K. Who Does First? The Story of Self-Experimentation in Medicine, p. 316.

[202] Reade MC, Young JD   Editorial 1. Of mice and men (and rats): implications of species and stimulus differences for the interpretation of studies of nitric oxide in sepsis. *British Journal of Anaesthesia* 90(2) Feb 2003: 115-118

[203] http://www.sciencemag.org/cgi/content/short/1076514; 19 Sep 2002.

[204] Int J Cancer 2002;99:238-244.

[205] Int J Cancer 2002;97:365-371.

[206] *Cancer* 2002;94:272-281.

[207] EurekaAlert! Public release date: 28-Aug-2002. "Eating soy during adolescence may reduce breast cancer."

[208] *Tobacco Control* 1999;8:156-160

[209] *Reuters Health,* November 9, 1999

[210] *Reuters Health*, October 6, 1999

[211] *JAMA* 1999;282:1539-1546

[212] *Reuters Health*, November 25, 1999

[213] *Circulation* 1999;100:1502-1508

[214] *Circulation* 1999;100:1260-1263, 1268-1273

[215] *N Engl J Med* 1999;341:1715-1724, 1759-1762

[216] *Reuters Health*, November 16, 1999

[217] John Casey, Medical Writer Dec. 10, 2001 (Medscape Health) http://health.medscape.com/cx/viewarticle/410938

[218] *J Mol Med* 2001;79:390-98

[219] Lancet 2001;358:2012-2013,2026-2033 and NEW YORK (Reuters Health) Dec 13, 2001

[220] *Stroke* 2002;33:1041-1047 Reuters Health 2002-04-29 15:41:40 EDT

[221] WESTPORT, CT (Reuters Health) Aug 24, 2001 and *Int J Cancer* 2001;93:601-607

[222] Reuters Health 2002-06-19 11:28:12-0400. "Second hand smoke causes lung cancer: international experts."

[223] Rampton, Sheldon and John Stauber. *Trust Us, We're Experts!* Penguin Putnam 2001.

[224] McNeill, John H. (Ed.) *Experimental Models of Diabetes* CRC Press LLC 1999 p 337-398

[225] *JAMA* 1999;282:1539-1546

[226] *Reuters Health*, September 1999

[227] *San Diego Union*, June 22, 1999

[228] *Journal of Clinical Investigation* December 15, 2000

[229] *Medscape*, June 12, 2000

[229] Dove, Alan, *NATURE BIOTECHNOLOGY* January 2001;19:25-28

[230] *Arch Pathol Lab Med*, Vol. 120, August 1996.

[231] *Pediatrics* 1993;92:872-875; *Pediatr Clin North Am* 1994;41:967-989; *Scand J rehab Med.* 1988:17(suppl);25-31.

[232] Reuters Health 2002-03-28 19:01;43 EST.

[233] *J Am Coll Surg* 2002;194:401-406 and Reuters Health 2002-04-25 12:16:41 EDT.

[234] *BMJ* 2002;324:761-763.

[235] *Science* 2002;295:1210.

[236] From Phil B. Fontanarosa, MD and George D. Lundberg, MD. Alternative Medicine Meets Science. *JAMA* November 11, 1998—Vol 280, No. 18 1618-19

[237] http://www.cebm.net/

[238] Meissner, Judith E. 1993. Reducing the risks of digitalis toxicity. Nursing 23:46

[239] Meissner.

[240] DiMasi, J. A., Hansen, R. W. & Grabowski, H. G. The price of innovation: new estimates of drug development costs. J. Health Econ. 835, 1-35 (2003) and *Nature Reviews Drug Discovery* 2003;2:247

[241] *Nature Biotechnology* 2002;21:470-71

[242] S. Grabley and R. Thiericke, eds. Drug Discovery form Nature. Springer-Verlag Berlin Heidelber 2000, p. 5

[243] Davis JM. Antipsychotic Drugs, in Kaplan HI, Sadock BJ, 9eds. Comprehensive Textbook of Psychiatry, Fourth Edition. Baltimore, Williams and Wilkins, 1985)

[244] Drews, Jurgen. *In Quest of Tomorrow's Medicines.* Springer 1998 p. 66

[245] Grabley and Thiericke, p. 3

[246] *J Nat Prod* 1997;60:52

[247] Drews, p 6,7

[248] *Nach Chem Tech Lab* 1997;45:159

[249] Bumol, TF, Ph.D. and August M. Watanabe, MD. *Genetic Information, Genomic Technologies, and the Future of Drug Discovery. JAMA 2001;285:551-555*

[250] Luttrell LM, Daaka Y, Lefkowitz RL. Regulation of tyrosine kinase cascades by G-protein-coupled recpetors. *Curr Opin Cell Biol.* 1999;11:77-183

[251] Drews, In Quest of Tomorrow's Medicines, p. 82

[252] Brimblecombe, Roger. *Drug Discovery World* Summer 2001 p. 7

[253] *Am Chem Soc* 1971;93:2325

[254] Associated Press, Jan. 22, 2002. "FDA Oks landmark liver drug; failed weed killer Orfadin fights rare baby disease.

[255] Mort, Mona. *Biocombinitorial techniques aid the development of small molecules to control the disease. (Don't know where this came from?)*

[256] Smith, Adam. "Screening for drug discovery: the leading question." *Nature* Technology Feature 25/07/02.

[257] Smith, Adam. "Screening for drug discovery: the leading question." *Nature* Technology Feature 25/07/02.

[258] Fulton, Michael J. "Survival of the Fittest in Drug Design. *Modern Drug Discovery*

[259] *ScienceExpress* 2001;10.1126

[260] Sali, A; Blundell, T.L. *J. Mol. Biol.* 1993, *234,* 779-815.

[261] *Science* 2001;293:2266-2269

[262] Public release date: 4-Sep-2002. Duke University Medical Center. "Duke researchers develop method to make safer drugs."

[263] Grabley and Thierecke, p. 31

[264] Grabley and Thierecke, p. 13

[265] Dorland's Electronic Medical Dictionary

[266] ASSOCIATED PRESS WASHINGTON, May 28, 2002

[267] Reuters 17:03 03-20-02

[268] Kaufman, Mark. "Decline in New Drugs Raises Concerns." The Washington Post 18 November 2002. www.washingtonpost.com/wp-dyn/articles/A3265-2002Nov17.html.

[269] *Nature Reviews Drug Discovery* 2003;2:167

270 Lazarou J, Pomeranz BH, Corey PN. Incidence of adverse drug reactions in hospitalized patients. A meta-analysis of prospective studies. JAMA. 1998;279:1200-1205.

271 FRANKFURT (Reuters Health) Jan 18, 2002

272 *Forbes* December 27, 1999 p190

273 Telegraph. Cost timebomb 'may kill supply of new drugs' By Roger Highfield, Science Editor (Filed: 17/09/2003)

274 Secret Paths by Mark Peplow www. newscientist.com 3 May 20031 *New Scientist*

275 Hodgson, John. "ADMET—Turning Chemicals into Drugs" *Nature Biotechnology* Vol. 19, August 2001, p. 772

276 Ibid.

277 American Chemical Society. The Role of Toxicology in Drug Discovery. ACS Short Course.

278 American Chemical Society. The Role of Toxicology in Drug Discovery. ACS Short Course.

279 Drews, In Quest of Tomorrow's Medicines. p. 129

280 American Chemical Society, Short Courses

281 Smith et al, The selection of marmoset monkeys in pharmaceutical toxicology; *Laboratory Animals* (2001) 35, 117-130

282 Focus: Toxicity Tests in Animals: Extrapolating to Human Risks; http://ehpnet1.niehs.nih.gov/docs/1993/101-5/focus.html

283 House of Lords Select Committee on Animals in Scientific Procedures Report, Volume 1 The Stationery Office Ltd. HL Paper 150-1 p70-72

284 American Chemical Society Short Course. The Role of Toxicology in Drug Discovery. August 16, 2001Boston, MA.

285 *Nature Biotechnology* 2001;19:722-26

286 Drug Metab Dispos 1996 Jun;24(6):634-42. Comparative studies of drug-metabolizing enzymes in dog, monkey, and human small intestines, and in Caco-2 cells. Prueksaritanont T, Gorham LM, Hochman JH, Tran LO, Vyas KP. Department of Drug Metabolism, Merck Research Laboratories, West Point, PA 19486, USA.

287 *Modern Drug Discovery* October 2003 p 14 and *N Engl J Med* 2003;349:474-485

288 *Nature* 1982;296:387-90

289 LONDON (Reuters Health) Dec 18, 20001

290 *JAMA* 2002;287:2215-2220. Lasser KE, Allen PD, Woolhandler SJ, Himmelstein DU, Wolfe SM, Bor DH. Timing of new black box warnings and withdrawals for prescription medications.

291 Reuters Health Jan 18, 2002

292 Rhonda Rowland CNN Medical Unit

293 *The Scientist* April 1, 2002 p22

294 Ibid

295 Alzheimer's Vaccine Permanently Shelved By Rick Weiss Washington Post Staff Writer Saturday, March 2, 2002; Page A03

296 Levine, S. "The Story of Patient 10," *The Washington Post* July 31, 2001:F1

297 Oklahoma NewsChannel 8. 16 November 2002. "FDA Issues Warning About Painkiller."www.ktul.com/new/stories/1102/63140.html.

298 Reuters Health 2002-07-15 16:10:26-0400.

299 GAO/PEMD-90-15 FDA Drug Review: Postapproval Risks 1976-1985.

300 *The Scientist* February 4, 2002 p22

[301] Toxicology flawed by "decades-old" paradigm 30 April 2002 22:00 EST by Apoorva Mandavilli, BioMedNet News

[302] *Nature Reviews Drug Discovery* 2003;2:233-40

[303] Drews, In Quest of Tomorrow's Medicines, p. 128

[304] Dr M. G. Palfreyman, Dr V. Charles and J. Blander, The importance of using human-based models in gene and drug discovery. DDW (Drug Discovery World), Fall 2002, p.33-40

[305] Dr M. G. Palfreyman, Dr V. Charles and J. Blander, The importance of using human-based models in gene and drug discovery. DDW (Drug Discovery World), Fall 2002, p.33-42

[306] Hodgson, ADMET—Turning Chemicals into Drugs, p. 724

[307] Evolving away from animal tests: Charles River Laboratories shifts to new technologies. By Naomi Aoki, Boston Globe, 2/27/2002 D1

[308] Lab Automation Article. Nov. 27, 2001 *In Silico* ADME Screening - An Introduction Laura Robinson M.B.A. LION bioscience, Inc. San Diego, CA 92121 Laura.robinson@lionbioscience.com, www.lionbioscience.com

[309] Tripos web site

[310] Hodgson, ADMET—Turning Chemicals into Drugs, p. 724

[311] *Drug Discovery & Development* January 2002 p 71

[312] Hodgson, ADMET—Turning Chemicals into Drugs, p. 72

[313] Borman, S. *Chem Eng News* 1990;68:20-23

[314] as quoted in *Nature Biotechnology* 2001;19:725

[315] as quoted in *Nature Biotechnology* 2001;19:725

[316] *New Scientist* June 30, 2001 p. 22

[317] Public release date: 4-Oct-2002. "'Virtual stomach' reveals pill's path."

[318] Prentis, R.A., Lis, Y., and Walker, S.R. Pharmaceutical Innovation by the Seven UK-owned Pharmaceutical Companies (1964-1985). Br. J. Clin. Pharmac. 1988, 25, 387-396. And Egan, W. J., Merz, K.M., Jr., and Baldwin, J. J. Prediction of Drug Absorption Using Multivariate Statistics J. Med. Chem.,2000, 43, 3867-3877. and Ghose, A. K.; Viswanadhan, V. N.; Wendoloski, J. J. Prediction of hydrophobic (lipophilic) properties of small organic molecules using fragmental methods: An analysis of ALOGP and CLOGP methods. J. Phys. Chem.,1998, 102, 3762-3772, 1998.

[319] Rogers D. and A.J. Hopfinger, "Application of Genetic Function Approximation to Quantitative Structure Activity Relationships and Quantitative Structure Property Relationships". J. Chem. Inf. Comp. Sci., 34, 854-866, 1994. and Rogers, D., "Genetic Function Approximation: A Genetic Approach to Building Quantitative Structure-Activity Relationship Models". In: QSAR and Molecular Modelling: Concepts, Computational Tools and Biological Applications. F. Sanz, J. Giraldo and F. Manaut, eds. Prous Science Publishers, Barcelona, Spain. 420-426, 1996. and Rogers, D., "Some Theory and Examples of Genetic Function Approximation with Comparison to Evolutionary Techniques". In: Genetic Alogorithms in Molecular Modeling. J. Devillers, ed. Academic Press, London, England. 87-107, 1996. and Hahn, M., and D. Rogers, "Receptor Surface Models. 2. Application to Quantitative Structure-Activity Relationships Studies". J. Med. Chem., 38, 2091-2102, 1995. and Dunn, W.J. and D. Rogers, "Genetic Partial Least Squares in QSAR". In: Genetic Algorithms in Molecular Modeling. J. Devillers, ed. Academic Press, London, England. 109-30, 1996. and Selwood, D.J., Livingstone, D.J.,

Comley, J.C., O'Dowd, A.B., Hudson, A.T., Jackson, P., Jandu, K.S., Rose, V.S. and Stables, J.N., J.Med.Chem. 33, 136, 1990.

[320] Dr Claude Reiss http://perso.wanadoo.fr/proanima/anglais.htm
THE ASSESSMENT OF HUMAN HEALTH SAFETY BY MEANS OF THE ANIMAL MODEL VIOLATES THE PRECAUTIONARY PRINCIPLE. Open letter to the members of the French Academy of Sciences, by the Scientific Council of Pro Anima

[321] Constans, Aileen. "Making Medicine Personal." *The Scientist* September 30, 2002,

[322] Genomic Medicine. Alan E. Guttmacher, M.D., and Francis S. Collins, M.D., Ph.D., Editors Inheritance and Drug Response by Richard Weinshilboum, M.D. *The New England Journal of Medicine* 2003;348;:29-37

[323] Aldridge, Susan, Ph.D. "Customizing Drugs to Individual Genetic Profiles. *Genetic Engineering News*, Volume 21, Number 14, August 2001, p. 29

[324] Holtzman NA, Marteau TM. Will genetics revolutionize medicine? N Engl J Med 2000;343;141-144.

[325] Kuivenhoven JA. The role of a common variant of the cholesteryl ester transfer protein gene in the progression of coronary atherosclerosis. N Engl Med. 1998;338:36-93.

[326] De Morais SM, Wilkinson GR, Blaisdell J, Nakamura K, Meyer UA, Goldstein JA. The major genetic defect responsible for the polymorphism of S-mephenytoin metabolism in humans. J Biol Chem. 1994;269:15419-15422.

[327] Nelson R. Genome pharmacy. Hospital Pharmacist Report. 2000;14:22-24.

[328] Relling MV, Hancock ML, Rivera GK, et al. Mercaptopurine therapy intolerance and heterozygosity at the thiopurine S-methyltransferase gene locus. J Natl Cancer Inst. 1999;91:2001-2008.

[329] Wolf CR, Smith G, Smith RL. Pharmacogenetics. BMJ 2000;320:987-990.

[330] *Science* 2003;302:588-90

[331] DRUG METABOLISM AND DISPOSITION Copyright © 1997 by The American Society for Pharmacology and Experimental Therapeutics Vol. 25, No. 10
In vitro Comparison of Cytochrome P450-Mediated Metabolic Activities in Human, Dog, Cat, and Horse Nathalie Chauret, Annick Gauthier, Jean Martin, and Deborah A. Nicoll-Griffith

[332] Chang M, Tybring G, Dahl ML, et al. Interphenotype differences in disposition and effect on gastrin levels of omeprazole—suitability of omeprazole as a probe for CYP2C19. Br J Clin Pharmacol. 1995;39:511-518.

[333] Bertilsson L, Aberg-Wistedt A, Gustafsson LL, et al. Extremely rapid hydroxylation of debrisoquine: a case report with implication for treatment with nortripytyline and other tricyclic antidepressants. Ther Drug Monit. 1985;7:478-480.

[334] Ingelman-Sunderberg M, Oscarson M, McLellan R. Polymorphic human cytochrome P450 enzymes: an opportunity for individualized drug treatment. TiPS. 1999:20:342-349.

[335] Joanne M. Meyer and Geoffrey S. Ginsburg, "The path to personalized medicine." *Current Opinion in Chemical Biology* 2002, 6:434-438.

[336] Joanne M. Meyer and Geoffrey S. Binsburg, "The path to personalized medicine." *Current Opinion in Chemical Biology* 2002: 6:434-438.

[337] Aldridge, Susan, Ph.D. "Customizing Drugs to Individual Genetic Profiles. *Genetic Engineering News*, Volume 21, Number 14, August 2001, p. 29

[338] Roses AD. Phamacogenetics and the practice of medicine. Nature. 2000;405:857-865.

[339] Wolf CR, Smith G, Smith RL. Pharmacogenetics. BMJ 2000;320:987-990.

[340] Public release date: 12-Oct-1001 New Scientist. "Special report: Personal Genomics.
[341] Warner, Susan, "Out of Reach." *The Scientist*. September 30, 2002, p. 35.
[342] Public release date 7-June-2002 "New robotic microscope helps scientists track cells over time." University of California, San Francisco
[343] *Companion Encyclopedia Of The History Of Medicine,* Bynum and Porter eds., Routledge 1993
[344] Asimov, I. *Asimov's Biographical Encyclopedia Of Science & Technology* 2nd edition. Doubleday & Company 1982
[345] *New Scientist* Feb. 7, 1998 p6
[346] *Scientific American Science's Vision: The Mechanics of Sight* 1998, p. 31-55.
[347] *American Family Physician* vol. 55, no. 6. May 1, 1997 p2219-28
[348] *New Scientist,* June 6, 1998, p20.
[349] *Discover,* July 1998, p. 86.
[350] *The Lancet,* 1999; 353:1585
[351] Tuggy, Michael L. MD, presented at the 1998 AAFP Scientific Assembly Research competition, San Francisco, September 1998.
[352] *Scientific American,* November 1999, p 91-97
[353] *JAMA* 1998;280:1510-1516.
[354] September/October issue of the journal *Health Affairs* in a special section titled, "The Value of Innovation
[355] *Trends in Biotechnology* 2002, 20:S1-S2
[356] *Med. Phys.* 22 (11), Pt 2, Nov. 1995
[357] *Med. Phys.* 22 (11), Pt. 2, Nov. 1995
[358] Nobel Foundation and Odelberg, W., op. cit.
[359] Ibid.
[360] Ibid.
[361] Ibid.
[362] *Science* vol. 254, Oct. 25, 1991 p518-19
[363] *The New York Times* October 7, 2003 and quoted in *New Scientist* October 11, 2003 p8.
[364] *Perspectives in Biology and Medicine* 36(1) Autumn 1992 p39-45
[365] *Perspectives in Biology and Medicine* 36(3), Spring 1993, p323-337
[366] James, L. K. (ed.) *Nobel Laureates in Chemistry 1901-1992* American Chemical Society 1993
[367] Ibid.
[368] Ibid.
[369] Ibid.
[370] Nobel Foundation and Odelberg, W., op. cit.
[371] James, L. K., op. cit.
[372] *Perspectives in Biology and Medicine* 36(3), Spring 1993, p323-337
[373] Nobel Foundation and Odelberg, W., op. cit.
[374] James, L. K., op. cit.
[375] Nobel Foundation and Odelberg, W., op. cit.
[376] James., L. K., op. cit.
[377] Ibid.
[378] Ibid.
[379] Ibid.
[380] *Journal of Computer Assisted Tomography* 1992, 16(1):1-2

[381] *The Scientist* July 23, 2001 p11
[382] Adams, Amy. "Supercomputing in the Life Sciences." The Scientist Vol. 16 Sept. 2, 2002.
[383] *The Scientist* July 23, 2001 p11
[384] *Circulation* 2001:103:2711-2716 and WESTPORT, CT (Reuters Health) Jun 01, 2001
[385] *Clinical applications of artificial neural networks* (Eds. Dybowski, Richard and Vanya Gant) Cambridge University Press 2001 p14
[386] Breslau, Karen. "Tiny Weapons with Giant Potential." Newsweek June 24, 2002, p72
[387] "Biomedical Scientist Testing Nanoparticles as Early Cancer Detection Agent." Public release date October 23, 2002 Georgia Institute of Technology
[388] Ananova Story filed: 19:01 Thursday 15th November 2001 and WESTPORT, CT (Reuters Health) Nov 15, 2001 and *Science* 2001;294:1537-1540
[389] Soares, Christine. "Virtually human." *New Scientist.* 16 June 2001.
[390] Public release date: 17-Sep-2002. "Engineers model blood flow. University of California, Davis.
[391] Public release date 26-Jun-2002 "Virginia Tech researchers receive $450,000 award to model cell division." Virginia Tech
[392] 2002-06-03 16:53:52 -0400 (Reuters Health) and *Neurology* 2002;58:1476-1482
[393] 2002-05-24 13:30:41 -0400 (Reuters Health) and *J Neurol Neurosurg Psychiatry* 2002;72:564-565,576-582.
[394] http://health.medscape.com/cx/viewarticle/416405 Brain Scan Helps Tell the Future of MS Michael W. Smith MD, Reviewed by Gary D. Vogin, MD
[395] PRESS RELEASE DATE: 23-MAY-2002 Contact: Joni Westerhouse westerhousej@msnotes.wustl.edu 314-286-0120 Washington University School of Medicine. Schlaggar BL, Brown TT, Lugar HM, Visscher KM, Miezin FM, Petersen SE. Functional neuroanatomical differences between adults and school-age children in the processing of single words. *Science*, 296, pg. 1476-9, May 24, 2002
[396] *Sarah Graham* http://www.scientificamerican.com/news/112801/3.html
[397] Story filed: 05:46 Friday 14th December 2001, Copyright: 2001 Ananova Ltd
[398] Stroke 2001;32:2543-2549 and WESTPORT, CT (Reuters Health) Nov 09, 2001
[399] Gina Shaw, Nov. 6, 2001 (CBS HealthWatch) and WESTPORT, CT (Reuters Health) Nov 08, 2001 and *JAMA* 2001;286:2120-2127
[400] Sarah Graham scientificamerican.com/news
[401] *Nature Medicine* Feb 2002 and *BusinessWeek* Feb 25, 2002 p 129
[402] http://health.medscape.com/cx/viewarticle/412797 Alzheimer's Diagnosis Breakthrough–New Imaging Technique Salynn Boyles, Reviewed by Gary D. Vogin, MD
[403] WASHINGTON (Reuters Health) Aug 02, 2001
[404] Public release date: 30-Sep-2002 "'Slice' scanner latest advance in early detection of heart disease." American Heart Association
[405] Reuters Health 2002-06-18 14:45:49-0400 "PET scans may help predict chemotherapy response."
[406] Public Release Date 17-Jun-2002. Contact: Karen Lubieniecki. Karenlub@aol.com 703-683-0357. Society of Nuclear Medicine. Abstract No. 128 "Prognostic Significance of 18F-FDG Uptake in Primary Osteosarcomas. C. Franzius,* S. Bielack, S. Flege, J. Sciuk, H. Juergens, O. Schober, University Hospital Münster, Münster, Germany; Department of Nuclear Medicine, University of Münster, Münster, Germany. (200926)
[407] Virtual reality therapy reduces hand impairment years after stroke 2002-02-01 14:48:46 EST (Reuters Health) By Faith Reidenbach

[408] *Am J Med Genet* 2002;109:167-170 2002-05-24 14:47:28 -0400 (Reuters Health)

[409] *Arch Otolaryngol Head Neck Surg* 2002;128:11-14

[410] Caryn Goldstein, Medical Writer, Article URL:
http://www.cbshealthwatch.com/cx/viewarticle/217850

[411] Craelius, William. "The Bionic Man: Restoring Mobility. Science Vol 295 8 February 2002 p1019

[412] *Times Higher Ed Supp.* Key basic research study proves fatally ambiguous. By Steve Farrar. Published: 21 November 2003

[413] ASSOCIATED PRESS. BALTIMORE, Nov. 11

[414] Van, Jon. "Surgeons on the Cutting Edge." Chicago Tribune, Business.Technology Section NW. May 1, 2000. P 1

[415] Colt HG, Crawford SW, Galbraith O. Virtual reality bronchoscopy simulation: a revolution in procedural training. *CHEST* 2001 120; 1333-1339

[416] http://www.cdc.gov/nchs/data/nvsr/nvsr51/nvsr51_05.pdf 6-23-03

[417] Government Executive. GovExec.com. Daily Briefing. November 3, 2003. Congress wants payoff from increased NIH funding. By Neil Munro, National Journal.

Index

ISBN 141202058-1

9 781412 020589